W9-CHP-914

The Best of
Learning & Leading
WITH TECHNOLOGY

Selections from
Volumes 31–35

Edited by Jennifer Roland

International Society for Technology in Education
EUGENE, OREGON • WASHINGTON, DC

The Best of **Learning & Leading with Technology**
Selections from Volumes 31–35

Edited by Jennifer Roland

Director of Book Publishing: *Courtney Burkholder*
Acquisitions Editor: *Jeff V. Bolkan*
Production Editors: *Lynda Gansel, Lanier Brandau*
Production Coordinator: *Rachel Bannister*
Graphic Designer, Book Design and Layout: *Signe Landin*
Copy Editor: *Mary Snyder*
Cover Design: *Tam Kidd*

Library of Congress Cataloging-in-Publication Data

Learning and leading with technology. Selections. 2009.
   The best of Learning & leading with technology : selections from volumes 31-35 / edited by Jennifer Roland. — 1st ed.
      p. cm.
   Includes bibliographical references.
   ISBN 978-1-56484-255-8 (pbk.)
   1. Computer-assisted instruction. 2. Computer literacy. I. Roland, Jennifer. II. International Society for Technology in Education. III. Title. IV. Title: Best of Learning and leading with technology.
   LB1028.5.L384 2009
   371.33'4—dc22

                          2009012647

First Edition
ISBN: 978-1-56484-255-8

Printed in the United States of America

International Society for Technology in Education (ISTE)
Washington, DC, Office:
      1710 Rhode Island Ave. NW, Suite 900, Washington, DC 20036-3132
Eugene, Oregon, Office:
      180 West 8th Ave., Suite 300, Eugene, OR 97401-2916
Order Desk: 1.800.336.5191   Order Fax: 1.541.302.3778
Customer Service: orders@iste.org
Book Publishing: books@iste.org
Book Sales and Marketing: booksmarketing@iste.org
Web: www.iste.org

Cover Photos: goldfish © iStockphotos/LiseGagne; block cube © iStockphotos/rzdeb; people equation © iStockphotos/rosendo; Second Life avatar © Linden Lab.

about ISTE

The International Society for Technology in Education (ISTE) is the trusted source for professional development, knowledge generation, advocacy, and leadership for innovation. ISTE is the premier membership association for educators and education leaders engaged in improving teaching and learning by advancing the effective use of technology in PK–12 and teacher education.

Home of the National Educational Technology Standards (NETS) and ISTE's annual conference and exposition (formerly known as NECC), ISTE represents more than 100,000 professionals worldwide. We support our members with information, networking opportunities, and guidance as they face the challenge of transforming education. To find out more about these and other ISTE initiatives, visit our website at **www.iste.org**.

As part of our mission, ISTE Book Publishing works with experienced educators to develop and produce practical resources for classroom teachers, teacher educators, and technology leaders. Every manuscript we select for publication is carefully peer-reviewed and professionally edited. We value your feedback on this book and other ISTE products. E-mail us at **books@iste.org**.

about the editor

Jennifer Roland's career in educational technology publishing began with a summer internship with ISTE in 1990. In her 12 years on staff, she worked on *Learning & Leading with Technology*, *Journal of Research on Computing in Education*, *Journal of Computing in Teacher Education*, *Journal of Computer Science Education*, *Journal of Online Learning*, and the full suite of Special Interest Group publications. Jennifer was instrumental in creating the online spaces for ISTE's periodicals and she helped edit ISTE books and conference materials.

In addition to educational technology, Jennifer writes about personal finance, entertainment, pets, and health and fitness. She holds bachelor's degrees in journalism and political science from the University of Oregon. She lives in the Portland, Oregon, area with her husband and their extended family and pets.

acknowledgement

Jennifer wishes to thank the *L&L* volunteers and staff for their insight and guidance in selecting the articles to include in this collection. And she extends special gratitude to the authors who allowed their works to be reused here and who provided wonderful, insightful updates when asked.

contents

preface by Leslie Conery x

introduction 1

chapter 1   **The First 30 Years of *L&L*** 3

chapter 2   **Issue Oriented** 7

The Best Defense is a Good Offense 9
Anita McAnear

Equity in Practice 10
Anita McAnear

The Magic of Emerging Technology 11
Anita McAnear

chapter 3   **Point/Counterpoint** 13

Is the Goal of K–12 to Produce Employees or Learners? 15
Francis D. Head and Randy Edwards

Is It Time for a National Student Tracking System? 18
June Atkinson and Ruth Reynard

Is Chatspeak Destroying English? 21
Linda Howard and Greg Monfils

chapter 4   **Features** 25

Statistics for Success 29
Robert Kadel

Digital Citizenship: Addressing Appropriate Technology Behavior 34
Mike S. Ribble, Gerald D. Bailey, and Tweed W. Ross

Digital Citizenship: Focus Questions for Implementation 39
Mike S. Ribble and Gerald D. Bailey

Are You the Copy Cop? 44
Doug Johnson and Carol Simpson

Get the Word Out with List Servers 53
    Laurence Goldberg

Avoid the Plague: Tips and Tricks for Preventing and Detecting
Plagiarism 58
    J.V. Bolkan

Designing the New School 63
    J.V. Bolkan, Jennifer Roland, and Davis N. Smith

Social Justice: Choice or Necessity? 69
    Colleen Swain and Dave Edyburn

Sowing the Seeds for a More Creative Society 75
    Mitchel Resnick

chapter 5   **Learning Connections** 81

Business Ed: Simulations as Action Learning Devices 85
    Dan Smith

Computer Science & ICT: Trash or Treasure? Evaluating a Web Site 88
    Kathy Schrock

Early Childhood: Digesting a Story 90
    Stacy Bodin

Foreign Language: Improving Students' Language Learning 92
    Lyn C. Howell and Robert Rose

Health: Dynamic Human Anatomy 94
    Ken Felker

Language Arts: Electronic Read-Arounds 96
    Rick Monroe

Mathematics: Dynamic Visualizations 98
    Margaret L. Niess

Multidisciplinary: Research, Deconstructed 102
    Leslie Yoder

Science: Students as Environmental Consultants: Simulating
Life Science Problems 104
    Megan Roberts and Janet Mannheimer Zydney

Social Studies: Kids Galore Helping Kids in Darfur 109
    Wendy Drexler

chapter 6   As I See "IT" 113

Teacher-to-Teacher Mentoring 115
    Kathleen Gora and Janice Hinson

The Mature Family 122
    Marilyn Brooks

Herding Cats 123
    Don Hall

chapter 7   Research Windows 125

Research into Practice 127
    John W. Collins

Ethics in Ed Tech Research 131
    Robert Kadel

Does Your District Need a Technology Audit? 134
    Howard Pitler

chapter 8   Media Matters 139

Substantive Searching: Thinking and Behaving Info-Fluently 141
    Joyce Valenza

Blogging and the Media Specialist 148
    Doug Johnson

Blogging and the Media Specialist, Part 2 150
    Frances Jacobson Harris

Wikipedia: Ban It or Boost It? 152
    Doug Johnson

chapter 9   Project-Based Learning 155

Building Better Projects 157
    Diane McGrath with Mark Viner and Allen Sylvester

Taking the Plunge 166
    Diane McGrath and Nancy Sands

Visualize, Visualize, Visualize: Designing Projects
for Higher-Order Thinking 169
Pearl Chen and Diane McGrath

chapter 10   **Connected Classroom** 175

A Space for "Writing without Writing" 177
Sara Kajder and Glen Bull

Folk Taxonomies 181
Glen Bull

Educational Crowdsourcing 183
Glen Bull

chapter 11   **Miscellaneous Columns** 185

Guest Editorial: A Proposal for Banning Pencils 187
Doug Johnson

ISTE in Action: Systemic Leadership 188
Idelma Quintana

Voices Carry: Reframing the Debate 189
Hilary Goldmann

chapter 12   **Product Reviews** 191

GTCO CalComp InterWrite PRS RF 193
J.V. Bolkan

EMTeachline Mathematics Software 195
David K. Pugalee and Margaret Adams

GeeGuides geeArt16 197
Savilla Banister

chapter 13   **Buyer's Guide** 201

Student Response Systems 202

Multimedia Laptops 204

Virtual Worlds 206

chapter 14 **Member Profiles** 209

Hungry Minds: Daphne Griffin. 211

Promoting Ed Tech Use in the Pacific Northwest: NCCE 212

Texas Instruments Strategies Add Up 213

Teaching Teachers to Create "Sticky" Learning: SIGTE. 214

chapter 15 **The Future of *L&L* by Kate Conley**. .215

color section **The Best of *L&L*: Art**

preface

ISTE's mission is to improve teaching and learning by advancing the effective use of technology in education. ISTE leaders and staff have known that one of the most effective ways to support educators in improving instruction and student learning is to provide practical, useful, classroom-based examples. And ISTE members have long appreciated *Learning & Leading with Technology* as the member benefit that helps bring them closest to the classroom with information they can use. Perhaps this is why, with each member satisfaction survey ISTE conducts, *Learning & Leading with Technology* continues to be the number-one most valued and most used member benefit.

Learning & Leading has benefited from having many of the best thinkers, researchers, teachers, and authors in the field as regular contributors. I can imagine what a difficult task it must have been for editor Jennifer Roland to pick the best of five years' worth of outstanding articles and columns. Although I don't think I'm quite ready to permanently archive the 27 years of ISTE's flagship periodical adorning my home office, I do look forward to having a compilation of *The Best of Learning & Leading with Technology: 2003–2008.*

Leslie Conery
ISTE Deputy CEO

introduction

Selecting the best articles from the last five years was quite a challenge—much more than I thought it would be when I first embarked on this project.

I began with the assumption that articles and activities that appeared in *L&L* were the best of the best. They had been reviewed by the staff and subject-matter experts, so the pedagogy and technology use was sound. Any concerns had been addressed before acceptance and publication. I also decided not to include news and new product announcements—these types of articles do not have a high archival value, and their worth is based more on the fleeting elements they cover than their writing.

With that in mind, I began narrowing down my selections. I decided to use a blog to help ISTE leaders and *L&L* readers nominate some of their favorites and discuss their nominations with each other. Based on the feedback I received, I added links to the PDFs of all of the articles to help blog visitors refresh their memories.

While readers were posting their comments on the blog, I also looked through the letters to the editor to see which articles had generated the most reader feedback over the years. I also went outside the ISTE universe and searched general education blogs to see which articles had generated discussion throughout the field.

I used nominations from my blog, feedback published in the magazine, and my careful reading of the issues to select a slate of nominations from each section of the magazine. The final step I took in making my initial selections was to ensure broad representation across volumes and issues. I wanted to avoid the trap of focusing solely on the newer articles. As the magazine and the field evolve, it is hard to argue that the most current information is the most relevant. But my goal was to ensure that this collection represented all five volumes. In the curriculum section, I also ensured that most curriculum areas and age groups were covered. I posted these on the blog for further feedback and help selecting the final articles for inclusion.

I wrote the chapter introductions to provide some background for the articles and columns. I also approached many of the authors included to see if they could provide short updates to accompany their articles. The author updates appear with the features, curriculum articles, and other articles as appropriate. They help provide a more recent context for some of the articles, which is useful in the fast-changing field of educational technology.

Jennifer Roland

chapter 1
The First 30 Years of *L&L*

The early history of *Learning & Leading with Technology* is inextricably linked with the history of David Moursund's career.

In the early 1970s, a group of Oregon educators, including Dave, met and formed the Oregon Council for Computer Education (OCCE). They received a National Science Foundation (NSF) grant to fund their work supporting computer education in Oregon. The NSF grant covered editorial and printing support from the University of Oregon. As part of that work, Dave decided to publish a magazine—the *Oregon Computing Teacher*—to focus the efforts of the fledgling organization.

The first issue, published in May 1974, was typewritten and stapled together with yellow cardstock covers. The editorial staff listed was Dave, Keith Garrett, Mike Neill, Kay Porter, and Rusty Whitney. Dave noted that he "served as editor-in-chief and did the work of drawing material together, preparing it for publication, and getting it published. The first issue … contained a variety of articles, including two by me."

"For the most part," Dave said, "the articles were written by me and by people from around Oregon that I knew. It was a constant struggle to get content. I 'leaned on' my students and other people who were doing good things. By and large, teachers do not like to write for publication." Dave continued in the position of editor-in-chief, although he said he began to grow tired of publishing the magazine. In 1979, Bob Albrecht, the founding editor of *Calculators/Computers* magazine, decided to cease its publication and offered the advertiser list and unpublished material to Dave. At a meeting of interested OCCE members at current *L&L* Acquisitions Editor Anita McAnear's home, it was agreed to form a new organization, the International Council for Computers in Education (ICCE), to publish the newly christened *The Computing Teacher*. Soon after, OCCE changed its name to the Northwest Council for Computer Education (NCCE).

On the new magazine, Dave continued to partner with the university, which provided space for the burgeoning nonprofit. He also enlisted his older children to help with the fulfillment duties, paying three cents per copy for affixing the mailing label and sorting as required by the post office. Membership (all subscribers to *TCT* were considered members of ICCE) and advertising revenue supported the staff.

During this time, there was another organization, the Association of Educational Data Systems that was a competitor to ICCE on some level. They published a research journal and had an annual conference, which was quite successful. In the early 1980s, however, conference attendance was down, and the organization merged with ICCE. ICCE continued to publish the journal under the title *Journal of Research on Computing in Education*.

Later in the 1980s, ICCE pursued another merger, with the International Association for Computers in Education. In 1989, the two organizations merged into the International Society for Technology in Education (ISTE). Dave continued his work as editor-in-chief, and the magazine staff expanded over the next few years. In addition, ISTE began publishing a new periodical, the *Educational IRM Quarterly*, which focused on the needs of information resource managers.

In 1995, ISTE decided to merge the *IRM* and *TCT* to create a new magazine that would serve the needs of both the classroom teachers and the IRMs, or technology coordinators, as they were beginning to be called. The new magazine was to be called *Learning & Leading with Technology*.

This was also the time that I started working on *L&L*. It sounds, reading this brief history, as if the first 20 years of *L&L* were a tumultuous time. There was a lot of change and a lot of consolidation among educational technology (ed tech) organizations, but from what I gathered from staff during those years, the changes were natural and appropriate and not full of a tremendous amount of angst. In fact, the change that worried Anita McAnear the most was the name change from *TCT* to *L&L*. She called it "scary, because we did have some name recognition with *TCT* and it was a hard transition for the old-time ICCE members."

From my perspective as an editorial assistant, it seemed to evolve just fine. The big challenge for the staff was continuing to serve the technology coordinators. This was accomplished through the creation of the For Tech Leaders column, which has morphed over the years into As I See "IT".

L&L kept plugging along, while minor changes were made to the research journal and the SIG publications. Long-time columnists Judi Harris (Mining the Internet), Fred D'Ignazio (Multimedia Sandbox), and Bob Albrecht (Power Tools for Math & Science/Starship Gaia) provided some stability to the long-term readers.

As we became more introspective as a staff, we noticed that many of our original writers, who had been maverick teachers sneaking computers into the classroom in the early days of *OCT/TCT*, were being promoted out of the classroom into leadership roles in buildings and districts. This changed ISTE's marketing strategy, as we focused on technology coordinators as our target audience. *L&L* continued to speak to the classroom teacher for the most part, with the assumption being that tech coordinators would copy and share articles with the appropriate teachers.

The makeup of the *L&L* editorial staff changed during this time, as well. In the beginning, the staff was mainly teachers and teacher educators with an aptitude for writing and editing. The newer hires tended to be professional writers and journalists with little background in the field of education. Kate Conley, who was hired by ISTE in the late 1990s, had both backgrounds, eight years of teaching experience and a master's degree in journalism.

As we neared volume 30, the changes in our readership, the field, and the staff necessitated some sweeping changes to the magazine. Some of our older columnists moved on to different ways of publishing and supporting the field, Dave Moursund parted ways with ISTE and *L&L*, and we began soliciting articles rather than using only blind manuscript submissions. We never lost our focus on the classroom teacher or the technology coordinator, but the range of voices we heard from began to broaden, as did the range of readers we served. During the five years collected here in this book, we discontinued many columns and created many new ones. *L&L* became the membership magazine, including news and articles about ISTE initiatives. Our methods for soliciting and shaping content became increasingly sophisticated.

These were exciting times in the best sense, and I look back on my time on the *L&L* staff with great pride and fondness. There were growing pains here and there, but the magazine we see now is a great testament to the passion of ISTE's leadership and staff, the writers who continue to volunteer their work to support the field, and the readers who learn from each issue and share their opinions through reader polls, discussions with their colleagues, and posts to online discussion forums and blogs. I look forward to seeing how the magazine develops in the future.

—

chapter 2

Issue Oriented

The Issue Oriented column has evolved over the years from a description of all of the articles in the magazine to a discussion of current issues and how certain articles in the magazine fit into that context. It has also become a focal point of discussion between the magazine and the readers.

This shift was made consciously as the staff tried to elicit more reader feedback and begin a lively discussion. It was great to watch the column grow and to watch Anita McAnear become more comfortable in her role as the face of the magazine. Her long-time involvement in ISTE and NECC meant she was a focal point for ISTE members, and this column gave her a tool to talk to those people outside of planning sessions and conference activities. The more she used this tool, the more Anita seemed to enjoy the opportunity.

And her enjoyment comes through in each column. In addition to highlighting discussions of the field, Anita has used her column to open the inner workings of the magazine to the reader. We shoot for a high level of transparency in technology, why not also in our ed tech sourcebooks?

We begin the articles with a call for second-order educational activities and assessments. In "The Best Defense Is a Good Offense" (April 2005), Anita discusses the unprecedented opportunities technology offers to support student learning, from differentiating instruction to engaging students through the use of tools they use in their personal lives. She ties the discussion into the theme of the issue—copyright and fair use—to help educators use the power of these tools in an appropriate manner and to model appropriate use for their students. (You'll find one of the articles discussing copyright in Chapter 4.)

We then move to discussion of another important issue in ed tech: the distribution of technology resources. Unless you are working in a

1-to-1 computing environment, you will have to grapple with differing levels of technology access in your classroom. How do you structure activities and assignments that harness technology tools while ensuring that no student is shut out of learning by lack of access to technology? Anita provides some ideas in "Equity in Practice" (April 2006).

Finally, we look at the power of emerging technologies in the classroom. Anita describes new technologies that seem magical in their ability to change learning and how they can be used for classroom activities and assignments in "The Magic of Emerging Technology" (November 2006). Many of these new tools, she points out, are free or very low in cost, allowing them to be easily integrated into classroom and at-home learning. Web tools in particular are important as students create blogs as a means of journaling about their learning, wikis to share learning among group members or classmates, and e-mail and VoIP (Voice Over Internet Protocol) to communicate with experts all around the world.

April 2005

The Best Defense Is a Good Offense

Keep the Focus on Knowledge Generation and Communication

Anita McAnear

Helping students become information seekers, synthesizers, analyzers, evaluators, innovative thinkers, problem solvers, decision makers, producers of knowledge, communicators, and collaborators is one way to create an environment that minimizes cheating, plagiarism, and copyright violations. In such an environment, you may also be able to take advantage of the tools digital natives regularly use, such as instant messaging, chat, and cell phones. As much as possible, eliminate testing of basic facts and skills and focus on helping students find and use the right tool or information source for the task at hand. You may not be able to eliminate high stakes testing, but if the school environment is focused on teaching for understanding, students should do well on any kind of test.

Projects, assignments, and lessons that get students asking questions and using the information they find to create something new, teach a concept to someone else, solve a problem, or contribute to a solution help prepare students for their futures. In such an environment, many unethical behaviors simply don't work. If the emphasis is on what you do with basic facts, then it doesn't matter if Jane asked her neighbor or used her cell phone to find out the information she needed.

Technology helps differentiate the delivery of information. If students are poor readers or not native language speakers, set them up for the text to read to them. If students can't remember their math facts, teach them to use spreadsheets to generate their own reference tables and give them a calculator, but include lots of estimating activities. Develop creative assignments with real-world connections for students to demonstrate their understanding.

Technology enables students to create their own music and art. There is a lot of wonderful music software. Is it available to your students? Do you have and use digital and video cameras as well as graphics tablets and drawing software? If students have access to tools that allow them to be creative, they are less likely to need copyrighted materials.

Technology does provide access to writing, art, music, and video that may be copyrighted. Moreover, this access is important for learning. As technology has made access and copying easier, the notion of copyright as well as attribution is increasingly important and is the responsibility of all educators. We hope this issue will clarify the fair use laws, alert you to gray-area situations that really aren't gray, and start productive conversations in your educational setting. In the inquiry-focused, knowledge-generating school environment, appropriate use should not be an uphill battle, but should be easy to emphasize and maintain.

Anita

April 2006

Equity in Practice

By Anita McAnear

Anita McAnear is L&L's acquisitions editor and national program chair for NECC. A former middle school math and language arts teacher, McAnear has been with ISTE since 1983.

You have classroom Internet access, and you have multiple digital tools and resources provided by your school district or local educational service agency. You are eager to try out and support new learning environments for students, and the necessary staff development is available.

You want students to be blogging; podcasting; researching via the Internet at home and in class; creating new knowledge by themselves and with their peers; creating digital products to communicate their knowledge; accessing your Web pages for assignments, background information, lessons, and digital resources; or possibly taking an online course. Learning can and should be 24/7. But that goal is a little difficult without 24/7 access to technology.

What if you are not involved in a one-to-one computer environment, and you know that not all of your students have access at home? What can you do that is equitable for all students?

Teachers can survey their students to see what they do have available at home. Don't limit this to a computer. But if students do have a computer, find out if they have Internet access and how many people have to share it. Do they have cell phones? If so, what features/services do they use? Do they or their parents have a PDA that no one is using? Do they have an MP3 player? Do they have a friend who lets them use his or her computer? Find out their perceived level of expertise with whatever they have. Who is a power user of their tools? Who wants to learn more? Who wouldn't mind helping a classmate with is or her technology? (Parts of this survey could be useful in wealthy schools and in one-to-one programs,

especially if students don't take the computers home.)

With this knowledge you can begin to work on solutions. As much as possible without highlighting who is a have and who is a have-not, involve your students in the solutions. Use the challenge as an opportunity to begin forging a learning community in your classroom.

You can start by enlisting students' help in finding resources—district or community organizations that refurbish and donate computers; businesses that want to donate used equipment; parents, friends, and neighbors with needed expertise; local library resources and hours; wireless hot spots in your area. Students will probably have many other ideas. If you are a middle/high school teacher, try it with just one class—perhaps your most motivated, or least.

Working out solutions will certainly take some creativity, but by now you should be armed with the knowledge you need and a great opportunity for getting to know your students. Taking advantage of the technology that students have will take some special knowledge, but most likely you can tell your students what you want to do and they can figure out how and teach you.

Administrators and tech coordinators can encourage and support teachers in these efforts at the district level. Beginning on page 15, Don Hall provides ideas for the building/district level. Teacher educators can be sure their teacher candidates are aware of equity issues and have ideas about solutions. We do all have a role to play in the equitable distribution of resources for students. We can't wait for funds to materialize for one-to-one for all students.

November 2006

The Magic of Emerging Technology

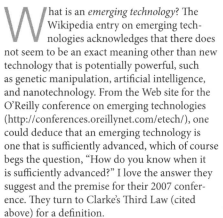

"Any sufficiently advanced technology is indistinguishable from magic."
—Arthur C. Clarke, *Profiles of the Future,* 1961

By Anita McAnear

Anita McAnear is L&L's acquisitions editor and national program chair for NECC. A former middle school math and language arts teacher, McAnear has been with ISTE since 1983.

What is an *emerging technology*? The Wikipedia entry on emerging technologies acknowledges that there does not seem to be an exact meaning other than new technology that is potentially powerful, such as genetic manipulation, artificial intelligence, and nanotechnology. From the Web site for the O'Reilly conference on emerging technologies (http://conferences.oreillynet.com/etech/), one could deduce that an emerging technology is one that is sufficiently advanced, which of course begs the question, "How do you know when it is sufficiently advanced?" I love the answer they suggest and the premise for their 2007 conference. They turn to Clarke's Third Law (cited above) for a definition.

As the O'Reilly planners classify potential speakers for their conference, they further clarify what they mean by magic: "If your magic makes complex things simple or makes the impossible possible, we want to know about it."

This makes sense to me, and I can understand this definition. Lots of technologies are magic to me, but the current show stopper is VOIP (voice over IP). That I can use Skype and my computer in Eugene, Oregon, to talk to Julie Lindsey, our curriculum specialist for ICT, in Dhaka, Bangladesh is magic. Never mind that her connection wasn't working very well; we still communicated for a few minutes before deciding that it needed to work a little better. Their system was being upgraded, and it should work much better the next time we try it.

What is emerging educational technology? This answer seems obvious: If the magic has potential for helping students learn, then it is an emerging technology. If it is also easy and transparent and cheap or free, then it is a sure-fire winner!

Happily for us, many of the new Web 2.0 tools and applications, such as blogs, wikis, audioblogs, and RSS, are just that. The tools also fit nicely with current theories on how students learn. Learning is a social activity. Student blogs can reveal student thinking and demonstrate growth over time and help with student metacognition or thinking about thinking. Wikis and blogs can help organize and manage knowledge. It is collaborative in that everyone can contribute. VOIP with or without built-in cameras can open the classroom to the world much more simply and cheaply than any previous technology.

Sometimes the learning curve is steeper with emerging technology, but it carries even greater learning rewards when students master difficult and complex concepts. I'm thinking of technologies such as Geographic Information Systems (GIS), probeware, robotics, 3D software, full-dome video (see p. 12), and serious games and simulations. Some of these technologies put real-world tools into the hands of students and allow them to work on real-world problems. Others allow them to create their own products and learn difficult concepts along the way. But they also demand knowledgeable teachers who must be able to use the tools and understand why they are magic and how the magic works. Many of these technologies are expensive, but open source software is emerging for some as well.

Our jobs are exciting but challenging. We need to be capitalizing on all these emerging technologies to make learning magic for our students and ensure that they understand that magic. ■

ISSUE ORIENTED

chapter 3
Point/Counterpoint

We created the Point/Counterpoint column to broaden discussion. With the Issue Oriented column, we had begun a discussion between the magazine and the readers. With Point/Counterpoint, we were able to foster discussion among the readers. In addition to the monthly debate, we began offering a poll on the *L&L* website. Readers could simply tick a box describing how they felt about the issue, or they could offer a description of why they came down on one side or the other. These responses were then published in a later issue—I've included the reader poll results and responses to ensure a complete picture of the issues.

First, we take a lofty perspective: the goals of K–12 education. In "Is the Goal of K–12 to Produce Employees or Learners?" (September 2006) Francis D. Head and Randy Edwards debate the seeming opposition between educational goals. This question actually came up in response to a previous Point/Counterpoint entry in which Chris Stephenson and Trudy Abramson debated whether there was still a gender gap in science, math, and technology disciplines ("Has the Gender Gap Closed?" May 2006). We noticed that in addition to their difference in opinion about whether the gender gap had closed, they also seemed to have a difference in opinion about whether education should be focusing on teaching skills related to learning or to employment. We then asked Francis and Randy to elaborate on this issue. They brought up important points about how the U.S. job market is stunted because of the lack of prepared workers and about the danger of vocational tracking of students in an educational system focused on employability. Readers came down vehemently in support of creating learners in the poll, but in the responses, a few readers pointed out the false dichotomy of the question. When we set up the Point/Counterpoint column, we knew that in most cases, the real answer would be somewhere in the middle. We believed strongly in the value of the discussions, and Point/Counterpoint generated more reader feedback than we had ever received before.

In our next debate, June Atkinson and Ruth Reynard discuss "Is It Time for a National Student Tracking System?" (May 2007). This topic comes up often in the literature about the education of children of migrant workers. A tracking system could keep such students from being lost in the system as they travel from area to area. In the context in which June and Ruth discussed it, a tracking system could be used to help educators assess their effectiveness in preparing students for higher education and the workforce. The reader response was evenly split. One of the great parts of these debates is the level of discourse that happens. In many debates, you will find responses that use only the arguments given in the original debate. However, the responses from *L&L* readers take the debate farther, exhibiting well-reasoned arguments and individual concerns. June discussed a project in her state that was helping all schools ensure that they were meeting the same high standards. And Ruth pointed out the dangers inherent in focusing only on easily tracked data such as standardized test scores. Reader responses brought new issues to the table, including the costs of such systems and the loss of local and state control over educational outcomes.

The final debate highlighted here centers on chat shortcuts ("Is Chatspeak Destroying English?" November 2007). Whenever we see a new development in technology, we inevitably see debate over whether it is a sign of the endtimes or the next big thing. *L&L* readers have debated whether social media and cell phones are useful tools within education. The influence of chatspeak on spoken and written English has happened very fast, maybe because we seem to be in a time of compressed change or maybe because it is such a boon to fast communication. It has shown up in advertising and mainstream media, not just tech-specific media. And, teachers are seeing students using it in settings when more formal language might be a better choice. Linda Howard argues against reliance on chatspeak in educational settings, pointing out that the increasing reliance on shortcuts and acronyms have no place in academic or business writing. Linda fears that students will not be able to separate their common parlance from their professional requirements and thus they will experience failures and disappointments in higher education and the workplace. Greg Monfils argued on the other side, reminding fellow educators of the ease with which students shift between languages, be they foreign languages, such as Spanish or German, or different written languages for different contexts. Readers overwhelmingly believed that the English language is safe from the onslaught of chatspeak, focusing on the power of harnessing new modes of communication as a means to enrich ourselves and engage our students.

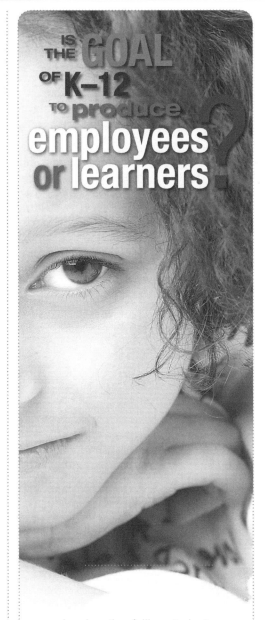

Is education failing students if it doesn't produce enough graduates willing to enter science, technology, engineering, and mathematics fields?

POINT/COUNTERPOINT

Employees

The modern workplace demands employees with a high degree of technical comprehension. We have a responsibility to prepare our students to enter the working world as technically capable employees. In the 1950s, most high school graduates did not go to college and could still find gainful employment. They went into the world with confidence, knowing that their diploma was backed with the skills required for a successful transition into the workforce. Today, our high school graduates enter the job market unprepared to meet the needs of our modern workplace. Many of these deficiencies relate to science, technology, engineering, and math (STEM), areas of learning most marketable for today's employers.

Today's international workplace requires the United States to compete with countries around the globe for employee placement. In math and sci-

By Francis D. Head

Learners

The goal of public education in the United States is to create well-rounded citizens, not to function as an institution of job training. To focus public education on workplace skill shortages is to deny the idealism of our Constitution and founding fathers, to shortchange our youth, and ultimately, ourselves. While some countries, Germany for example, send students into vocational and college-prep tracks, we in the United States have resisted that approach and have taken a more egalitarian tact.

A huge attraction of the United States is the idea that you can become anything. In that sense, public education works as an equalizer, toning down class differences and mitigating the impact of poverty. A broad education creates the *potential* for a child raised in poverty (and according to UNICEF, that's more than 22% of U.S. children) to rise to the highest heights. Thomas Jefferson wrote of public education, "[We proposed

By Randy Edwards

Continued

Continued

ence, our fourth graders are among the best in the world. By the time these students get to the eighth grade, they are in the middle. By 12th grade, these students are at the bottom compared to those from other industrial nations of the world. At the same time, the U.S. General Accountability Office reports that STEM-related jobs have increased by 23%. As the number of technical jobs increases, the number of high school graduates prepared to work in these fields decreases. The deficit seems to be filled by either exporting jobs or importing workers.

There is an argument in education that we should be developing learners and not employees, but it seems that we are not doing an adequate job of creating either. According to an ACT report, *Crisis at the Core: Preparing All Students for College and Work*, in 2004 only 22% of the 1.2 million ACT-tested graduates met all three of the ACT College Readiness Benchmarks in English, math, and science. When a student receives a high school diploma in the United States, it should come with the confidence that the graduate is prepared to enter either the workplace or college.

The argument that schools should ignore workforce needs also is not valid because the two are not mutually exclusive. Preparing students to enter the workplace in STEM fields involves substantial learning capabilities. If students continue to college, they are better able to meet the requirements of secondary education and hold meaningful jobs while in college. These skills, combined with the specialization of their college courses, prepares them even better for their chosen career. Take accounting, for example. A high degree of computer literacy is required whether you are

Today, our high school graduates enter the job market unprepared to meet the needs of our modern workplace.

an accounting clerk with a high school diploma or an accountant with a college degree.

The main point here is that by preparing students to graduate with substantial skills in science, technology, engineering, and math, we are providing them with the edge they need for success in life. Ultimately we are preparing them for life, and by having those STEM skills they are ready for the journey.

Francis D. Head is the technology coordinator for St. John the Evangelist Catholic School in Hapeville, Georgia. He is responsible for technology infrastructure and collaborative teaching. After 15 years in the corporate workplace, he transitioned to education and is currently pursuing a master of education degree in instructional technology.

---

a plan] to avail the commonwealth of those talents and virtues which nature has sown as liberally among the poor as rich, and which are lost to their country by the want of means for their cultivation."

If public education focused heavily on vocational training and workplace skills, would it provide those skills equally to rich and poor alike? Of course not—the vocational aspects will be heavily skewed toward poorer students and schools. Would schools be able to fund such skills programs and keep them current in our dynamic economy? That's iffy at best.

If we were to train students for workplace skills, what sort of jobs and skills? Economist, former assistant U.S. Treasury secretary, and *Wall Street Journal* editor Paul Craig Roberts has written extensively about the U.S. job market. He reports that based on U.S. Labor Department statistics, the vast majority of job growth (72% in April) is in domestic services. Month after month, the leading job-growth areas are in fields like bartending, waitressing, other low-paying service jobs, and nursing. That's the reality of new jobs today. Do we really want our schools focused on training workplace skills for those jobs?

In advanced technology industries, Roberts reports that the United States now imports more technology than it exports. Ask anyone in commercial tech fields to summarize the past few years from a jobs perspective and their report is likely to be depressing.

So how can schools best prepare and encourage students for STEM careers?

We must prepare students by giving them a broad background of knowledge, with a heavy emphasis on fundamentals. We need to teach students to think, to research, and to be *critical*

A broad education creates the *potential* for a child raised in poverty (and according to UNICEF, that's more than 22% of U.S. children) to rise to the highest heights.

thinkers. We need to nurture their inquisitiveness. By focusing on this, we will create citizens that can adapt to any future job market.

And those "business skills" that I keep hearing so much about? Well, employers will have to do what they've always done—pay to train their workers. We should not allow that cost of doing business to be socialized, to burden the taxpayer, and to detract from our schools' primary goal.

Randy Edwards is a computer consultant and a former computer science professor who has taught about computers and the social sciences in public and private schools. He has worked in both the commercial software industry and in Ed Tech positions ranging from a district technology coordinator to a college director of technology.

November 2006

READERS respond

Employees 22%

78% Learners

Is the Goal of K–12 to Produce Employees or Learners?

More than 75% of those who responded agree that the goal of K–12 is to produce lifetime learners who can adjust to the ever-changing workplace.

Create Fearless Learners

Our job today is to produce eager and adaptable learners. Since we can only blindly try to predict the jobs that will be available to our students 12 years from now, we must focus on producing fearless students who are able to quickly learn the skills necessary for whatever task is presented to them.

Mary Catton
American Academy Charter School
Lone Tree, Colorado

Produce Employees

The United States is the only industrialized nation in the world completely dependent on immigration to fill jobs in science and technology. One reason is the U.S. K–12 philosophy: focus on students merely meeting minimum graduation requirements rather than providing the SciTech skills needed to succeed in today's global economy.

Bjorn Norstrom
Colchester Middle School
Colchester, Vermont

Yes to Both

K–12 Education should prepare students to be successful employees and successful learners. However, the goal of preparing students to be lifelong learners is of greatest benefit and is the more sustainable skill. In times of change—and we are in times of change—the learning, not the learned, inherit the earth. A learner can learn to be a successful employee, but an employee who is

not a learner will not be a successful employee long.

Don Knezek
ISTE
Washington, DC

Manage the Gap

Our job is to help students learn to manage the gap between what they know and what they need to know. Ethically, we can do nothing less when the half-life of what we've learned decreases continually. If we do not develop learners, we will not develop employable people.

Dorothy Fuller
Black Hills State University
Spearfish, South Dakota

Neither Is the Primary Goal

Employability and the ability to learn are both admirable, yet neither should be the primary goal of K–12 education. Rather, the goal should be to educate 21st century citizens who have the intellectual, digital, and social skills that promote an ethical and humane stewardship of their local and global communities while enhancing the quality of life, liberty, and pursuit of happiness for all.

Joe Gotchy
Teacher/Consultant
Auburn, Washington

Remember the Mantra

The over-used mantra "lifelong learners" will always be the key for education. Business tells educators that they plan on retraining 90% of their work force upon hiring. Our students will

serve six different employers, on average. They must be learning-efficient to be successful professionally, socially, and personally.

Howard J. Martin
Austin Independent School District
Austin, Texas

If You Had to Choose

In which would you want to confidently place our economic future? Employees that are capable of continuous learning are essential for the survival of the ever-changing marketplace and for the security of the standard of living we sustain in the United States.

Martha Kennelly
Mid East Suffolk Teacher Center
Ridge, New York

Times Are Changing

As long as the world doesn't change, producing employees would be adequate. Producing learners, however, provides employers with the human resources to meet their changing needs.

Timothy P. Williams
Manheim Township School District
Lancaster, Pennsylvania

Let Students Decide

The goal is to educate the whole child ultimately empowering them to choose the world of work or pursue academic studies. It is not about limiting their options during the K–12 years, but teaching skills to find success in whatever they choose.

Emmy Hartney
St. John the Baptist Middle School
Draper, Utah

May 2007

Is It Time for a National Student Tracking System?

In recent testimony before Congress, Bill Gates called for a Center for State Education Data to aggregate information on student achievement. However, given the differences in students' socio-economic situations across the United States, as well as varying curriculum and academic standards across districts, is a national system to track academic progress feasible?

Yes

The growing debate around the creation of a national system for the secure exchange of key education data has far-reaching implications for PK–20 educators. Although some view this as an educational issue, in North Carolina, we view data access as an economic issue. *Tough Choices or Tough Times*, by the National Commission on Education and the Economy, reports that in the last 30 years the cost to educate each student has increased 240%, yet student achievement levels remain about the same. The cost of education in the United States ranks second highest in the world, yet we have one of the highest dropout rates. The commission's authors caution, "The problem is not with our educators. It is with the system in which they work."

Our ultimate goal is much broader than simply tracking students. The PK–20 education entities in North Carolina recently embarked on an important project, called the *NC Education Insight Project*, that includes access to student data

June Atkinson

No

Tracking might be helpful when crises strike, as an efficient way to access some information for placing students. This is all it is, however: a simple administrative support. What typically happens, once any sort of student tracking is introduced, is that it is used to definitely reflect student achievement. Educational success is complex to track when done well. If we remove the complexity and opt for a clean and fast system, we miss the point of education completely, and we end up marginalizing more students than we help.

Learning is ongoing and can never be reflected in a simple grade or any kind of simplistic data system. Socioeconomic status, learning style, age, gender, race, language, and other factors have long been recognized in educational research as important variables in anyone's learning progress. Why do we insist on finding a simple solution to a complex issue?

Although there is a certain practicality about keeping records of students—who they are, where they live, and

Ruth Reynard

Continued

across three systems. We want a system that leverages our existing databases and allows North Carolina's PK–20 educators to eliminate information silos, integrate and analyze data, and make informed decisions about programs and practices that will prepare students to be more productive citizens in the 21st century. To evaluate performance of graduates in the workplace, our *NC Education Insight Project* will also include relevant data from the Employment Security Commission and the NC Board of Nursing. These additional data will allow us to assess the performance and success of graduates as they leave the system.

The initial outcome will be unprecedented insight into two areas in which North Carolina is currently experiencing critical shortages: teaching and nursing. The North Carolina Department of Public Instruction (NCDPI), the North Carolina Community College System (NCCCS), and the University of North Carolina General Administration (UNCGA) can determine which policy initiatives show the best evidence of increasing student achievement, optimize performance in each system, and enhance operational efficiency statewide. Security and privacy are key concerns. Authorized personnel will be granted access to data based on assigned permissions and state and federal guidelines.

The *NC Education Insight Project* will clearly lead to an unprecedented level of informed decision making among educational entities in North Carolina, but a number of important questions can only be answered if we ultimately have access to a nationwide data system: Are our students academically prepared to enter schools and colleges in other states or do they need remediation? How do our teachers perform when they enter the workforce in other states? What happens to students who leave the state? Will displaced students be counted as dropouts? Which higher education programs are producing the most effective teachers?

Our initiative began with a collective decision by leaders at NCDPI, NCCCS, and UNCGA. Rather than working alone, they optimized performance of the state PK–20 system by locking arms, leveraging federal reporting requirements, and working collaboratively to find answers and gain insight that will benefit the state's students throughout their education—and beyond. This effort will only be complete when we can integrate data from other states in a national system. Now is the time!

June St. Clair Atkinson is the North Carolina State Superintendent of Public Instruction. She received a doctorate in Educational Leadership and Policy from North Carolina State University in 1996, and has made presentations to business and other educational groups in 43 states.

other personal demographics as well as reporting on their progress through school—where is the connection with evidence of learning? These are very different objectives. The reality is that teachers are driven by standardized tests, which only tell us how students respond to and take tests, not what they know.

Tests tell us how those students who have a similar way of knowing to the test maker can respond to or take the test. Other students with differing learning styles remain marginalized. Preparing students for tests also does not ensure learning is taking place—only information exchange, organization, and memorization. Measuring learning is a very different objective and must be based on measurable learning outcomes.

Once the course work and various learning options have been covered, the student must produce something—a project, a paper, a presentation, a skill demonstration, a construction of some sort, or a portfolio—to show that learning has taken place. All of the learning must be integrated into the final product or products. How can a test ever be a production of student learning? Students do not create tests; teachers and administrators do.

If test results are the only way in which student learning is tracked for administrative purposes, then nothing is known about the actual learning taking place. Additionally, if the tracking data are used to either progress or remediate a student, then the student falls victim to a faulty and biased process. For example, if groups of students perform similarly on a standardized test, then the test also becomes discriminatory. That is, there may be groups of students who are badly resourced in a particular area, and all would perform poorly in a standardized test. The tracking then shows those students as a group doing badly. Decisions made from this biased data will result in whole groups of students being marginalized and labeled. At this point, the result of tracking is far from accurate or helpful.

Although student tracking may provide some administrative help, those data should not be used to tabulate student progress or predict student achievement unless those data also include various forms of reporting from teachers in a more holistic manner. That is, if teachers can include data from various demonstrations of learning by students, then those data can be analyzed for educational purposes. Without that level of complexity, numbers mean nothing.

Ruth Reynard holds a PhD in curriculum, teaching and learning from the Ontario Institute for Studies in Education, University of Toronto. She was an associate professor of education for almost eight years. Currently she is director of faculty for Career Education Corporation in Illinois.

September/October 2007

READERS respond

POLL RESULTS

Is It Time for a National Student Tracking System?

Poll takers and those who sent letters were evenly divided on this issue. Variations in state educational systems and costs topped the list of concerns.

No 49% Yes 51%

Has To Happen Eventually

Digital technologies are decreasing the importance of geography as an educational constraint. Increased family mobility is causing stresses on inter-district sharing of student contact and academic learning information. We are going to have to confront this issue sometime. Why not sooner rather than later?

Scott McLeod
CASTLE, Iowa State University
Ames, Iowa

Cost Is Too Great

What will it cost and what are the benefits? If the benefits don't outweigh the costs, it should not be done. Many of us have experienced the implementation of statewide identifiers for student tracking and probably would agree that the benefits do outweigh the costs. However, in a national system of tracking where you don't have uniform curriculum, uniform laws governing education etc., etc., the cost/benefit relationship gets considerably skewed to the cost side. Not worth it—yet!

James H. Dillon, Jr.
Cranston Public Schools
Cranston, Rhode Island

Would Be Beneficial

A secure national student tracking system would have a great deal of benefits, including the ability to illustrate to the nation the true need for additional funding and intervention, particularly in overcrowded, rural, and low-socioeconomic schools, and aid teachers and schools in accessing specific performance data for transfer students.

Ashlee Copper
Ketchikan Charter School
Ketchikan, Alaska

Weakens State Control

No, the complexities due to the variation of all the states educational systems would be too difficult to organize without a huge expense. Also each state has different state assessments, and criteria. Not all schools have the technology to establish and contribute to such a system. Much national standardization would need to be done, and states would feel that their rights would be weakened too much.

Karl Sprenger
Penn State University INSYS Department
University Park, Pennsylvania

Time To Standardize

It is simply time to standardize, as a nation, the results we expect students to achieve, the standards we expect teachers to relay, and the plethora of consistent tests we need to follow in measuring student achievement. A simple yet optionally complex and report-generating national database is absolutely necessary.

Douglas Belk
Mississippi Educational Computing Association
Pascagoula, Massachusetts

Will Only Label Students

No! Enough is enough! All we do anymore is teach to the test. And if you don't do well enough on the test, you get a label and a plan to fix your problem. Who decides I have a problem? Does it matter if I'm happy? Have you taught me anything I WANTED to learn? No, tracking is a way of providing a label to children, a label they don't need. Bring back recess!!

Steve Martin
Newberry County School District
Newberry, South Carolina

Time Is Being Wasted

Absolutely! We're wasting valuable hours creating a system internally that should be standardized across the board to accommodate students transferring from and to schools from around the country. Some might feel that Big Brother is watching—He is! So, why not give us access to the information he already knows?

Jeremy Shorr
Aurora City Schools
Aurora, Ohio

POINT/COUNTERPOINT

Is Chatspeak Destroying English?

Yes

When students are thoroughly immersed in the culture of instant messaging, meaningful written expression may be hindered because their mindset is that of the shared culture of other students, and the common language is chatspeak, not traditional English. Chatspeak is destroying students' command of written English, in the sense that whatever we engage in for a long period of time will most likely become commonplace.

I am concerned whether students are learning the skills to fully express themselves through writing as they move toward adulthood. Every generation has something that is uniquely their own, and that is wonderful; however, a time comes when we all have to grow and evolve into our true character, and many young people will have a difficult time drawing the line between acceptable and unacceptable dialogue in everyday life, especially in written communications. Good writing skills are essential as high

Linda Howard

No

A student of mine recently asked via e-mail, "hey, i cant find hw n the conf can u help." I did. Shortly thereafter, she wrote a lovely paper devoid of chatspeak.

The kids know the difference. I strongly suspect, based on my experience at a laptop school where kids communicate with each other and with their teachers in chatspeak, that their subversion of standardized English has no appreciable effect on their command of written English. They codeswitch. Nor do I believe that their command of written English would *increase* appreciably if they would only *forego* chatspeak and strive to exhibit a command of written English at all times.

They know the difference. Indeed, I'd go so far as to say that their command of chatspeak is directly proportional to their awareness that the fashion of chatspeak subverts traditional rules of written English. They know the difference and it's fun for them when we get aggravated and act as if they *don't* know.

Greg Monfils

Continued

Continued

school students go on to college in traditional settings or online, and they will need to fully express their opinions and expound on subject matter in a way that compels them to think and engage with others on a deeper level.

The shortcuts and acronyms that make instant messaging, text messaging, and online chatting so popular have no place in academic, business, and other formal writing settings where it is essential that all individuals involved are using language that is clear and concise. Students may very well become so familiar and comfortable with chatspeak that it will be difficult to switch gears and construct adequate, meaningful academic papers and other assignments. It is one thing to use the vernacular that is common to a particular micro society, but at some point, students must know when it is time to alter written communications so that their

For most students, the reality of the larger society that they share with others may not come until they have had disappointments in higher education and job interviews.

words are understood by all who read them. We may have different sets of linguistic conventions according to our ethnicity, family, friends, and our work and school communities, but at some point it is time to realize that the English language must be used effectively to understand and to be understood. When it comes to students and their use of chatspeak, it will be more difficult for many to switch gears to effective and meaningful writing. For most students, the reality of the larger society that they share with others may not come until they have had disappointments in higher education and job interviews. The shortcuts of

chatspeak are a welcome convenience when keying data into the cell phone or online chat rooms, but they have no place in the larger society, where effective writing skills are a must. My main concern is that students, especially those needing to polish their writing skills, will hinder their writing abilities to the point that they will be adversely affected when faced with the task of providing meaningful written elaboration.

Linda Howard earned a BS in Information Technology from the University of Phoenix Online, and is presently working toward her MS in Education from Capella University with a concentration in Instructional Design for Online Learning.

But we *should* know that they know. After all, we teach them different languages all the time. We don't fear that a Spanish class will diminish a student's command of English. And a teenager experimenting with a sprinkling of profanities in her conversation with peers will not suddenly forget how to converse properly with her grandmother.

The Urban School of San Francisco, where I work, is a laptop school. Every kid gets one upon enrolling at Urban. The entire community communicates through e-mail quite a bit. As an English teacher, I get homework questions and other concerns. These e-mails are often written in appalling chatspeak filled with shortcuts, neologisms, inelegance, and mistakes. But they are more than sufficiently communicative.

Do I find chatspeak inelegant, even annoying to the point of aggravation? Sure, sometimes, but that makes it all the more attractive to teens who,

We don't fear that a Spanish class will diminish a student's command of English.

by any means at their disposal, will codeswitch to create a private language that excludes members of my generation who will most likely find their code aesthetically wanting. And to the extent that we rail against it, well, that makes it even more attractive to kids.

Yes, we've standardized grammar, spelling, and so on since Chaucer, but kids live to challenge standards. It doesn't mean that they don't know what the standards are. As in most things, they will drop their petty rebellions and attend to the standards in time. If we're lucky, they'll provided a few sensible updates to the standards as they charmingly mature into adulthood.

If chatspeak is leeching into papers, it's probably due to a small bit of re-

belliousness as opposed to obliviousness. The kids want to see if they can get away with it and, perhaps, help to make a change in something so drily traditional as spelling.

And for that matter, why shouldn't "you" be spelled "u"? We don't spell "I" "aye" or "eye," do we? We could also agree to spell "eye" "I." If you agree, you might say, "I I." And I know no reason why we don't spell "know" "no." Indeed, Word wouldn't let me spell "know" as "no" in the third word of the last sentence.

But yeah, substituting numbers 4 words is really annoying.

Greg Monfils is the Freshman/Sophomore Academic Dean for the Urban School of San Francisco, where he also teaches English. He has taught English and history in middle school and high school for 15 years.

February 2008

READERS respond

L&L wants your opinion!
Send comments to letters@iste.org.
Participate in our monthly reader poll at
http://www.iste.org/LL.

POLL RESULTS

Is Chatspeak Destroying English?

Poll results and comments suggest that most feel
chatspeak is not destroying English

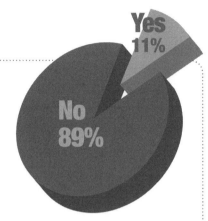

No More Than Rock 'N' Roll

The fact that modern digital communicants utilize chatspeak is no more destroying English than rock 'n' roll destroyed music (though rap may yet—LOL). Savvy humans nuance their language style according to its effectiveness, and I'd wager that formal English will always have its place (Probs).

Scott Merrick
University School of Nashville and
Vanderbilt Center for Science Outreach
Nashville, Tennessee

Chatspeak Enriches the Language

The English language, like any other, is subject to evolution caused by movements of people and now communications technology. There are about 540 million words in the English language, about five times the number that Shakespeare had to work with. Semantic compression has been a useful tool for Latin (et al.), modern English (etc.), Morse code (SOS), and cell phones (c u l8r). Does this destroy language? No, it enriches it, allowing it to adapt to the spirit of the times.

Graham Brown-Martin
Handheld Learning
London, England

Language Is Always Evolving

No, chatspeak is part of the evolution of the English language. It is facilitating better communication through a more succinct use of words. A new tool, Twitter.com, is a form of chatspeak where a message is delivered in 140 characters. Consider also the international perspective of what correct

English is. Already, different forms of English are accepted throughout the world; therefore, chatspeak can be considered an alternative way of communicating that identifies the user with their friendship and peer group.

Julie Lindsay
Qatar Academy
Doha, State of Qatar

Makes Me LOL

OMG, evry genRAshun goes thru dis cuz da oldies don get it—hipEEz, valEE girlz, hIp HoP n ebonics, n now chatspk. All deez thangs R reking english but iTz StILl hErE cuz U hafta no it fer skool n jobz

Scott Laleman
Schertz-Cibolo-Universal City ISD
Schertz, Texas

It Can Be Used Inappropriately

The problem with chatspeak is that students do NOT know when to code switch as Mr. Monfils talked about (Point/Counterpoint, Nov. 2007, pp. 8–9). Students have a hard enough time getting focused on writing—chatspeak only adds to the detritus that has to be shaken out of the rough drafts, which students are loathe to do unless under extreme duress.

Bonnie Maye
El Segundo Middle School
El Segundo, California

Consider Chatspeak a Useful Tool

I believe that text-messaging has proven itself a powerful tool in unifying many factions in a diverse population. The use or nonuse of social networking tools does not pose a degradation

of English skills, and does in fact increase student interest in written communication.

Karon Tarver
Fort Worth ISD
Fort Worth, Texas

Chatspeak May Be Counterproductive

When e-mailing friends, chatspeak, aka netspeak, helps to write more quickly. But I started with good writing and grammar skills. I believe that chatspeak undermines the kinds of writing we are teaching in schools that is being tested on high-stakes tests.

Esther Bobowick
Cooperative Educational Services
Trumbull, Connecticut

Formal Language Will Survive

Chatspeak is not destroying the English language. Younger generations may use it for simple e-mails, instant messaging, or texting, but that's about it. When it comes to the real world, businesses are not going to allow chatspeak in formal writings and documents. Chatspeak is also derived from Leetspeak, which originated in the mid '90s on IRC (Internet Relay Chat) servers. This has been around for 20 years and it will remain commonplace for small messaging.

Jason Roussin
Windsor C-1 School District
Imperial, Montana

Features

The feature well, as this section of the magazine is called, is the life-blood of the magazine, the place where authors present new pedagogy, discuss the current state of ed tech, and provide systemic looks at projects. It is where the true leading takes place, as the best and brightest in the field share their expertise with the readers.

It is also the place where the staff spends a tremendous amount of time planning for ideas, helping authors achieve their goals, and ensuring that pieces fit together in a cohesive whole and that all stakeholders are being served. And finally, it is the place that allows the most freedom. Although each article is part of a larger puzzle, it is also able to stand on its own. Because of that, these are the articles that are most discussed in the field and most shared through course packets and magazine swapping.

I am proud to see articles from *L&L* show up on resource lists, syllabi, and blogs. Our authors really are shaping thought on ed tech issues and ensuring that future educators learn from their successes and missteps.

In our first article, Robert Kadel helps all educators better understand how they can use the data they are already mining to show the successes of their various educational interventions ("Statistics for Success," March 2004). Rob's article came at the perfect time. At the beginning of the No Child Left Behind (NCLB) era, schools were being pressured to use data-driven decision making and prove the effectiveness of all educational interventions without a tremendous amount of preparation and guidance. But many classroom teachers had little to no experience analyzing data and discussing statistics. Rob took a scary topic and made it accessible by even the most math-phobic teacher. He used real-world examples to show the data that was already being generated in classrooms and described how to use Excel, which was installed on nearly all computers in schools, to analyze it.

Based on the success with which he demystified the topic, we asked Rob to become the Research Windows columnist, a post he held until 2008. And though we are still heavily embedded in the NCLB era, much has changed since this article was first published, and Rob provides a nice overview of the changes in his author's update.

We then move to a two-part series in which Mike Ribble, Gerald Bailey, and Tweed Ross provide a framework for teaching ethics in a technology-enhanced world ("Digital Citizenship," parts 1 and 2, September and October 2004). This series was one of the first that specifically addressed what was then NETS•S 2, Social, Ethical, and Human Issues (it is now NETS•S 5, Digital Citizenship). The framework made it easy for teachers to provide students with an ethical compass to inform their decisions regarding technology use. One of the most important points in the first article is the need to model appropriate use. How many of us grew up with parents who had a "do as I say, not as I do" attitude toward discipline? And how well did that work? It certainly did not work for me, and I know that it would not work with today's kids! Really, how can we expect our students not to engage in cyberbullying behavior when a quick Google search could reveal the nasty flame wars we have gotten involved in? By practicing ethical uses of technology, we prove that the behavior we are asking students to engage in is possible and desirable. The second article is very practical, with Mike and Gerald providing guiding questions to help students discuss specific ethical situations and come up with their own answers. Mike and Gerald later wrote a book on digital citizenship, *Digital Citizenship in Schools*, which ISTE published in 2007. Through this work, they made some adjustments to the framework, which they describe in their authors' update.

The next article was a long time coming. We had been hoping to feature copyright issues for years, but we had a hard time finding the right authors with the right combination of expertise. We decided to host a theme issue on the topic, with articles covering different aspects. In "Are You the Copy Cop?" (April 2005), Doug Johnson and Carol Simpson describe common violations of fair use in educational settings, giving the all-important why they happen and how to prevent them. The discussion of the "whys" was particularly interesting to me, and as I read the article, I thought back to my own years in school and how many fair use violations I had witnessed, even though my teachers would never have thought they were violating copyright regulations—so many gray areas exist in fair use. This article has been a staple of course packets and fair use resource lists since its initial publication. And, in that time, the "copyleft" movement has affected current thought on fair use, making Doug change his opinion about copyright and fair use. His author's update describes resources to further the discussion of fair use and the classroom in an open source era. However, there has been no change in legal precedent regarding fair use, which Carol points out in her author's update. This debate has been the most exciting thing I've come across in compiling this collection, and I hope to watch the discussion continue to evolve.

We move next to a discussion of how to use electronic means to foster home–school communication ("Get the Word Out with List Servers," Laurence Goldberg, February 2006). This article is part of *L&L's* focus on technology coordinators and on the ways technology can ease the burden of administrative tasks. There is more to a school than just the classroom, after all. And the vast amounts of paper generated, from permission forms to report cards, leave a lot of room for items to get lost either on their way home in a backpack or at home before they can be signed and returned. Laurence describes the process his district went through as they shifted from paper to e-mail to communicate. Of particular interest is the system they chose to handle list updates, bouncebacks and opt-outs, which if not done right, can be more time- and resource-intensive than the paper methods. Reader Alison Statton said in a letter to the editor that she was "inspired and enlightened" by this and other articles in this issue. In his author's update, Laurence provides a little more context and some guidance in selecting the proper format for your communication with parents and guardians.

We travel back to the classroom to deal with an issue that has seemed even more prevalent in the Internet age: plagiarism ("Avoid the Plague: Tips and Tricks for Preventing and Detecting Plagiarism," J.V. Bolkan, March 2006). But plagiarism existed before the Internet, and it will continue to exist after we laugh at the primitive nature of the Internet as it exists now. Jeff addresses these concerns and gives real-world examples of how teachers are addressing them through technological means and through simply teaching ethical computer behaviors and crafting assignments that do not lend themselves to easy plagiarism. The focus on assignment generation is the most important idea presented. A good assignment with a narrow focus makes it harder for students to find previously written papers on a topic, requiring multiple methods of presentation (paper, multimedia presentations, oral reports, etc.), which adds another layer of prevention.

When the *L&L* staff got the chance to visit new school sites in the Eugene, Oregon, District 4J, we learned a lot about the differences between building a school for current and future technology and retrofitting old buildings to include technology ("Designing the New School," J.V. Bolkan, Jennifer Roland, and Davis N. Smith, April 2006). In particular, the level of research and planning into every aspect of the buildings to improve student learning was amazing. In addition to a wireless technology infrastructure and ready access to computers, projectors, and other necessary technology tools, the architects and educators involved used research on appropriate lighting, acoustics, and classroom design in their blueprints. It was very interesting to see schools built to incorporate so many of the elements *L&L* authors had been advocating all these years. The lessons learned in the two school buildings profiled in the article were presented to help other school systems plan their own building projects.

Our next article elevates the discussion of technology use and explores the long-term effects on students and on the structure of our society ("Social Justice: Choice or Necessity," Colleen Swain and Dave Edyburn, March 2007). The authors take a completely novel approach to assessing technology use, arguing that by choosing not to use technology or not to progress to higher-order uses, teachers put their students at a lifelong disadvantage by failing to prepare them for a technology-based world of higher education and work. The true digital divide, Colleen and Dave argue, is not in access but in application. To illuminate their argument, they use examples of technology use that would have been considered perfectly acceptable when computers were first being used in classrooms. The computers were rewards for students who were farther ahead, and programs that provided intellectual stimulation to gifted students were often the only time the classroom computers were turned on and used. However, it is now obvious that these uses of computers reinforce the status quo and increase the divide between the haves and the have-nots. Colleen and Dave offer tools to help teachers ensure that technology integration in their classrooms is equal and helps all students further their education. This article generated some really interesting discussions on blogs, with many readers relating the arguments to their own experiences in higher education. In particular, blogger Laura Sugano discusses her return to college after years in the workforce and how behind she was in terms of technology skills. Those experiences inform her day-to-day classroom practice and highlight the importance of appropriate use of technology with her students.

The final feature article describes emerging technology tools designed to support creative expression and higher-order thinking in the context of the core content areas ("Sowing the Seeds of a More Creative Society," Mitchel Resnick, December 2007–January 2008). Many recent U.S. educational reforms have been targeted at improving students' performance in core areas (math, science, reading) in relation to other countries in the world. In fact, many writers in *L&L* over the years have bemoaned the lack of science and technology education in the United States. But the renewed focus on achieving national standards and satisfactory educational progress has left behind the need for students to develop critical-thinking and lifelong-learning skills so they can adapt to the constant changes in our society. The tools Mitchel describes allow teachers to fulfill their responsibilities to prepare students for standardized tests, while also fulfilling their personal obligation to create learners, not just workers.

March 2004

Statistics for Success

Statistical analysis of student data is a lot easier than you think and more useful than you imagine.

By Robert Kadel

Subject: Assessment, data-driven decision making

Audience: Teachers, teacher educators, technology facilitators, staff developers

Grade Level: K–12 (Ages 5–18)

Technology: Spreadsheets

Standards: *NETS•T* IV (http://www.iste.org/standards/)

To her surprise, Ms. Logan had just conducted a statistical analysis of her 10th grade biology students' quiz scores. The results indicated that she needed to reinforce mitosis before the students took the high-school proficiency test in three weeks, as required by the state. "Oh! That's easy!" She exclaimed.

Teachers like Ms. Logan are everywhere. You may be a lot like her yourself—you have lots of data on your students: quiz scores, homework grades, attendance records, and so on—but aside from reporting such information to your school, you don't know what else to do with it.

But conduct a statistical analysis? Why in the world would you want to do something like that? Well, aside from making you the life of staff par-

ties, you might be surprised at just how much you can help yourself and your students with some simple statistical procedures. Using statistics to look at student data can help you to prioritize your time and energy, give you a picture of student progress, and allow you to understand the relationships between, say, attendance and achievement or homework completion and achievement.

Statistics do not have to be the big, bad monster you may have thought of when faced with the course in college. The basic concepts are simple. Student quiz scores are data; the class average on a quiz is a statistic. Consider what you would learn if you had class averages on six quizzes covering six different topics. This information could tell you where your students

Continued

Continued

are doing well and where they need remediation.

Furthermore, suppose you have two classes of students, where one class is using new software in addition to the textbook for exploring science concepts while the other class is using just the textbook. Calculating the quiz averages across six different topics for *each* class can help you discover areas where the software is more effective and where it is not.

That said, we can now turn to using Excel to take on just this type of analysis. You can use other spreadsheet programs; most work very similarly to Excel. Figure 1 shows a simple, sample grade book: 12 students' scores for six different quizzes in a high school biology class. Of course, the concept works for virtually any curricular area.

First, let's consider average quiz scores. Click to highlight the box (a.k.a. a "cell") at the bottom of Column B, the column of numbers labeled "Intro & Scientific Method." Then click the "Paste Function" button (it has *fx* on it). A dialog box opens that says "Paste Function." In that box, click "Statistical" on the left, and then click "AVERAGE" on the right. Then click "OK."

Because you clicked in the cell at the bottom of Column B, Excel automatically assumes that you want to find the average of the numbers above it. That's why it puts B2:B13 in the "Number 1" blank. Note that cell B1 has the heading, the name of the quiz.

You can change this either by typing new cell references, such as B2:B11, to get the average for just the first 10 students, or C2:C13 to get the average score for the quiz on Spontaneous Generation Theory. Finally, click "OK" calculate the average quiz score. (In this case, 84.16667.)

Now here's the really easy part. Move your mouse so that the cursor

hovers over the lower-right corner of the cell that shows the average quiz score. The cursor will turn into a plus sign (Figure 2). This means that you should click-and-drag the cursor to the right until you've highlighted all the cells at the bottom of each column of quiz scores. When you release the mouse button, Excel will automatically fill in those cells with the average quiz scores for each topic.

If it looks a little busy to you because of all the decimal places, make sure all those cells are still selected, then go to the "Format" menu, select "Cells…," and then on the "Number" tab, select "Number." From there, you can change the number of decimal places to 1 or 2 and have a much more manageable view of the averages you just calculated.

So what areas need the most remediation before the students take their year-end science exam? With just six subjects listed here, you can probably eyeball the correct response. If you have many more, you may want to create a chart to help you get a graphical representation of the statistics.

Creating a chart in Excel is reasonably easy to do, but it takes some planning. Start by doing two things. First, click-and-drag your mouse across the cells in Row 1 of the spreadsheet where the titles of the six lessons appear (from "Intro & Scientific Method" to "Mitosis"). Then click the Copy button or go the "Edit" menu and select "Copy." Next, click on an empty cell anywhere on this spreadsheet (or on another spreadsheet). Then click the Paste button or go to the "Edit" menu and select "Paste."

You've copied your lesson titles, and now you need to copy the averages you just calculated. This procedure is almost the same (select the cells with the averages in them, click Copy), but you need to go to the

"Edit" menu and choose "Paste Special…" when you get the dialog box shown in Figure 3. Select "Values" and then click "OK."

Now that you have those groups of cells next to each other, you can create a chart quite easily. First, click-and-drag your mouse from "Intro & Scientific Method" to "55" to select all the cells. Click the Chart Wizard button or go to the "Insert" menu and select "Chart…" The first dialog box in the Chart Wizard asks you to select a "Chart sub-type." I suggest leaving it at the default setting for now, which is a two-dimensional bar chart. Then click "Next." The second dialog box is easy, because you've already set up your data for it. This is where you would select multiple rows and columns of cells to create your chart; but because you've already put your lesson titles together with their average scores and then highlighted that group of cells, Excel defaults to that selection for the chart. So you can click "Next" here too, and move on.

The third dialog box allows you to change a number of chart options. On the "Titles" tab, the blanks for chart title, category axis, and value axis are blank by default. Type in some information here and you'll see the preview of your chart update to include a title. You may wish to explore the options on some of the other tabs; for example, the Data Labels tab will allow you to put the number you are graphing (average quiz score) at the top of each bar.

When you are finished with the Chart Options box, click "Next." The final dialog box asks if you would like to have Excel create the chart on a new sheet or insert it into the existing worksheet. I suggest you choose "As new sheet:" for the time being. (You can experiment with the layout of your chart when embedded into the current worksheet at a later time.)

Continued

Continued

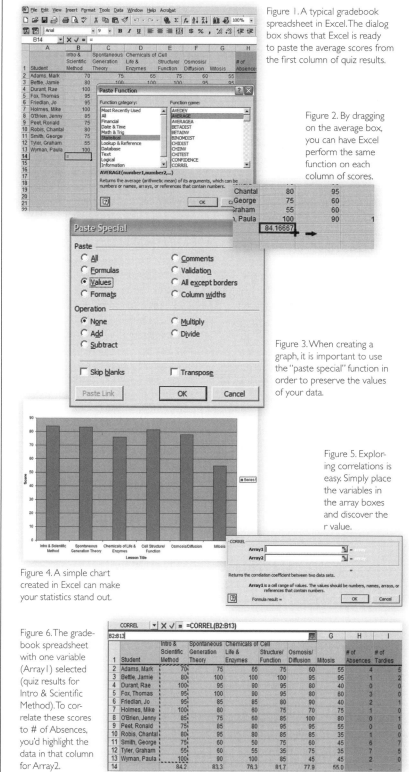

Figure 1. A typical gradebook spreadsheet in Excel. The dialog box shows that Excel is ready to paste the average scores from the first column of quiz results.

Figure 2. By dragging on the average box, you can have Excel perform the same function on each column of scores.

Figure 3. When creating a graph, it is important to use the "paste special" function in order to preserve the values of your data.

Figure 5. Exploring correlations is easy. Simply place the variables in the array boxes and discover the r value.

Figure 4. A simple chart created in Excel can make your statistics stand out.

Figure 6. The gradebook spreadsheet with one variable (Array1) selected (quiz results for Intro & Scientific Method). To correlate these scores to # of Absences, you'd highlight the data in that column for Array2.

Click "Finish" and you'll have a chart that looks like the one in Figure 4.

Looking at the chart, one can conclude that students need some extra attention in learning mitosis. They may also need some help with "Chemicals of Life & Enzymes" and "Osmosis/Diffusion," but clearly mitosis is the priority here.

Correlations

Let's cover one more area where Excel can be helpful, and that's in understanding the relationship between two different kinds of student data. Statisticians call this correlation, and it's a very handy bit of information. First, I'll cover the statistical basis, and then I'll show you how to calculate a correlation in Excel.

The concept of correlation comes from taking two things you can measure, such as quiz scores and attendance, and seeing if there is a relationship between them. Lots of people believe that there is a relationship between attendance and grades, and usually it's that as absences increase, grades decrease. But that's not always the case, and if you want to know for sure, you need to look at your data and calculate a correlation.

The "correlation coefficient" (also called "r") is a number between -1 and +1. If r equals 0, there is no relationship between the two variables. If r equals +1, then there is a perfect positive relationship between the two variables. When we say a positive relationship, we're not characterizing the relationship as a good thing. In correlation, positive simply means that as one variable increases, the other also increases. For example, you'd probably see a positive correlation (an r that is greater than zero) between the number of hours students in your class spend on homework and their quiz scores. If r equals -1, then there is a perfect negative relationship between the two variables. Again, negative is not a judgment. It simply

Continued

Continued

means that as one variable increases, the other decreases. For instance, you'd probably find a negative correlation (an r that is less than zero) between student absences and quiz scores.

If you haven't already figured it out by now, r falls between -1 and +1, but almost never actually reaches 1 (+ or -). But the closer r is to -1, the stronger the negative correlation between the two variables. Conversely, the closer r is to +1, the stronger the positive correlation.

Two important notes: First, always remember that correlation is not necessarily causation. In other words, just because two variables show a correlation, it does not necessarily mean that one causes the other. We can theorize that an increase in student absences will cause a decrease in quiz scores; but the correlation coefficient alone is not enough to confirm this. Why not? Let me demonstrate with an example: there is a strong, positive correlation (an r greater than zero and close to +1) between the number of storks living in an area in the U.S. and the number of babies born in that area. Do you want to conclude that more storks are bringing more babies? Probably not. In this case, there is actually a *third variable* influencing both of the first two variables—the degree of land development in an area. Storks are more likely to live in rural areas where they can nest close to nature. In the U.S., rural families typically have more children than families living in suburban or urban areas.

The moral is: just because two variables appear to be related, just because they have a correlation coefficient close to +1 or -1, don't assume you've found a cause-and-effect relationship.

The second important note is that correlation should only be performed on data that statisticians call interval/ratio data. These are variables such as quiz scores, age, height, income, tem-

perature, and so on. With this type of data, there is a clear indication of what is higher and what is lower: 70 degrees is warmer than 40 degrees; a 6' tall man is taller than a man who is 5' 6"; a student who scores 90 on a quiz has outperformed a student who scores 60. You cannot use variables such as sex/gender, race/ethnicity, special education classification, or eligibility for free or reduced meals in correlation because no single category for a variable is any better or higher than any other category. These variables do not consist of interval/ratio data.

So that's the theory. Now we can use Excel to calculate it. Using the same spreadsheet of biology quiz scores, absences, and tardies, let's find out if there really is a relationship between absences and quiz scores. First, click on any empty cell on the spreadsheet. (This is where Excel will put r once it's calculated.) Then click the "Paste Function" button just like you did when calculating the average. You'll get the same dialog box as before, and again, click "Statistical" on the left. Then click "CORREL" on the right. Then click "OK." You'll see a dialog box that looks like Figure 5.

Here, Excel is asking you to name the two variables that you want to compare ("Array1" and "Array2"). It really doesn't matter which variable, quiz scores or absences, you put in which array. But for this example, I'll put quiz scores in Array1 and absences in Array2. To do this, click the button for Array1. The dialog box will shrink down and allow you to click anywhere on the spreadsheet. Now, look at Figure 6. Let's say you want to select quiz scores for the lesson "Intro & Scientific Method," you'd click on the "70" (Mark Adams' score) and drag your mouse down to the last "100" (Paula Wyman's score). (Note that you do not want to select the 84.2 average score that you calculated earlier.) Once you've made this

selection, click the button to return to the CORREL dialog box. You'll notice that Excel has now filled in the information it needs for Array1. For Array2, repeat the same procedure a to select the students' absences, from Mark Adams' 4 absences to Paula Wyman's 2 absences.

Return to the CORREL dialog box, then click "OK," and in the empty cell you originally selected for Excel to put r, you will see your correlation coefficient. Given the data above, r equals -.60. This tells us that there is a moderately strong negative correlation between quiz scores and absences. In other words, when one goes up, the other goes down.

Try the same procedure, but with different combinations of variables (different quiz scores, or with absences, or number of tardies). You can also combine what we've covered in this article—insert a column between Mitosis and # of Absences or use the blank cells after # of Tardies, then use the function button to calculate each student's average quiz score over the course of the six lessons. Then correlate this result with absences or tardies to see if there is a relationship between overall quiz performance and absences or tardies.

This is just an introduction to the kinds of statistics that you can calculate based on data as readily available as your grade book. By simply exploring your student data, you can glean a wealth of information about your students, their needs, your priorities, and, just like Ms. Logan, you will find analytical steps to success.

Rob Kadel is the founder and a general partner of Kadel Research Consulting, LLC located in Columbia, MD. His firm focuses on the evaluation of educational programs in technology, school reform, and community involvement. With Rob's graduate degrees in sociology and his focus on educational research, the evaluation of technology-supported education became a natural fit.

author's update **Robert Kadel**

When ISTE published this article in March 2004, much of the emphasis was on the use of Microsoft Excel as a means for practitioners to analyze their student data and learn from it. Since then, the use of data-driven decision making (which, in my opinion, is an overused term) has evolved in that there are a great many programs that allow for analysis of student data. Most ed tech learning applications have data collection and processing components. With the national emphasis on standardized test scores, most districts—if not all—now provide test results to practitioners at the school, classroom, and individual level, including analyses of specific items that allow teachers, administrators, and parents to identify gaps in student learning and to address those needs. With such information available, one might be tempted to conclude that there is no shortage of data upon which to make decisions. I would argue otherwise. Yes, standardized test data abounds. But information on student aspirations, attainment, behavior, and 21st-century skills—just to name a few—is still sorely lacking. Thus I invite practitioners to continue to think about how to collect information in these areas and to use the data that they already have on hand. Whether you use Excel, FileMaker, Apple's Numbers, or some other method for storing and tracking data, there are a number of other measures of "success" that I believe will receive more of the spotlight in the coming years.

September 2004

Digital Citizenship
Addressing Appropriate Technology Behavior

By Mike S. Ribble,
Gerald D. Bailey,
and Tweed W. Ross

Subject: Appropriate technology use

Grades: K–12 (Ages 5–18)

Standards: *NETS•S* 2; *NETS•T* VI;
NETS•A VI (http://www.iste.org/
standards/)

Supplement: http://www.iste.org/LL/

Continued

Continued

R ecently, the popular press has pointed to increasing evidence of misuse and abuse of emerging technologies in U.S. schools. Some examples include using Web sites to intimidate or threaten students, downloading music illegally from the Internet, plagiarizing information using the Internet, using cellular phones during class time, and playing games on laptops or handhelds during class. How can we address these issues?

ISTE's National Educational Technology Standards (NETS) give us a starting point. The standards for students, teachers, and administrators all address social and ethical issues. For example, NETS for Students 2: Social, Ethical, and Human Issues, covers three very broad areas:

1. Students understand the ethical, cultural, and societal issues related to technology.
2. Students practice responsible use of technology systems, information, and software.
3. Students develop positive attitudes toward technology applications that support lifelong learning, collaboration, personal pursuits, and productivity.

All three of these areas are very important and help form students' technological development.

However, ISTE created these standards to guide in-school behavior. With increasing reports of student misuses of technology, student behavior in and out of school has become an issue for educators. They must prepare students to be members of a digital society or digital citizens. In this article, we discuss nine areas of digital citizenship and provide strategies for teachers to employ and teach appropriate behavior. Next month, we provide questions and answers to help technology coordinators and administrators implement digital citizenship.

A Definition of Digital Citizenship
Digital citizenship can be defined as the norms of behavior with regard to technology use. As a way of understanding the complexity of digital citizenship and the issues of technology use, abuse, and misuse, we have identified nine general areas of behavior that make up digital citizenship.

1. *Etiquette:* electronic standards of conduct or procedure
2. *Communication:* electronic exchange of information
3. *Education:* the process of teaching and learning about technology and the use of technology
4. *Access:* full electronic participation in society
5. *Commerce:* electronic buying and selling of goods
6. *Responsibility:* electronic responsibility for actions and deeds
7. *Rights:* those freedoms extended to everyone in a digital world
8. *Safety:* physical well-being in a digital technology world
9. *Security* (self-protection): electronic precautions to guarantee safety

Digital citizenship speaks to several levels of responsibility for technology. Some issues may be of more concern to technology leaders while others may be of more concern to teachers. Topics within digital citizenship are wide and varied, so you will need to use these topics as a "buffet" and take what you need, realizing that the other themes are there.

Examples and Strategies
Etiquette. Digital behavior makes everyone a role model for students. The problem with teaching digital technology is not all the rules have been written about uses for these devices. As new technologies have proliferated, users have not had the opportuni-

ty to "catch up" with all of their uses. Some rules or policies are assumed, while others have been created by an individual user or group. According to a 2003 Cingular Wireless survey of users and mobile phone etiquette, 42% in the South Atlantic region of the United States said they would answer a ringing phone while having a face-to-face conversation. (***Editor's note:*** Find this and other resources mentioned in this article on p. 10. The online supplement contains further resources on the issues addressed here.) When students see adults using technologies inappropriately, they can assume it is the norm. This leads to inappropriate technology behavior on the part of students.

Inappropriate Etiquette
• Students use handhelds or instant messaging (IM) to send non-class-related messages back and forth in class.

Strategies
• Follow rules and policies established by the school or district for appropriate technology use.
• Use case studies or scenarios (such as those included in the paper "Steal This Test!" posted on our Digital Citizenship site) to illustrate appropriate and inappropriate ways of using technology.
• Model appropriate uses of technology in and out of the classroom.

Communication. Cell phones, IM, and e-mail have changed the way technology users communicate. These forms of communication have created a new social structure of who, how, and when people interact.

Inappropriate Communication
• Students use cellular phones as the new "digital clique" to exclude other students, for example, excluding

When students see adults using technologies inappropriately, they can assume it is the norm. This leads to inappropriate technology behavior on the part of students.

Continued

Continued

Educators need to encourage students to use technology in a responsible way to prevent various physical injuries.

certain students from their cellular phone books.

- Students use IM and e-mail short-hand in class assignments. Using poor grammar and inappropriate slang or abbreviations can lead to bad habits in formal writing.

Strategies
- Model good use of electronic communication (e.g., sending messages that are to the point, avoiding short-hand when it is not appropriate).
- Encourage students to use digital communication, but correct them when they are doing something inappropriate.
- Use e-mail in situations where short responses are most appropriate.
- Use cell phones for learning purposes (e.g., accessing information in real time).

Education. Technology-infused teaching is becoming more commonplace every year. Technology in the classroom is becoming as transparent as the chalkboard and pencil. However, teaching how to use this technology has not grown accordingly. Technology-infused teaching does not always include teaching about appropriate and inappropriate uses of technology.

Inappropriate Education
- Students use cell phones or hand-helds to get test/quiz answers from other students.
- Teachers do not teach students how technology can be used to find credible resources and materials.

Strategies
- Create activities and exercises that allow students to use PDAs to retrieve, store, and share information in a responsible fashion.
- Encourage students to come up with new and alternative uses for the Internet and digital technolo-gies (e.g., IM or online discussion boards).
- Provide learning opportunities in different technology modes (e.g., Web sites, chat rooms, course management systems).
- Teach information literacy (e.g., identifying, accessing, applying, and creating information) by using technology-infused projects.

Access. Technology provides many opportunities for large numbers of people to access and use alternative forms of communication. But not everyone has the ability to use or access the tools in the new digital society. Often these opportunities are only available to a small group of students, even though the price of technology is rapidly dropping and access to technology is greater than ever before. The disparity of who does and does not have access to technology in America is widening. A 2003 report by the U.S. Department of Education showed that only 41% percent of Blacks and Hispanics were using a computer in the home compared to 77% percent of Whites.

Inappropriate Access
- Schools ignore or overlook the digital needs of disenfranchised groups.
- School districts do not provide specialized technologies for special populations (e.g., unavailable because of "lack of funds").
- Teachers fail to accommodate those students who do not have access to technology.
- Teachers "shy away" from assignments that require technology for fear that students do not have access.

Strategies
- Explore Web sites and materials to learn more about accessibility issues. The World Wide Web Consortium, SNOW, and the Special Needs and Technology page are good places to start.
- Identify students who have special needs or circumstances and explore ways to accommodate their technology needs (e.g., assistive technology). SERI's Special Needs and Technology Resources page can help you identify technology tools.
- Advocate the creation of Web sites that enable everyone to have equal access both in language and structure.
- Advocate for technology access for all students irrespective of disabilities. For example, either adhere to the World Wide Web Consortium's guidelines for Web site creation or ask that those in your school or district who create Web pages adhere to these guidelines.
- Provide time for students to use school technology to work on assignments.
- Allow students to work together on assignments (i.e., pair students with no or limited access to technology with others who have significantly greater access).

Commerce. Online purchasing is rapidly becoming the norm, and students need to understand this process. According to the *E-Commerce Times* report "There's Money in Teen Web Surfers," 29% of teens research products on the Internet before purchasing them in stores. If our goal is to produce literate citizens, then a discussion of digital commerce is important.

Inappropriate Commerce
- Students purchase goods online without knowledge of how to protect their identity (identity theft).
- Students fail to realize the consequences of poor online purchasing practices (e.g., impulse buying). Although poor purchasing practices are common to face-to-face and electronic exchanges, students are at greater risk online because of ease of access, unscrupulous sellers, and targeted maketing.

Continued

Continued

Strategies
- Engage students in a dialogue about using technology to purchase goods and services.
- Engage students in a discussion about good and bad experiences of purchasing goods online.
- Ask students to read comparison shopping Web sites such as CNET or AddALL to analyze comparative shopping strategies.
- Teach students about the dangers of identity theft and how to protect themselves.

Responsibility. At an early age, students found it easy to locate and download material from the Internet. However, they have not learned what is appropriate or inappropriate, legal or illegal when using the Internet. For example, a 2003 Business Software Alliance report indicated that two-thirds of college faculty and administrators say it is wrong to download or swap files while fewer than one-quarter of students at the same colleges say it is wrong. Recently, the Recording Industry Association of America (RIAA) filed suit against students and others for downloading music illegally. This action has caused technology users to think twice about what is appropriate and legal.

Inappropriate Responsibility
- Students download illegal MP3 music from sites.
- Students copy material off the Internet for class projects without giving credit to the author.

Strategies
- Use materials from Junior Achievement to illustrate the cost of illegal downloading from the Internet.
- Open a dialogue on students' feelings regarding their material being downloaded without permission.
- Discuss with students the school's codes of conduct as well as specific laws as they relate to illegal use of technology and the consequence/

cost for the breaking those rules/laws.
- Begin discussion on student perceptions of ethical/unethical technology use.
- Discuss fair use and copyright laws.

Rights. When creating or publishing anything digitally, students have the same copyright protection as any other content creators.

Inappropriate Rights
- Schools do not protect the rights of users working with school technology.
- Students violate school acceptable use policies (AUPs) because they view them as unfair.

Strategies
- Teach faculty about student digital rights.
- Teach students about their digital rights.
- Engage the school community in discussion of why school and district policies regarding technology exist.
- Provide students with information about appropriate and inappropriate use of technology in school.
- Engage students about the differences between rights in school and outside school when using technology.

Safety. Students need to be aware of the physical dangers that are inherent in using technology. Carpal tunnel syndrome is one (though not the only) such danger. Eyestrain and poor posture are not uncommon in technology-related activities. Educators need to encourage students to use technology in a responsible way to prevent various physical injuries. Having proper ergonomics can help protect students from long-lasting problems related to unsafe use of technology.

Inappropriate Safety
- Teachers are unaware of possible negative physical effects of technology on students.
- Teachers do not teach ergonomics when using technology.

Strategies
- Explore Web sites (e.g., UCLA's ergonomics site) to learn new ways for using technology safely.
- Make sure that rooms are well lit, and provide appropriately sized furniture for the technology use.
- Make students aware of the long-term physical effects of certain technology use.

Security. As more and more sensitive information is stored electronically, a corresponding strategy to protect that information must be created. Students need to learn how to protect electronic data (e.g., virus protection, firewalls, off-site storage). Protecting one's equipment is not only a matter of personal responsibility but also necessary for protecting the community (e.g., keeping one's virus software up to date). However, digital security goes beyond protecting equipment. It includes protecting ourselves and others from outside influences that would do us physical harm.

Inappropriate Security
- Students and educators assume there is no need to protect electronic data.
- Students and faculty fail to maintain current software updates or patches on their home computers that protect us from viruses
- Students do not protect their identities while using e-mail, chat, or IM.

Strategies
- Contact organizations (e.g., i-SAFE America) to obtain materials about

Protecting one's equipment is not only a matter of personal responsibility but also necessary for protecting the community.

Continued

Continued

protecting online users.

- Research what your school does to provide protection from possible outside digital harm.
- Teach students to back up data and protect their equipment from damage.
- Teach students how to conduct regular checks for viruses or other software intrusions using approved software. The National Cyber Security Alliance stated that 67% of broadband users don't have properly installed and securely configured firewalls.

Conclusion

Digital citizenship has become a priority for schools that see technology integration as a major teaching and learning strategy for preparing students to live and work in the 21st century. Using the NETS to help understand how technology should be used in the curriculum and applying digital citizenship to help define students' behavior will facilitate the development of well-rounded, technology-savvy students.

As the years pass and new digital technologies appear, a framework of codified principles will be harder to create. Society will need guidance on how to act with respect to technology. Laws will be enacted, but they will not be enough. Groups and organizations (including schools) have created rules and AUPs, but they, too, fall short. There has been no universal agreement on how we should act in relation to digital technologies. Will reaching an agreement be easy? Quite the opposite; it will be very difficult to come to a consensus on how everyone will deal with digital technology. We must begin somewhere, and because the schools encompass our future, this is where the discussion begins. In his 1975 book *Fifty-Four Landmark Briefs and Arguments of the Supreme Court of the United States,* U.S. Supreme Court Justice Thurgood Marshall helps place the importance and urgency of teaching digital citizenship in proper perspective:

> Education is not the teaching of the three R's. Education is the teaching of the overall citizenship, to learn to live together with fellow citizens, and above all to learn to obey the law.

Resources

Reports

Business Software Alliance. (2003). Internet piracy on campus. Available: http://www.bsa.org/customcf/popuphitbox.cfm?ReturnURL=/resources/loader.cfm?url=/commonspot/security/getfile.cfm&PageID=2396&CFID=88560&CFTOKEN=87295225.

Cingular Wireless. (2003). *Cingular Wireless survey reveals regional differences in courteous use of cell phones.* Available: http://www.cingular.com/about/latest_news/03_10_27

Enos, L. (2003). Report: There's money in teen Web surfers. *E-Commerce Times.* Available: http://www.ecommercetimes.com/perl/story/12095.html.

National Cyber Security Alliance. (2003). Fast and present danger: In-home study on broadband security among American consumers. Available: http://www.staysafeonline.info/press/060403.pdf

Ribble, M. S., & Bailey, G. D. (n.d.). *Steal this test!* Available: http://coe.k-state.edu/digitalcitizenship/CompassArt.pdf.

U.S. Department of Education, National Center for Education Statistics. (2003). *Computer and Internet use by children and adolescents in 2001.* Available: http://nces.ed.gov/pubsearch/pubsinfo.asp?pubid=2004014

Web Sites

AddALL: http://www.adall.com
CNET.com: http://www.cnet.com
i-SAFE America: http://www.i-safe.org
Junior Achievement's Digital Citizenship materials: http://www.ja.org/programs/programs_supplements_citizenship.shtml
Mike Ribble and Gerald Bailey's Digital Citizenship Site: http://coe.ksu.edu/digitalcitizenship/
SERI's Special Needs and Technology Resources: http://www.seriweb.com/tech.htm
SNOW: http://snow.utoronto.ca/technology/products/
Special Needs and Technology: http://www.educationnews.org/special_needs_and_technology.htm
UCLA Ergonomics: http://ergonomics.ucla.edu/
World Wide Web Consortium: http://www.w3.org

Mike S. Ribble serves as the instructional services coordinator for the College of Education at Kansas State University. He has worked as a network manager at Northeast Community College in Norfolk, Nebraska. He was an assistant principal and before that a science teacher at Bishop Carroll High School in Wichita, Kansas.

Dr. Gerald D. Bailey is professor of educational leadership in the College of Education at Kansas State University. His areas of specialty are technology leadership and staff development. Prior to earning his doctorate at the University of Nebraska, he worked as a classroom teacher, demonstration teacher, and supervisor in the Lincoln (Nebraska) Public Schools.

Dr. Tweed W. Ross is associate professor of educational technology in the Department of Educational Administration and Leadership and director of the Catalyst Center at the College of Education Kansas State University. His research interests include the ethical issues of information technology and the preparation of undergraduate preservice educators to use information technologies in K–12 classrooms.

October 2004

Digital Citizenship

Focus Questions for Implementation

By Mike S. Ribble and Gerald D. Bailey

Subject: Appropriate technology use

Grades: K–12 (Ages 5–18)

Standards: *NETS•S* 2; *NETS•T* VI; *NETS•A* VI (http://www.iste.org/standards/)

Continued

Continued

A re you irritated at the thoughtless technology-related interruptions in public places? Are you tired of having to "police" staff and/or students who use technology inappropriately? Are you concerned that schools ban certain forms of technology in schools only to see students using and misusing it after the last school bell rings? A growing consensus among technology leaders is that we must begin educating teachers, students, and administrators in the day-to-day use of technology. Simply put, personal misuse and abuse of technology have reached epidemic proportions in school as well as in our daily lives. Digital Citizenship must become part of our school culture—not just a class or lesson but the way we do business in education.

The following discussion briefly reviews the nine categories of digital citizenship we described in the September issue of *L&L* 2004. (See "Digital Citizenship: Addressing Appropriate Technology Behavior," pp. 6–11.) The nine categories emerged from an extensive search of hundreds of articles that spoke to the issue of digital citizenship, which can be defined as the norms of behavior with regard to technology use. (***Editor's note:*** See Resources on p. 15 for a partial list.) We follow that with focus questions and suggestions by category for how administrators and tech leaders can begin to create education environments conducive to teaching digital citizenship. Also see Creating

> **Personal misuse and abuse of technology have reached epidemic proportions in school as well as in our daily lives.**

an Action Plan on p. 14 for several overall strategies for getting started.

1. *Etiquette:* electronic standards of conduct or procedure
2. *Communication:* electronic exchange of information
3. *Education:* the process of teaching and learning about technology and the use of technology
4. *Access:* full electronic participation in society
5. *Commerce:* electronic buying and selling of goods
6. *Responsibility:* electronic responsibility for actions and deeds
7. *Rights:* those freedoms extended to everyone in a digital world
8. *Safety:* physical well-being in a digital technology world
9. *Security* (self-protection): electronic precautions to guarantee safety

Focus Questions

Etiquette. How do technology leaders maximize a culture of high technology use while minimizing poor technology etiquette? Technology leaders must provide a solid example for faculty and students. Students and teachers should be required to silence (i.e., mute or vibrate) or turn off their own electronic equipment (e.g., cell phones, personal digital assistants or PDAs) during class. Students and teachers should not play games or use instant messaging on portable lap-

tops, desktops, or PDAs during class. Users need to remember that what they do in public affects others.

Where and when should digital etiquette be taught? Outside school, violations of digital etiquette are ignored or tolerated by members of society. Inside schools, we create rules (AUPs) and regulations or even ban the technology being used inappropriately. The nine themes of digital citizenship should be discussed and understood in relation to all curriculum areas.

Communication. How does a school district create a digital citizenship program that affords students the opportunity to make good decisions when faced with many options? Technology leaders need to provide timely training on what is available and appropriate. The training of teachers, staff, and students on the precepts of digital citizenship should be ongoing throughout the school year.

What form of communication is most appropriate under any given set of circumstances? Use face-to-face communication instead of electronic communication when the situation involves sensitive, personal, or negative information. Electronic communication is used to convey basic information for the sake of efficiency and effectiveness.

Education. Students need just-in-time information. This process requires sophisticated searching and processing skills (i.e., information literacy and

> **Digital citizenship can be defined as the norms of behavior with regard to technology use.**

Continued

Continued

Creating an Action Plan

Though there is no step-by-step plan for dealing with teaching digital citizenship, technology leaders should consider the following strategies:

1. Make digital citizenship a priority in your district and building technology plan by explaining its importance in society.

2. Empower your technology leadership teams by providing examples of problems that occur in the 10 areas of digital citizenship. Discuss and debate the areas, especially the positive examples.

3. Enlist all stakeholders by explaining the urgency—both in schools and out—of teaching digital citizenship. Engage parents in dialogue using the focus questions for all 10 areas of digital citizenship.

4. Empower technology leadership committees to identify and prioritize the steps needed to deal with digital citizenship in curriculum, staff development programs, and board policy, by providing a clear understanding of what technology and literacy skills are needed in this new digital society.

technology skills). In other words, learners must be taught to learn anything, anytime, anywhere because society has begun to learn in this manner. How do technology leaders teach necessary technology standards? Schools and school districts need to develop information literacy and technology skill curriculum materials matched to content standards and a plan to implement that curriculum.

How do schools begin to work with business, military, medicine, and government as well as other segments of the workplace to achieve a mutual understanding of technology needs and uses for productive citizenship? Schools can develop plans, programs, and/or partnerships for preparing electronic workers for technology-rich work environments. Digital citizenship involves educating a new breed of person—information workers with a high degree of information literacy skills. Educators need to take notice outside their field for help.

Digital Access. Digital exclusion of any kind minimizes the growth of human beings in an electronic society. Many factors contribute to the digital divide, including economic, social, and even personal reasons. How do technology leaders ensure that everyone has equal access to technology regardless of gender,

race, age, ethnicity, and physical or mental challenges?

Technology leaders must be aware of and support electronic access for everyone to create a foundation for digital citizenship. Providing the resources to allow everyone to participate in a digital society is necessary. Both elementary and secondary students need to have access to up-to-date computers, software, digital cameras, and so on. Assistive technologies such as page readers for word processing, spreadsheets, and Internet use should be provided for students with special needs. School libraries are open to the public after school and on weekends, which allows for access students may not have at home.

How do we provide equal access for those who cannot or choose not to use technology? Some people have the resources to allow them to participate in the digital society. Others cannot afford the technology. Still others may choose not to use the technology. Schools and society must provide access while leaving the choice to become a participating member in the digital community up to the individual.

Digital Commerce. The rise of the digital economy does not change the issue of right and wrong, but it does make buying and selling goods easier, which magnifies the issue of illegal activities. How do technology leaders ensure that students learn how to operate in the new digital economy? Students must be taught how to make wise decisions for purchasing goods legally and the consequences of not doing so.

What are the new technical skills required to participate in a digital economy? Students should be taught how to electronically purchase goods with emphasis on privacy, identity theft, and credit card protection. They can be shown how to shop for the best bargains using specific research strategies, such as buying a book online.

Digital Responsibility. Digital responsibility deals with the ethical use of technology. What is ethical or unethical in a digital community (inside school and outside school)? Students should not be able to steal or cause damage to other people's work, identity, or property. Creating Web sites that are belittling and/or slanderous to others is destructive behavior. Hacking into another person's computer information, downloading music illegally, plagiarizing, or creating and distributing worms, viruses, or Trojan Horses are unethical acts regardless of whether school or personal property is involved.

How do school leaders focus on the positive side of technology integration without over-emphasizing rules and regulations? Students can be taught about ethical and unethical technology behavior in a manner that allows them to make decisions and understand the consequences of

In other words, learners must be taught to learn anything, anytime, anywhere because society has begun to learn in this manner.

Continued

Continued

> Students should be taught how to electronically purchase goods with emphasis on privacy, identity theft, and credit card protection.

those decisions. Students, teachers, administrators, and parents can work with community members to create a forum for dialogue about ethical and unethical technology behavior in the workplace.

Digital Rights. Basic rights are extended to every digital citizen. Digital citizens should have the right to privacy, free speech, and so on. What are digital rights for administrators, teachers, students, parents, and community members? Students can be taught about basic freedoms such as speech, privacy, and right to property and how they apply to technology use. Students can work with local, state, national, and international agencies or citizens to learn how digital rights are violated or protected. Schools can work with local businesses or agencies to establish internships and community service programs that focus on digital rights.

What school district and classroom policies must be in place to protect the digital rights of everyone? Basic digital rights must be addressed, discussed, and codified in the school district.

Digital Safety. Eye safety, repetitive stress syndrome, and sound ergonomic practices are included in the digital safety category. Students must be taught that there are inherent dangers of technology use. How do a board of education, superintendent, and principal initiate a digital safety program without unduly alarming the school community? The school district can implement a program dealing with safe use of equipment and give each teacher responsibility for teaching digital safety.

How can a technology staff development program be initiated to ensure that the entire district is aware of and skilled in digital safety measures? Digital citizenship includes a school culture where technology users are taught how to protect themselves through education and training.

Digital Security (self-protection). It is not enough to trust other members in the community for our own safety. In our own homes, we put locks on our doors and fire alarms in our houses to provide some level of protection. The same must be true for digital security. We need to have virus protection, backups of data, and power surge control devices on our equipment. Students should be taught how to use surge protectors in their homes with their own computers, to back up data, and to use passwords to protect their electronic work.

How can a technology staff development program be initiated to ensure that the entire district is aware of and skilled in digital security measures? School districts could develop partnerships with local, state, and federal agencies to protect users online. The school district could create a plan for protecting district data in case of emergencies or attack by hackers (e.g., backup systems).

Conclusion

The debate and necessary dialogue about digital citizenship are long overdue. If we hope to create citizens who know right from wrong and appropriate from inappropriate behavior in the 21st century, technology leaders must make digital citizenship a top priority in their school districts. The old adage seems quite appropriate when gauging the importance of digital citizenship education: "If not here (schools), where? If not now, when? If not you, who?"

Resources
Articles
Fryer, W. A. (2003). A beginner's guide to school security. *Technology & Learning, 24*(2), 9.

Hafner, K. (2003). *Eluding the Web's snare.* Available: http://www.nytimes.com/2003/04/17/technology/circuits/17shun.html?ex=1063339200&en=b2b9d72b27138633&ei=5070.

Harmon, A. (2003). *New parent-to-child chat: Do you download music?* Available: http://www.nytimes.com/2003/09/10/technology/10MUSI.html?th.

Harmon, A. (2003). *Digital vandalism spurs a call for oversight.* Available: http://www.nytimes.com/2003/09/01/technology/01NET.html?ex=1063339200&en=6c9adcbdd0cb5f11&ei=5070.

Mitchell, W. J. (2003). Designing the space. *Syllabus, 17*(2), 10.

Reuters. (2003). *Blaster suspect a typical teen?* Available: http://www.wired.com/news/technology/0,1282,60263,00.html.

Rimer, S. (2003). *A campus fad that's being copied: Internet plagiarism.* Available: http://www.nytimes.com/2003/09/03/education/03CHEA.html?th.

Salpeter, J. (2003). Professional development: 21st century models. *Technology & Learning, 24*(1), 34.

Toppo, G. (2003). *Who's watching the class? Webcams in schools raise privacy issue.* Available: http://www.usatoday.com/usatonline/20030811/5396054s.htm.

Web Sites
PBS's Digital Divide series: http://www.pbs.org/digitaldivide/themes.html.

World Wide Web Consortium's Curriculum for Web Content Accessibility Guidelines: http://www.w3.org/WAI/wcag-curric/.

Mike S. Ribble serves as the instructional services coordinator for the College of Education at Kansas State University. He has worked as a network manager at Northeast Community College in Norfolk, Nebraska. He was an assistant principal and before that a science teacher at Bishop Carroll High School in Wichita, Kansas.

Dr. Gerald D. Bailey is professor of educational leadership in the College of Education at Kansas State University. His areas of specialty are technology leadership and staff development. Prior to earning his doctorate at the University of Nebraska, he worked as a classroom teacher, demonstration teacher, and supervisor in the Lincoln (Nebraska) Public Schools.

authors' update
Mike Ribble and Gerald Bailey

Since the publication of the articles on digital citizenship in September and October 2004, there have been some updates/modifications to some of the information. The most significant changes were in the nine elements that provide the framework for digital citizenship. When evaluating the original nine elements it became apparent that some of those concepts could be combined while yet other elements were needed. These changes provide a more adequate coverage of the issues within digital citizenship. Today the nine elements and definitions of digital citizenship are:

Digital Access: full electronic participation in society

Digital Commerce: electronic buying and selling of goods

Digital Communication: electronic exchange of information

Digital Literacy: process of teaching and learning about technology and the use of technology

Digital Etiquette: electronic standards of conduct or procedure

Digital Law: electronic responsibility for actions and deeds

Digital Rights and Responsibilities: those requirements and freedoms extended to everyone in a digital world

Digital Health and Wellness: physical and psychological well-being in a digital technology world

Digital Security (self-protection): electronic precautions to guarantee safety

We are constantly evaluating the nine elements to determine if additional work or modifications need to be made. Feedback from educators and district representatives confirm that many users are pleased with the way the elements are organized at this time.

In summer 2007, two events coincided to help support and expand the concept of digital citizenship. First, ISTE refreshed the National Educational Technology Standards for Students (NETS•S). The Social, Ethical, Legal, and Human Issues standard was changed to Digital Citizenship. This change helped to show the importance of the digital citizenship concept. Second, ISTE published the book *Digital Citizenship in Schools*, which included updated content and materials on this topic. These events have helped digital citizenship to continue to develop in schools and districts. In 2008, the NETS refresh continued for teachers and it includes digital citizenship as one of the updated standards. ISTE also published the book *Raising a Digital Child* on digital citizenship for parents under its new imprint, HomePage books, in early 2009. We believe that this move into educating parents about digital citizenship will support the work in schools and create more communication between these groups about appropriate technology use.

April 2005

Are You the Copy Cop?

Why Copyright Violations Happen in Schools and How to Prevent Them

By and large, educators are honest and ethical. Yet, copyright violations such as those described in the following scenarios are all too common in many, if not most, schools:

- Teacher Gray shows Disney's *The Little Mermaid* to reward her students for scoring exceptionally well on a recent test.
- Teacher Black adds images taken from various Internet sites to a multimedia presentation he uses to complement his lecture on Egypt.
- The district purchases a single-use license for Photoshop, but Technology Coordinator Green installs it on all the computers in a classroom.
- Teacher Scarlet downloads songs from a file swapping service to listen to while working on her lesson plans.
- Media Specialist White transfers an educational film to videotape because the district has decided it will no longer support its 16mm projectors.
- Teacher Brown copies short stories and essays from a variety of magazines, textbooks, and Web sites to create an anthology for his AP English class.

Interpreting, and to some extent enforcing, copyright policies has long been regarded as a responsibility of the school's library media specialist. Intellectual property, before schools adopted computers and connected to the Internet, was found primarily in print and audiovisual formats—both types of resources largely controlled by the school's librarian. The librarian is among the few educators whose professional training includes information about copyright, and he or she has traditionally been viewed as the local expert on intellectual property issues.

By Doug Johnson and Carol Simpson

Subject: Copyright, ethics, intellectual property

Standards: *NETS•S* 2; *NETS•T* IV; *NETS•A* IV (http://www.iste.org/nets/)

Continued

Continued

However, with intellectual property increasingly available in digital formats, the role of the library media specialist as the "copyright cop" is untenable. All educators who deal with technology need to understand the legal and illegal uses of intellectual property if a school hopes to both keep free of copyright lawsuits and provide ethical models for students to emulate.

Why Does Abuse Happen?

Why does intellectual property not merit the same respect among educators as physical property? Our experience shows many factors influence educators' behavior with respect to copyright.

Ignorance and Misperceptions. Formal training slights educating teachers about copyright. NCATE's Unit Standards (http://www.ncate.org/documents/unit_stnds_2002.pdf) do not address copyright, and only two of NCATE's affiliate accreditation organizations (ISTE and AECT, linked from the NCATE Program Standards page, http://ncate.org/standard/programstds.htm) include an understanding of copyright as one of their competencies. For example, NETS for Teachers standard VI asks teachers to "model and teach legal and ethical practice related to technology use." And AECT's Initial Standard 3.4 focuses on policies and regulations "that affect the diffusion and use of intructional technology," including copyright law. This situation results in a number of poorly understood concepts about the use of intellectual property in schools.

Fair Use. Educators too often interpret fair use as "any use so long as it is done in school" or "if it benefits the kids, it must be okay" or "we aren't making any money on it." But even CONFU (that's Conference on Fair Use, not just CONFUsion abbreviated) determined in their final report that there is:

> no simple test to determine what is fair use. Section 107

Editor's note: This article is intended to provide a discussion of copyright problems and solutions and *not* as specific legal advice.

Continued

Continued

of the Copyright Act sets forth the four fair use factors which should be considered in each instance, based on particular facts of a given case, to determine whether a use is a "fair use": (1) the purpose and character of use, including whether such use is of a commercial nature or is for nonprofit educational purposes, (2) the nature of the copyrighted work, (3) the amount and substantiality of the portion used in relation to the copyrighted work as a whole, and (4) the effect of the use upon the potential market for or value of the copyrighted work.

Beyond the four-factor test of fair use prescribed in the law, there are several guidelines that are generally agreed to be fair use. Each of the guidelines affects a specific type of use, such as using copyrighted materials in multimedia presentations. The perceived difficulty in determining whether a use meets the statutory fair use rules as above, or the various guidelines, dissuades many educators from even making a good faith attempt to question whether their use of intellectual property is legal.

Information on the Internet. Plenty of myths surround copyright, especially as it relates to information found on the Internet. Brad Templeton, chairman of the Electronic Frontier Foundation, lists 11, including "If it doesn't have a copyright notice, it's not copyrighted." (***Editor's note:*** See Copyright Resources on p. 22 for this and other URLs.)

Intangible Property. Except in the case of open source software, when you buy a piece of software (e.g., Photoshop), you are actually buying the right to use the software, not the software code itself, on a fairly restricted basis. The software license (often viewable only in a small window while the product loads) describes the specific uses you are allowed.

The Digital Millennium Copyright Act of 1998 and the Multimedia Fair Use Guidelines (1996) attempt to address copyright changes that new technologies and media have brought about, but the effects of these have not been widely discussed in the professional literature that teachers actually read. Because so many teachers have practiced copyright carte blanche for so long, attempts to correct their bad habits may not be met with the nicest response.

Ease and Convenience of Copying. Violating copyright is now faster and easier than it has ever been. A computer program, file, or digital image copies in seconds, whereas copying print materials requires a trip to the photocopier to laboriously reproduce the source, one page at a time. Peer-to-peer file sharing services, video digitizers, and even the simple copy and paste commands all contribute to the ease of violating copyright laws. Teachers gleefully demonstrate to students how simple it is to find a fetching graphic and "keep it on your computer to use whenever you like." The development of large libraries of the works of others, without payment or permission, has resulted in a climate of entitlement.

Often teachers are pressed for time and simply feel they must violate copyright because there is no other option. A common example of this type of activity is showing entertainment videos to keep students occupied during rainy day recess, for perfect attendance rewards, or for assorted babysitting activities such as when teachers are behind in their grading.

Intangibility of Intellectual Property. Were I to walk into a Wal-Mart store and tuck a camera under my coat and walk out, it is obvious that I have

Continued

Continued

deprived Wal-Mart of its property and of the revenue they could earn by selling it. I have the camera; Wal-Mart does not. However, were I to borrow a friend's installed copy of Photoshop, install another copy of it on my computer, and then return the physical program to my friend, the deprivation of property becomes an abstract concept instead of a physical reality. The friend has his program back, so nothing is really missing, is it?

The intangibility of intellectual property often leads people to view copyright violations as a "victimless" crime. Denying an intellectual property holder his potential profit is not deemed as serious as depriving a physical property holder of a currently held physical possession. Besides, schools can't afford to actually purchase all the software they truly need, so making an extra copy "for the kids" doesn't hurt anyone because the person who bought the software still has his or her own copy. Some rationalize, saying that training kids on commercial software might even promote sales of the software to the kids' parents.

On an even more abstract level is understanding that even when there is no loss of remuneration, intellectual property holders still have the right to control the use of their property, especially regarding use of materials that may no longer be available for purchase (out of print or out of production) or works that have never been available for sale (e.g., photographs, letters, e-mail messages).

Perception of Copyright as a Blue Law. Some copyright violations are so often committed and of such long-standing practice that many educators are genuinely surprised that they are copyright violations, such as showing movies that do not have a public performance license as a reward, adding copyrighted material to a Web site without permission, using a

transparency of a copyrighted cartoon in an inservice workshop, copying workbook pages from sample copies, or adding unlicensed music in the background of a movie. Even administrators will retort, when informed of some blatant offense, "You show me one school that has been successfully sued for that!"

Difficulty and Cost of Obtaining Copyright Permission. Given enough time and usually the willingness to pay for the right, most intellectual property holders will allow some use of copyrighted materials. But determining how and to whom the request should be made, waiting for a response (even by e-mail), and paying any required charge for the use is often more confusing, time consuming, and expensive than many teachers are willing to undertake. Publishers and other copyright owners don't make compliance simple for educators, and frequently refuse to answer questions about permissions and licensing. Eventually educators tire of the game and just ignore the option.

Poverty and Emotional Appeals. Teachers view their job as a means of bettering the lives of children and improving society. But illegal activities, even when done for good causes or because of poor funding, are still illegal. It's that old "ends don't justify the means" problem. A fair-use analysis includes much more than simply a finding of nonprofit educational use.

Civil Disobedience in Reaction to Protections. Laws that grant greater and longer copyright protections to owners, more sophisticated physical copyright protection schemes, and increased consolidation of ownership of intellectual property by powerful for-profit corporations all heighten the perception among users that the laws unfairly protect the wealthy. In times when educational funding is viewed by many as inadequate and

Continued

Continued

decreasing, a certain Robin Hood mentality develops. The idea that the large corporation in the big city will never know what is happening in the small towns pervades decisions on using copyrighted materials.

Copyright Complexity. Copyright has so many shades of gray, without a law degree one can never be certain he is making a correct interpretation, and even lawyers disagree. Even teachers or administrators who diligently try to follow the letter of the law may find themselves in a copyright quagmire. Why bother to obey when you are just going to get into trouble anyway? In areas of new technology, none of the old rules fit, so if you were inclined to play by the rules, what rules should you apply? New regulations, such as the TEACH Act, come down with no interpretation on areas of internal conflict, so school personnel are forced to interpret complex legislation in ways that beg to become a test case in court.

Mixed Messages. Conflicting district policies and practices also play into the puzzle. "Do I follow district policy on copyright, or do I copy these materials that will help our students score higher on the standardized test?" When one can't figure a way to understand the copyright regulations, it is simpler and more expedient to ignore them. Seeing administrators ignoring copyright (through neglect or ignorance) only fuels the conviction of teachers and paraprofessionals that carte blanche is appropriate, despite what the Board policy may state. The fact that few copyright actions against schools are publicized compounds the idea that copyright is no big deal. However, if you speak privately with school officials in a local area, virtually everyone can identify a school in the area that has received a cease and desist letter or been the target of an actual copyright suit within in the past 15 years. School-

library.org hosts a voluntary database of copyright actions in its Copyright Resources section.

What Can We Do about It?

Library media specialists, technology directors, and administrators are unlikely to prevent every violation of copyright law and abuse of intellectual property in their schools, but that does not mean they should not make good faith efforts to do so. In fact, it makes very good sense to make all reasonable efforts to ensure compliance with copyright laws related to activities common in schools.

When a school is identified as being a party to a legal action involving copyright infringement, one of the factors considered is how blatant the infraction appears to be. If, for example, the school were allowing students to download and share MP3 music files at a music swap fest sponsored by the student council, a court might find that the school was complicit in any infringing activity. If one teacher installs software for which the school does not own a license, the district might not be liable if the district can show that the teacher knew the rules and the district took appropriate steps to prevent the installation of unlicensed software. However, if the district technology office installs such software in an entire school or across the district, there would certainly be reason to complain of flagrant disregard of copyright requirements and the district would have legal responsibility for the infringement.

So how can we address the issue without becoming "Big Brother"? Here are some common sense recommendations on dealing with the thorny issue of copyright.

Get Information into Teachers' Hands. Copyright is a complex and evolving subject, and schools need to teach and provide information about proper intellectual property use as a part of ongoing staff development

Continued

Continued

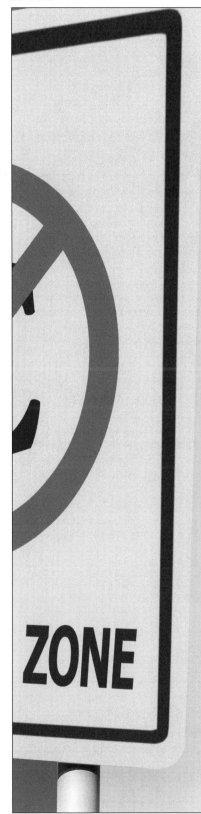

efforts. Schools can and should provide short, readily understood guides regarding copyright of all materials, especially those in digital formats. Groton (Connecticut) Public Schools has an online copyright manual, and the University of Texas System has developed an online Copyright Crash Course that schools may wish to model. (The Crash Course is geared toward university users, but the school exemptions still hold true for PK–12.) Basic copyright notices should be placed on circulating software, videos, Internet terminals, and photocopiers. Some notices will protect the school from lawsuits if particular types of infringements take place. *Copyright in Schools* contains sample language. Technology and library newsletters to staff should address intellectual property issues.

Intellectual Property Rights Benefit Users and Creators. Copyright laws benefit individuals in two ways. First, teachers and students themselves may be creators of intellectual property for which they would like control and the potential for remuneration. (Schools may own the rights to teacher-developed materials, under work-for-hire guidelines.) Second, those who create intellectual property (e.g., software) are more likely to support and continue to develop that property if there is a financial reward for doing so. These concepts should be understood by all school staff members as well as students.

Conduct Audits and Monitor Photocopying. The Mankato (Minnesota) School District where co-author Johnson works uses Apple Remote Desktop to scan the more than 2,000 district computers for executable programs every two years. The technology staff then compares the programs found with the licenses on file. When a program is found on a computer for which the district does not have a license, the technology office sends a letter to the user of that computer, carbon-copied to the building principal, asking the user to provide proof of purchase of the program for its files, purchase the program and then send a copy of the license to the office, or remove the program from the computer. Were the district to be audited, these actions will help show due diligence in enforcing copyright. The Software and Information Industry Association (SIIA) identifies additional software programs that can perform similar audits (http://www.siia.com/piracy/audit.asp).

Personnel in district print shops or who run building photocopiers need to have a firm understanding of copyright laws. If a teacher requests copies of an item that may be copyrighted, it should be returned to the building principal for his or her signature before the print job is completed. Photocopying consumable materials is a common infringement that should be monitored closely.

Maintain Budgets That Allow Legal Purchase of Needed Materials. A budget for software, a process for selection and adoption of software, and the purchase of building or district licenses when feasible all decrease the likelihood of illegal software use. If teachers use videos for reward purposes, the district should purchase public performance licenses. Royalty-free music and clip art with few use restrictions should be available to teachers and students. Extracurricular activities, not having the same fair use protections of direct teaching in the classroom, need extra guidance and supervision in their use of copyrighted materials such as videos for lock-ins or other social events, music for dances, and images/music for fundraisers such as CD-ROM yearbooks.

Designate a Copyright Expert. Schools need a "go-to" person when copyright questions arise. These people should have the budget to

Continued

Continued

receive training in copyright issues as they pertain to schools and access to resources such as co-author Simpson's book *Copyright for Schools* to help them answer questions. These folks also need the backing of the administration if an unpopular answer is provided to a copyright question. The district needs a copyright coordinator who will monitor licenses, conduct periodic audits, and act as the registered copyright "agent" identified in the Digital Millennium Copyright Act's online service provider protections. Such a position can protect the district from infringement suits resulting from copyrighted material posted on school Web pages. The IT department may want someone on the staff to take SIIA's seminar to become a certified software manager to verify compliance with licensing requirements and tracking (http://www.siia.com/piracy/seminars.asp).

Serve as Models of Ethical and Legal Behavior. You do not need to work with young people very long before realizing that they learn more from your behavior than from your words. If we wish to develop moral, law-abiding citizens, we as educators must act ethically and legally ourselves. Copyright should be a part of the information literacy and technology skills curriculum. The topic should be dealt with seriously, and with respect. Using a "nudge, nudge, wink, wink" curriculum that says "just use discretion, and you won't be caught" conveys the message that infringement is perfectly fine. It says that the end justifies the means. If you were to voice those sentiments to the school board to approve as goals of a program, they wouldn't fly; yet they may be current practice. Perhaps a technology skills curriculum audit is in order, along with the software audit.

Walking the Talk

Following copyright laws in schools comes down to a few radically simple ideas. The first is a concept that may not have been considered in many schools: copyright is federal law. Schools are quite serious about many federal laws and regulations. The Americans with Disabilities Act, for example, is well respected and enforced. In our civics classes, we regularly tell students that when you don't agree with a law, you work to change it. However, we appear not to practice what we preach when it comes to copyright.

Second, obeying copyright is an ethical necessity. Although following the current copyright act may not be the most popular course of action with teachers, the fact that students are observing us and modeling their behavior on ours is the single most important reason to obey the law.

Finally, copyright compliance is the right thing to do. Ethical use is a difficult concept to teach in many schools, simply because of the religious connotations that are attached. But in this context, we are considering the theft of someone's work and property. What some educators don't always realize is that writers make their living creating educational materials; if they don't sell their creations, they cannot make a living.

Congress provided certain exemptions from the requirements of copyright so that schools could use limited amounts of published and marketed materials to assist in teaching students. The exemptions were not intended to take the place of purchased materials, nor were they designed to contribute to extracurricular activities. The intent was to give the schools an assist when they just needed "a little something." Unfortunately, we have come to believe that "if a little is good, a lot is better." Having an understanding of the limits of copyright and fair use is essential to sound business practices in schools as well as sound educational and ethical practices. Knowing the limits and the rules will help responsible educators protect their schools and their personnel from legal action concerning copyright.

Doug Johnson has been director of media and technology for the Mankato (Minnesota) Public Schools since 1991. Doug is a veteran author whose works have appeared in books, journals, and magazines. Doug serves on ISTE's board of directors and as volunteer editor of L&L's Media Matters column.

A public school educator for 25 years, Dr. Carol Simpson has taught every grade from kindergarten through graduate school. Currently, she is an associate professor in the University of North Texas School of Library and Information Sciences and a fellow in the Texas Center for Digital Knowledge. She is the author of Copyright for Schools: A Practical Guide *(4th ed., Linworth, 2005) and* Ethics for School Librarians: A Reader *(Linworth, 2003).*

author's update
Doug Johnson

This article still accurately reflects traditional thinking about copyright instruction and enforcement in schools.

There have recently been, however, some powerful and thoughtful trends that have changed my thinking about copyright and how we deal with it in schools. I would encourage all educators to read these materials:

Aufderheide, Pat, Renee Hobbs, and Peter Jaszi. "The Cost of Copyright Confusion for Media Literacy." Center for Social Media. www.centerforsocialmedia.org/files/pdf/Final_CSM_copyright_report.pdf

Aufderheide, Pat and Peter Jaszi. "Recut, Reframe, Recycle: Quoting Copyrighted Material in User-Generated Video." Center for Social Media. www.centerforsocialmedia.org/resources/publications/recut_reframe_recycle

Hobbs, Renee, Peter Jaszi, and Patricia Aufderheide. "Ten Common Misunderstandings about Fair Use." Temple University Media Education Lab. http://mediaeducationlab.com/index.php?page=274

Hobbs, Renee. "Fair Use and the Educational Guidelines: FAQ." Temple University Media Education Lab. www.mediaeducationlab.com/index.php?page=275

Johnson, Doug. "Beating the No U-Turn Syndrome: Modifying Our Approach to Copyright Instruction and Enforcement." https://dougjohnson.wikispaces.com/NUTS

Lessig, Lawrence. *Free Culture*. Penguin, 2004.

Stallman, Richard M. "Did You Say 'Intellectual Property'? It's a Seductive Mirage." Free Software Foundation. www.fsf.org/licensing/essays/not-ipr.xhtml

My personal view is that when teaching both students and teachers about copyright, we need to stress the outer limits of fair use, not just the "safe harbors," if we are to avoid producing a nation of intellectual property scofflaws.

author's update
Carol Simpson

Because my role in this discussion seems to be the contrarian, I will politely point out that just because someone suggests that schools *should* have more access to copyrighted material doesn't (1) change the law, (2) change the way courts interpret the law, or (3) change the way administrators respond when faced with a copyright enforcement action. Because 99.99% of all copyright actions (probably more when considering schools) are settled out of court, factor 3 appears to control what copyright philosophy governs schools. For example, when faced with a copyright infringement action because titles of licensed video appear in an online catalog, administrators chose to bow to all the demands of the producers rather than engage in a court fight that would have probably enhanced the fair use rights of schools and libraries, as I reported in the February 2008 issue of *Library Media Connection*. But they chose not to do that because fighting is expensive and schools don't have enough money to teach students, much less pay lawyers and court costs.

Many of the suggestions Doug cites to justify use beyond safe harbors are wonderful ideas, and certainly educationally valuable. Unfortunately there is no case law to support most of them. To get legal precedent sufficiently authoritative for a lawyer to make such recommendations to a school client would require at least two layers of exceptionally expensive litigation. As far as administrators are concerned, they want to avoid the intellectual and financial drain that litigation requires. Financial considerations will almost always outweigh the fight for a principle, at least in this arena.

I wrote a law review article on the case cited above for the summer 2008 issue of the *SMU Science and Technology Law Review*. In it, I demonstrate how simple it would be for Congress to change the law to make such use exempt for schools and libraries. The likelihood of such a small amendment passing in this political climate is minuscule because schools don't contribute to congressional candidates, and students don't vote. Producers, however, do both, employ hundreds of taxpayers, and generate money for the economy. Until Congress decides that education is worth more than re-election, business will have the upper hand, and schools can only be assured of those limits explicitly outlined—safe harbors. Kudos to those who press the limits; but they should be prepared to fight in court for their principles.

February 2006

Get the Word Out with List Servers

>>>>>> By Laurence Goldberg

In my school district of about 7,300 students in suburban Philadelphia (Abington SD), electronic mail list servers are now being used, along with other methods of communication, to disseminate information quickly and widely. We began by manually maintaining lists of e-mail addresses. It soon became apparent that we needed a more hands-free method of allowing parents and community members to receive information. This is when we moved to a list server model.

A list server is simply an automated list of e-mail addresses used to communicate with people on certain topics. Users can join or leave list servers themselves, without any intervention on the part of the schools. We first began testing using one of the free online services; however, the sign-up method was confusing, and the commercial advertising was distracting. Instead, we settled on a self-

Continued

Continued

maintained software package (in this case, GFI Mail Essentials) to create group lists that could be accessed directly. The list server software is relatively simple to install and maintain, running as an intermediary server to a mail server running a program such as Microsoft Exchange.

Hopefully it won't come as a shock that sending home photocopied handouts in student folders is no longer a cutting-edge method of communication. How many of those fliers actually make their way to parents, and how many end up crumpled at the bottom of an overstuffed backpack? And of those that survive the journey home, how many get lost when they fall off the magnet clip and slip into the neverland of dustballs and loose change under the refrigerator grille?

Happily, list servers are a better way. These days, even in less advantaged school districts, many households are equipped with computers and e-mail access. Even parents who do not have access at home often have access at work or through a local library or community center. School districts are only beginning to take advantage of this valuable method of communication.

Most schools now have their own Web sites. Yet without dedicated staff that can invest substantial time in maintaining current information and updates, school Web sites often provide only general, relatively static information. And Web sites are based on pull technology, meaning that viewers must take the time and effort to seek and download the information they need. Push technology, by contrast, sends the information out to the target audience. For schools to really get the message out to their target audience of parents, students, and community members, they need to use effective push technology. E-mail is one of the most basic methods of pushing essential communication.

Just as schools have developed telephone chains and postal mail directories, some schools have developed lists of e-mail addresses. The problem with this is that it places an additional burden on school staff, and the lists never remain accurate for very long. People change ISPs or e-mail accounts frequently, and misspelling a single letter in an e-mail address can prevent a parent from getting mail. Moreover, when the school is responsible for maintaining a mailing list, it opens itself to criticism if some parents are inadvertently left off. In some cases, if senders are careless and enter multiple individual addresses in the To field, they will reveal personal addresses to all recipients, which can

> ISTE's List Server Communities

ISTE members have a variety of organizational list servers available to them. Access to the lists and other community-building tools is under the Membership section of the ISTE Web site (http://www.iste.org). From the Membership page, choose My Communities and explore the options your membership plan affords.

Among the most commonly used community tools are the list servers. Nearly every one of the ISTE SIGs (special interest groups) maintains a list server so that members can share insights, discuss hot topics, and help each other out.

ISTE's list server software allows members to choose direct e-mail delivery of each list message, daily or weekly digests, or no e-mail delivery (you can retrieve messages from the community Web area).

The ISTE list servers are configured to be interactive. This means that members of the list are allowed to post messages to the group, even messages with attachments. However, as with most lists, you cannot post directly to individuals. The other members, of course, will not be able to respond directly to you either. This is usually considered an advantage of the list server model because it diminishes the number of "private" conversations that can clutter a forum area.

>>>>>>> *J.V. Bolkan,*
Senior Editor, L&L

Continued

Continued

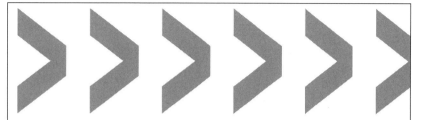

lead to spammers' harvesting the list of addresses and then bombarding them with spam.

We created a list server for parents and students of each of the nine schools, and an additional list server geared toward residents without children, interested community members, or anyone seeking information on the entire district. We publicized the list servers in various ways: with fliers sent home with students, hard copy newsletters, school Web sites, and the local cable television station. Those interested in subscribing need only send a blank e-mail message to a special account and then reply to an automated confirmation message. If subscribers type in an incorrect address, they will know because they won't get the confirmation—and the list server will notify us of the unsuccessful attempt. Incorrect or discontinued addresses are automatically removed from the system. Subscribers can leave the group by unsubscribing in a similar manner. The beauty of the system is that it can accommodate thousands of subscribers with little or no maintenance.

When principals or administrators wish to send a message out, they must use a generic account as the sender. This way, the sender will not be identi-

fied as an individual and will not be flooded with response messages. For example, at Abington School District, there is a generic account for each school that is used as the originating mailbox. If the originator accidentally tries to send messages from his or her personal mailbox or an unauthorized sender attempts to send to the group, the message is rejected and never reaches the group. Subscribers are not able to send messages directly to other group members, nor are their e-mail addresses revealed to one another, or third parties. Rights are assigned to authorized senders for each list server. We also created a catch-all group that contains all of the district list server members, so that certain individuals such as the superintendent could reach the entire wired community with a single message.

At first, things took off slowly. It took a while for a couple hundred subscribers to sign up, and when they did, the messages from the school were only trickling out. School newsletters, meeting and event reminders, board information, and other communication started flowing across the list servers to those early adopters. Then the first snows came, and suddenly there was a burst of activity. Although Abington already posted

For schools to really get the message out to their target audience of parents, students, and community members, they need to use effective push technology.

Continued

Continued

> It is incumbent upon public school districts across the United States to do a better job of reaching out and reporting back to their communities.

weather-related information on the community cable station and Web site, along with notifying local media outlets of this information, we were happy to be able to offer a convenient and instantaneous way to disseminate information directly to parents. On a snowy morning when we called our first late arrival of the season, list server subscribers who checked their e-mail were among the first to know. This quickly drove subscription rates up and got the word out as to the effectiveness of the list servers. And because we use Web-based e-mail, authorized senders can reach the entire subscribed school district community at any time from any Internet-connected location. The power of this should not be underestimated at five o'clock on a winter morning, or any time quick and effective communication is essential.

As a district actively involved in major construction and fundraising projects, Abington is also now able to more effectively disseminate information regarding these endeavors. The superintendent uses the list server to send out newsletters highlighting district awards and accomplishments. Other possible uses of the list servers include informing residents about issues related to district funding, legisla-

tive changes, and school quality measures. With increased emphasis on accountability through standardized testing and the mandates of NCLB, it is incumbent upon public school districts across the United States to do a better job of reaching out and reporting back to their communities. We must be able to effectively communicate with constituents, educate them on the issues that challenge us, call them to action when needed, solicit their input and support, tell them of our accomplishments and achievements, and remind them of the value they're receiving for their investment. It is no longer sufficient for us to be effective educators and administrators; we must also be active promoters and public relations experts. The list server method of communicating is just one tool in the well-equipped technology tool belt we must all wear in a fully wired and connected educational community.

Laurence Goldberg is a certified network engineer and director of technology and telecommunications for the Abington School District in Philadelphia, Pennsylvania. He has more than 15 years' experience working with technology in education and other organizations.

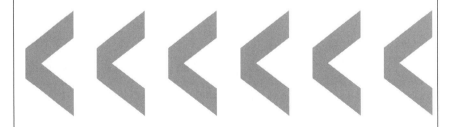

author's update
Laurence Goldberg

Format Wars

One of the unexpectedly significant issues we had to contend with as our list server usage grew was that of adopting an acceptable format for messages. Schools tended to want to simply attach to messages the flyers or letters they had prepared, creating large documents that might be rejected by some mail services or would be inaccessible if recipients did not have the appropriate software for reading the attachments. Our community relations department wanted everything to be richly formatted, colorful, and full of images so that it would be the most appealing. IT staff pushed for plain text messages devoid of any special formatting, worried about compatibility issues, rejection of messages, and network traffic from the more graphics-rich messages. And our superintendent wanted everyone to get the message with the smallest number of clicks—but wanted it to look great too. In the end, we settled for HTML-formatted text in the body of the message, with no attachments. A few recipients using older software or programs set to block HTML messages may have trouble viewing it properly, but we decided this was the best compromise, one that balances esthetics with functionality. Best advice: decide on your priorities early on and work out consistent formatting standards that everyone can live with.

March 2006

Avoid the Plague

Tips and Tricks for Preventing and Detecting Plagiarism

By J.V. Bolkan

Plagiarism is an ugly word. Copying someone else's work and attempting to claim credit for one's self is an act that involves a number of ethical failings—theft, laziness, coveting, and lying among others. Even in a complex world where many behaviors can be described as falling into ethical gray areas, few educators (or editors) have any tolerance for plagiarism. Yet, according to some studies, more than half of all college undergraduates admit to engaging in plagiarism. (*Editor's note:* Find these studies and other resources on p. 13.)

Many educators blame the Internet for what they perceive as the rise of plagiarism. Although the Internet certainly enables more efficient plagiarism, blaming it for widespread copying is akin to blaming a bank robbery on the presence of cash in the building. It is a factor, of course, but not the root cause of the behavior.

Just as with bank robbery, the solutions to plagiarism must be multifaceted. Efforts must be directed at prevention as well as detection and punishment. Banks don't leave piles of cash stacked by the front door. Educators should take care to make assignments that hinder plagiarists. It is also important to remember that it isn't just vaults and security guards stopping bank robberies. The vast majority of people wouldn't rob a bank even if they could. They understand that it is illegal and unethical. ISTE's NETS for Students includes an ethics standard:

Social, Ethical, and Human Issues

- Students understand the ethical, cultural, and societal issues related to technology.
- Students practice responsible use of technology systems, information, and software.
- Students develop positive attitudes toward technology uses that support lifelong learning, collaboration, personal pursuits, and productivity.

Educators should strive to reinforce the ethical ramifications of plagiarism. Setting a tone is important. "I establish my disdain for plagiarism early in the course and therefore (hopefully) set a tone for academic integrity, which will be reiterated each time research is required for an assignment," says Carlan Kephart, an English Instructor at North Eugene (Oregon) High School.

Deterrents

In-depth discussion of plagiarism has another deterrent benefit. It is a popular misconception that the reports and papers available from online "paper mills" are easy A's. In fact, the quality of papers offered online for plagiarists is quite uneven. It can be an extremely effective lesson to actually download a few sloppy examples and critique them with your class—a student willing to cheat to get a good grade may not be so eager to take the risk and spend the money just to get a mediocre or poor mark.

Although emphasizing ethics will diminish the instances of plagiarism, unfortunately, it isn't always enough of a deterrent. Fortunately, other methods of prevention are available. According to University of Oregon Journalism School instructor Mark Blaine, "I try to design assignments so that they have as much of a fingerprint as possible. The more unique each student's work is, the less likely they'll

Continued

Continued

report," they aren't as likely to copy someone else's work because they're going to have to learn the content anyway. Motivation, of course, is the key. Motivated and engaged learners are much less likely to take shortcuts. If they're only in your classroom to get a grade and move on, the potential for plagiarism will be greater.

be to cheat by lifting someone else's paper." For instance, it is pretty easy to find an online report on the topic of "the ocean" but a report on ocean beaches in Hawaii would be more of a challenge, and a report on the effects of a new resort hotel built on Waikiki might be impossible to find.

Another strategy that has proven effective is to require students to submit the various stages of their research. Although completed reports are quite easy to find online, very few are offered with outlines, early drafts, and lists of alternate and unused sources. Of course, determined plagiarists can recreate these, but they're likely to discover that the effort is equal to or even more laborious than crafting an original report.

A related strategy is to require at least one recent source. Most papers found online are at least a few years

old and include references and citations that are even older. Again, determined plagiarists can work around this requirement, but often, the research and effort needed to update an older paper's citations is enough of a deterrent.

The final deterrent strategy, solid assessment and good teaching, can't be over emphasized. If students understand that they will be graded not only on the artifact they produce (the paper) but also on their understanding of the topic expressed in an oral report, or an essay on "the making of my

> **"Unfortunately,** I think we only get **the really clumsy [students]** with Googling."
> —*Mark Blaine*

Continued

chapter 4   Features

Continued

Detection

A plan for detecting plagiarism can also serve as a deterrent. For instance, Blaine lets students know that he does at least rudimentary checking for plagiarism. "We do Google things and let students know we're going to do it. Sometimes it works."

As with any security system, the best strategy is to employ both obvious and hidden methods. The obvious steps, such as Googling random sections of a report, serve both as deterrent and detection methods. However, if you tell them exactly how you use all the anti-plagiarism tools at your disposal, you may be ensuring that determined cheaters won't be caught.

Google is far from a sure-fire method of rooting out plagiarism. "Unfortunately, I think we only get the really clumsy ones with Googling," says Blaine. Although Google searches an incredible number of Web pages, it can't look into password-protected sites. Because potential buyers typically can't see the papers for sale online until they enter a password or credit card information, those papers are also protected from Google's search routines.

Despite Google's limitations, it is the choice for Kephart. "It can be pretty costly to get a school license" for commercial programs, "and when Google works just fine, I don't see the need to spend the money." Even with the digital tools available, Kephart relies more on herself, "when I do assign an outside writing assignment, I make sure that I've had a chance to really get to know the students' writing in class, first. Once I know their writing style, getting away with a plagiarized paper is virtually impossible. Even when students have only used paragraphs of material from someone else's essay—even a mere sentence—I can tell that it is not theirs."

There are much more sophisticated tools for rooting out plagiarism. Most of these tools are commercially based, and some are even quite controversial. Perhaps the most widely discussed and heavily used commercial anti-plagiarism tool is Turnitin. The self-described leader in "enterprise solutions" to the problem of plagiarism, Turnitin offers a variety of use and payment options. Essentially a combination of search engine technology (akin to Google) and a database registry, even critics of the service acknowledge its effectiveness at discovering instances of cheating.

It is the database portion of Turnitin that is somewhat controversial. When an educator submits a paper to the service, it is added to the database and compared to all the other papers previously submitted, as well as checked against the service's Google-like Web search engine. The fact that the service copies the entire submission into its database and then uses that content as part of its commercial operation is the source of the controversy. Detractors claim the service is violating copyright law by using the student papers in their entirety for commercial purposes, often without consent. Proponents answer with a

Online **cheating** is a **huge concern** not only for **educators**, but for **students** as well.

Continued

60   The Best of Learning & Leading with Technology

Continued

number of arguments, including the fact that the service does not distribute or ever make those papers available. Most universities that subscribe to the service require students to sign waivers saying they understand that their papers will be submitted to the database.

Although the debate over the legal and ethical merits of services such as Turnitin continues, there are other services that are simply unethical. Before choosing an anti-copying service, you'll want to do some careful research. Demonstrating an evil ingenuity, at least one anti-plagiarism service has managed for a time to profit from both sides of the problem. Charging a modest fee to educators, this service did indeed detect plagiarized articles, but it only reported on those articles plagiarized from its competitors in the online research paper selling business. If a paper appeared to be original, this service would then copy the paper to its archive of papers for sale. In essence, unwitting educators were paying to submit papers to the very service they were trying to discourage.

Punishment

It is impractical, if not impossible to have an effective punitive policy in place without strong deterrence and detection policies. Furthermore, without a policy in place, deterrence is not as effective, and detection is unlikely to be a priority.

Statistics on the Plagiarism.org Web site paint a dire picture of the current plagiarism and academic environment. According to the site, nearly half of the students in one survey believed teachers ignored cheaters, and in another, 90% believed cheaters are never caught or adequately disciplined. Perhaps, in part because of these beliefs, large majorities of high school and undergraduate students admitted to having

cheated in various polls cited on the site. Although the Plagiarism.org site appears to be tightly affiliated with the commercial Turnitin.com anti-plagiarism business, there is little doubt online cheating is a huge concern not only for educators, but for students as well.

Conclusion

Although it is difficult to accurately gauge just how pervasive plagiarism is and whether the Internet has made the problem worse, as more than one wag has noted, it is the unoriginal sin. Eradicating cheating isn't likely to ever be accomplished, but there are tools and techniques that can help keep the educational environment much more honest.

Resources

Commercial Tools
EVE2 (Easy Verification Engine): http://www.canexus.com/eve/
Glatt Plagiarism Services: http://www.plagiarism.com/
SafeAssignment: http://www.mydropbox.com
Turnitin: htpp://www.turnitin.com

Ethics Resources
Computer Ethics, Etiquette, and Safety for the 21st Century Student by Nancy Willard. ISTE, 2001.
Copyright for Schools: A Practical Guide (4th ed.) by Carol Mann Simpson. Linworth, 2005.
"Plagiarism Tool Creates Legal Quandary" by Andrea L. Foster. *Chronicle of Higher Education.* Available: http://chronicle.com/free/v48/i36/36a03701.htm

General Resources
Penn State Cyberplagiarism Page: http://tlt.its.psu.edu/suggestions/cyberplag/
Plagiarism.org (sponsored by Turnitin.com): http://www.plagiarism.org
University of Alberta Guide to Plagiarism and Cyber-Plagiarism: http://www.library.ualberta.ca/guides/plagiarism/
University of Texas at Austin's Preventing and Detecting Plagiarism: http://www.lib.utexas.edu/services/instruction/faculty/plagiarism/

J.V. Bolkan is a senior editor for L&L. He's been writing original articles about technology for more than 20 years.

author's update

J.V. Bolkan

Ironically, I'm sure my article on plagiarism has been copied more than any other article I've written in *L&L*. Fortunately, as far as I know, the copies have all been authorized. I was a bit surprised, and gratified to discover that the article had been assigned to a number of preservice student teachers as a topic for discussion. The article has also been cited numerous times. I'm convinced that much of the success of this article was due to the excellent graphic treatment given to my words by Tamara Kidd and Elizabeth Scandalios—rats will get anyone's attention.

Beyond the catchy images and title, I do think the topic was and remains important. But even more importantly, I think the article resonated because the subject really addresses one of the overarching issues with technology. Without a doubt, having computers with ready access to the Internet enables a host of potential problems in the classroom, plagiarism included. However, it is just as true that plagiarism only flourishes in a classroom using outmoded teaching methods.

I wish I could take credit for the ideas, but all I did was ask questions and talk to a number of educators who had "solved" the plagiarism problem, then assembled those ideas into an article. Two sources were especially helpful and generous with both time and insight, Carlan Kephart from North Eugene (Oregon) High School, and Professor Mark Blaine from the University of Oregon's excellent journalism school.

I hope the article remains a useful and practical guide to the problem of plagiarism. Even more, I hope the concept behind the article—that for most of the problems that come with technology, there are opportunities to rethink how we teach, as well as methods that not only mitigate the problems but can improve teaching and learning—is fully embraced.

April 2006

Designing the New School

By J.V. Bolkan, Jennifer Roland, and Davis N. Smith

PHOTOS BY TAMARA KIDD AND BETH SCANDALIOS

Lots of things have changed since the baby boomers began overfilling postwar schoolhouses in the 1950s. The sparkling new buildings erected across the United States to handle the population surge have lost their luster, and in many cases, their functionality. This isn't new information; in a 1995 General Accounting Office report, nearly half of U.S. schools lacked the basic wiring to support computers, modems, and other modern communication technology. In the decade since that report, infrastructure needs have expanded dramatically. Replacing these buildings has become a priority for school districts. Eugene, Oregon's 4J district is fairly typical. It plans to open its fourth replacement school in as many years when the 2006–07 school year begins, and L&L staff visited the two newest buildings in the district.

Madison Middle School opened in fall 2005, and across town the new Cal Young Middle School is taking shape in the shadow of the current building. District and site-based staff were extremely gracious with their time as we toured Madison days before its opening and later took a rainy tour through the Cal Young construction site. Many of the lessons and insights the various participants shared with us should be of interest to personnel in other districts embarking on similar building projects.

Modern Needs for Modern Schools

Although a new school building shares almost all the obvious characteristics of one built in the 1950s—or even the 1920s—the infrastructure needs of 21st-century students and teachers have changed dramatically. In the 1950s, television was still relatively young, and its potential as an educational technology almost unimagined. Computers were still nearly as large as an entire school, and they were years from being introduced to students. The predominant technologies were the chalkboard, filmstrip, and movie projector. A modern school needs to have a robust network structure that can be easily upgraded, plenty of electrical outlets, rich multimedia and communication features, and safety and security equipment. It also needs to be accessible to a much higher degree than was common in the 1950s and incorporate modern design and ergonomic factors. And, it must still be designed to last through 40 or 50 years of hard use. Finally of course, it had better fit inside the inevitably tight budget.

Continued

Continued

At Madison, common areas were designed to allow pods of students to congregate and collaborate.

Joel Lavin, a science teacher at Madison who was part of his school's design team, says that planning for forward-thinking uses of technology is critical to a tech-integrated school's success.

"Teachers are mainly using computers for literacy, Internet research, and presentations," Lavin says. "We want to get kids doing presentations to each other. We want kids to use Inspiration for reading and reporting skills. All kids have e-mail. All kids have wireless access. We are trying to get them to interact more with each other electronically at school. We know they interact out of school electronically already."

Although details will change from district to district, many of the challenges encountered and lessons learned in 4J are likely to be repeated in other regions. For instance, the need to balance staff, student, and community expectations within a budget is a universal concern. Getting input from all these stakeholders is only part of the equation; weighing the importance of stakeholder opinion is much trickier. "It's all about the students," may sound very noble, but if a district shortchanges the needs of the staff so that they can't efficiently teach, how well are the students really being served?

Likewise, satisfying teachers and other staff but alienating the community can lead to long-term problems in a public school system. Ensuring that children with diverse experience with technology have robust access is vital.

"As I work with my students more, I notice a clear digital divide," Lavin says. "Kids with iPods, picture phones, and so on have integrated computers in their lives in the classroom and out of it. Kids without these things have a harder time using technology in the regular classroom."

It is easy to over-focus on computers and other digital equipment as the keys to the digital divide, but the fundamental technology of a school building can be a huge factor in closing or expanding the gap. For example, oft-ignored technology such as lighting and acoustical design can have concrete effects on student learning. According to studies by the California Board of Energy Efficiency, student test scores are 15% to 26% higher when classrooms are designed with daylighting. Likewise, student assessment results have shown to be closely tied to the acoustic properties of the classroom. Declines of nearly 30% in reading scores have been found when classrooms have poor acoustics. Both of the new middle schools were designed to bring maximum natural light into every classroom, and all classrooms are built with sophisticated multi-speaker sound systems that ensure consistent audio levels for all students throughout the room.

Because a new school is a multi-decade commitment with a large and diverse set of stakeholders, the pressure to do it right is intense.

Planning Is Crucial

Each of the new schools began with an exhaustive planning stage involving an advisory team composed of district and school staff, local parents, and districtwide community volunteers. Although each of the four replacement projects overlapped somewhat in their planning process, even fundamental decisions were made on each school independently. One community volunteer, Rodney Price, helped design the style of Madison's new building. "Madison was based on a classroom cluster theory, where subject matter rooms are grouped around a common area. The school district and Madison principal were

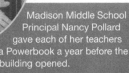

Madison Middle School Principal Nancy Pollard gave each of her teachers a Powerbook a year before the new building opened.

Continued

Continued

very committed to getting a modern school with outstanding classroom facilities and also accommodating the extras like band and athletics," which Price, a coach and former school band member, thought were important.

Opposed to a top-down philosophy, 4J's site-based schools are allowed to choose what technology to purchase, how it's used, and who uses it. But according to Kim Ketterer, 4J's educational technology district specialist, the site-based concept is far from purely implemented. The district houses network fileservers for the school in its central offices. Naturally,

COWs are an essential component of the district plan. Madison broke the shrinkwrap on theirs in September 2005.

with the district housing the actual fileservers for the schools, specifications for the fiber optic connections from the schools were made by district personnel. "Most of the input for infrastructure and networking actually came from the school district administration staff," Price says.

The district also offers staff training personnel, such as Ketterer, but district staff are only able to provide support and training on specific equipment and software. However, the major top-down influence is the districtwide commitment to online testing at every grade level. The district provides each elementary, middle, and high school a computers on wheels (COW) set with at least 12 Windows-based laptops so that students can be tested online. Although school staff can choose Macintosh, Windows, or handheld computers for use in their classrooms, the testing with the COWs is mandatory.

"Having COWs makes it possible to have students use spreadsheets and word processing for labs," says Angie Ruzicka, a science teacher at Cal Young, "and my two wireless laptops and a projector make it possible to access digital resources I didn't before, except for my own use."

Cal Young principal Sara Cramer shows off the design of her new building.

However, mandatory testing with COWs could also lead to bottlenecks.

"As more people want kids to use laptops, it is going to be frustrating to get access," says Ruzicka. "Right now I'm one of a small group that uses the COWs, so that has been nice. For it to be totally integrated you have to feel like you have access when you need it, and not have to change your instructional plan to fit availability."

A Tale of Two Sites

Because of the input from their respective advisory committees, the two middle schools, despite being opened within a year of each other and built by the same general contractor, are not twins. They do share several major technology elements. For instance,

Funding History

The genesis for these two schools was "a conversation [District 4J carried on] with our community that will help us develop a shared vision for education in Eugene," writes superintendent George H. Russell in his 1999 initial proposal for a Schools of the Future Committee (SOFC). The committee as Russell envisioned it would bring together education leaders, college of education faculty, students, parents, businesspeople, and members of the community to decide how education in District 4J should look in the 21st century.

The district supported Russell's vision and pulled together 29 community members, including

the mayor; the dean of the University of Oregon College of Education; representatives from the Chamber of Commerce, the Eugene Education Association, the Oregon School Employees Association, and the Eugene Administrators' Association; and school board members. They kicked off their project in September 1999 by inviting noted educational futurist Willard Daggett to speak. Daggett advised the SOFC to leave their expectations at the door and embark on the process with no prior assumptions.

The committee worked over the next 10 months to create a set of recommendations that guide a process to build new schools over the next three

decades throughout District 4J. The district then formed a Strategic Facilities Planning Advisory Committee (SFPAC) in March 2001. This 31-member group operationalized the recommendations the SOFC. This group's membership included principals, parents, students, facilities staff, a mechanical engineer, and a budget committee member.

The SFPAC placed a bond measure on the May 21, 2002, election ballot that included money for four new elementary school buildings and Madison and Cal Young Middle Schools. Voters approved the measure with 67.4% in favor, and the schools began their planning.

—*Jennifer Roland*

Continued

Continued

Built-in projectors in every classroom are already changing the way some teachers teach.

Madison made sure its music program benefitted from the state-of-the-art technology. They included acoustic tiles and speaker systems among traditional band equipment.

both schools are designed to provide full wireless networking throughout the building and surrounding grounds.

The commitment to robust networking, both wired and wireless, in the buildings was never seriously challenged. However, another feature common to both schools—projection systems in every classroom—was not so straightforward.

"We were hoping to have projection systems," says Madison principal Nancy Pollard. "However, the decision that we would in fact get them came very late in the building project. Teachers are in various stages of using their projection

systems. We will continue to provide training and collect and share ideas regarding best practices and uses." Each classroom includes a mounted NEC VT676 multimedia projector (reviewed in *L&L*, March 2006, p. 40).

Particularly in the elementary and middle schools, the most prevalent machines for staff are Apple Powerbooks. At Madison, creative budgeting and a strong belief in the value of technology enabled Pollard to purchase a Powerbook for every teacher a year before the new school opened. Total wireless coverage in the building has further increased the flexibility of the staff's laptop systems.

According to Ketterer, laptops are a key ingredient to getting full buy-in from teachers. "When they (teachers) can take the systems home, they

tend to learn and become more motivated to use the technology in the classroom." Ketterer also believes in providing as many digital cameras as possible to teachers, citing the creativity and enthusiasm the devices help foster.

The importance of staff buy-in and 4J's site-based emphasis have combined to differentiate the schools somewhat. Madison has an obvious emphasis on arts with a flexible, multi-use performance space and a high-tech, equipment-rich music room. Cal Young construction features an advanced multimedia lab and video emphasis.

Both Price and Grant Bowers, another member of the Madison planning team, worked with their kids to ensure that the new building would meet their needs. In fact, Bowers says he brought his daughters to some of the planning meetings. Price's younger son still attends Madison and, Price says, "is pleased with it." Price's older son and both of Bowers' daughters have since graduated, and all are jealous of the current students.

Rich Rewards

As with any new system, it takes a while to work the bugs out. "There are many glitches with our tech systems and wireless that we are working out with our district CIS folks," Pollard says. "I'm sure it will be a year of such glitches." Pollard says Madison's teachers and staff are working with district personnel, including Ketterer and others, to develop the school's technology plan, as well as activities and training as a part of the school's ongoing improvement plan.

Meanwhile, teachers and students at Madison and Cal Young are seeing benefits from the infusion of technology into the schools' planning from the ground up. According to Lavin, his

Construction on the new Cal Young building continues as students spend their final year in the old building.

Continued

Continued

Student-created art plays
a part at Madison, from the
chairs in the library to the
tiles in the bathrooms.

21st-century classroom at Madison has already changed the way he teaches.

"It gives me more access to visual and auditory learners," Lavin says. "I can use a stereo system to reach kids in the back of my room. I can show movies that all can hear and see. I can teach research techniques on various search engines and encyclopedias that pop up all the time. I can use digital streaming media on demand, no video tapes required. I can find images for kids to use in the classroom for projects that are safe and copyright safe."

Jason Erickson, a sixth grade block teacher at Madison, agrees. "I am able to teach from various points in the room. I have a Bluetooth keyboard and mouse, and with the use of my laptop and overhead projector, I'm able to teach most of my lessons without using the white board. I'm mobile, and can easily roam about the room, instead of being stuck in the front."

"I can get kids to interact in a positive way with each other by sharing information," Lavin concludes. "I can have students give each other help technologically with projects. I'm using textbooks a little less, using the projection system a lot, and enjoying finding resources I never knew I could use before."

Financial Issues

Replacing a school building is an expensive and time-intensive project. Often, initial community support is ambivalent at best. Nostalgia for an old building, resistance to new or increased taxes, intra-district politics, and a host of other potential roadblocks are all factors a district must face when contemplating building a school on the ashes of an older one.

Ultimately, there really is no choice. Because a school building can have such a profound effect on student learning, parents with children in substandard facilities have been successful in bringing lawsuits against districts and states across the country, forcing them to upgrade schools. (***Editor's note:*** See Education Commission of the States briefing at http://www.ecs.org/clearinghouse/60/26/6026.htm.)

Another huge concern is the higher costs associated with older buildings. In addition to significantly higher maintenance costs, new schools are estimated to be at least 25% more energy efficient than older schools. In 2003, the U.S. Department of Energy estimated overall energy costs for operating schools at more than $6 billion annually. A potential savings of $1.5 billion a year in energy costs is significant, and with the cost of power already well above 2003 levels and expected to continue rising, many districts cannot afford to put off replacement projects.

Conclusions

Now more than ever, a school is much more than bricks and mortar. Approximately half of the school districts in the U.S. currently need to replace at least one school. The key to successful implementation begins long before foundations are laid. Strong direction from the district, heavy involvement from the community, and attention to the needs of school staff all are required to create buildings that will bring out the best in our students.

J.V. Bolkan is a senior editor for L&L with more than two decades of publishing experience.

Jennifer Roland is a senior editor for L&L. She holds bachelor's degrees in journalism and political science and has been with ISTE since 1994, working on L&L and ISTE's research journals and Special Interest Group publications.

Davis N. Smith is an associate editor for L&L. He is also the copy editor and layout designer for ISTE's research journals, JRTE and JCTE.

author's update
J.V. Bolkan

When I first pitched this story idea to editor Kate Conley, 1-to-1 laptop programs were still fairly rare, but they were what everyone seemed to be discussing. From the nuts-and-bolts of financing and maintaining a full laptop program to the huge topic of training teachers and reworking the curriculum, ideas and debates were raging.

When I heard that one of the local school districts (Eugene, Oregon, 4J) was building a pair of new middle schools that would feature full campus-wide wireless, I knew I wanted to do an article. A little research showed that Eugene wasn't unique in needing desperately to update, overhaul, and replace schools. The mid-century baby boom was now more than 50 years behind us, the schools built for those students were getting old.

Kate jumped at the idea. She quickly expanded on the concept and soon the entire staff was involved. Although I was the lead author, it was truly a team article. The entire staff arranged to visit both schools. In addition to the three bylined authors, acquisitions editor Anita McAnear and Kate, along with our design team of Tamara Kidd and Elizabeth Scandalios, all trekked out to the construction sites.

In the back of my mind, I've got to admit I'd been hoping we'd find that they'd built "the school of the future"—holodecks for full immersion lessons, voice-activated everything, the entire sci-fi setting! Instead, the school had piles of textbooks in the classrooms, regular (if new) desks for writing (with pen and paper), and not a friendly robot in sight.

It wasn't until long after the article appeared in print that I began to appreciate the real story. The very fact that building a "digital-ready" school wasn't controversial or even terribly newsworthy is a powerful statement that I didn't appreciate fully at the time. Those of us immersed in the revolution that technology promises education way too easily get frustrated at the pace of change, wondering when and even if, change will occur. Stepping back, it is obvious—the foundations have and continue to be laid.

For *L&L*, this was a foundation-building article in a different sense. This article was among the first staff-written features the magazine had done. Although the magazine will always be primarily contributor driven, the magazine benefits greatly when the staff is able to interact with educators and contribute to the discussions.

March 2007

By Colleen Swain and David Edyburn

Social Justice
Choice or Necessity?

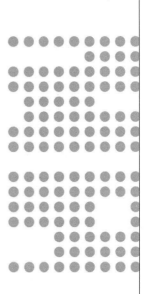

When a teacher chooses whether to use technology in the classroom
as a means of engaging students in challenging curriculum,
should the decision be considered simply a personal choice?

Continued

Continued

Given the power of instructional technology and the ubiquitous nature of technology in society and the workplace, what are the social implications associated with teachers' decisions to use, or not use, technology to enhance teaching and learning? Despite current U.S. educational goals and the documented effect of the achievement gap, little attention has focused on critical issues associated with the use of instructional technology as a social justice tool. This article will explore the social justice implications of instructional technology and provide educators with a framework for understanding the effects of their decisions in using instructional technology in the classroom.

A Social Justice Issue

What does social justice mean? In his book, *Principles of Social Justice,* David Miller states "Very crudely, I think, we are discussing how the good and bad things in life should be distributed among the members of a human society." Access to instructional technology is not enough for today's students. Students must be technologically fluent and able to use technology to solve problems with various sources of information, create new representations of their knowledge, and enhance their learning through the diverse strategies afforded by technology. Students without these skills are at a decided disadvantage in terms of future educational and employment opportunities in our global, technological, and information-based society.

Our students will most likely obtain jobs we cannot even imagine. In 1992, the U.S. Department of Labor's SCANS report noted that at least 80% of all jobs in the next two decades would require workers to be technologically fluent. This means if workers are not well prepared in using technology to succeed in the workplace, they will be forced to take low-paying jobs with limited potential for advancement.

At many universities, admission standards for incoming freshman continue to rise. Even if an incoming freshman is highly gifted, if he or she is not extremely familiar with using technology in the learning environment, that student is at a decided disadvantage the second he or she steps onto the university or college campus.

Continued

Continued

An important aspect of adopting a framework of social justice when using technology in the classroom is for the educator to be reflective about how it is used in the classroom.

Examining the Framework

Although the following examples provide poor instances of technology use from a social justice perspective, they do clearly illustrate important concepts in the framework for using a social justice lens to view the effectiveness of technology use in the classroom.

- Students only use technology to assess their comprehension of books or to prepare for the state standardized tests using drill-and-practice programs.
- Students are expected to hand-write the first draft of a report so they can type it into the computer when the class goes to the computer lab.
- Only students who have demonstrated mastery of the basic factual content of a unit are allowed to use technology applications for problem solving and simulation to expand their understanding of the concept.
- The teacher asks his or her students to share use of computers in the classroom or learning center but does not structure the activity to ensure that all students enjoy equal hands-on access to the computers. Left to themselves, the boys end up obtaining twice as much hands-on time as the girls.
- The schools' teachers assign students with lower grades or achievement scores to use computers to develop such "vocational" skills as keyboarding and word processing while engaging more highly achieving students in using the computers for more advanced problem solving.

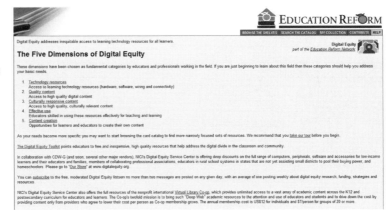

The National Institute for Community Innovations hosts the Digital Equity Portal, an excellent resource for getting started.

What framework can be used when thinking about technology use in the classroom from a social justice perspective? We believe that technology is equitably implemented when it is:

- available
- used routinely
- used in ways that reflect real-world applications of interest, complexity, and power
- used to enhance learning opportunities for all students
- used to monitor teacher/students progress over time.

Gaining Classroom Access

Although computer access in U.S. classrooms continues to improve, there are still classrooms that have no or limited access. So how can educators work to change this? One of the most powerful resources is the Digital Equity Portal and Toolkit (For this and other URLs, see Resources on page 18). The Digital Equity Portal has more than 150 strategies and resources for addressing key aspects of the digital divide. Many of the associated issues (access to hardware, software, digital content, connectivity, and support) do have solutions. There are computer refurbishment Web sites where schools can obtain computers and also ways to get deeply discounted computers. There is also a growing collection of free or open source software available. Educators must search for ways to make instructional technologies accessible in the class and a normal part of the learning process. The free Digital Equity Toolkit contains the "greatest hits" of such practical strategies and any educator can recommend a resource to the toolkit by e-mailing digitalequity@iste.org. You can also conduct an audit of the readiness level of your school by using the School Technology and Readiness (STaR) chart.

Continued

Continued

Locating Powerful Resources

Once you've gained access to technology, you need resources for using it effectively. There are a variety of excellent instructional technology resources, but it is often time-consuming and difficult for educators to locate them. The Digital Equity Portal and Toolkit mentioned earlier is an excellent place to start a search for exemplary digital resources. It is critical that students use instructional technology to learn concepts deeply and have the opportunity to learn and present their understanding using a variety of multimedia formats.

New resources continue to become available to educators, so it is important to evaluate each resource in terms of how it allows students to learn the concept deeply, enhances higher-order thinking opportunities, presents their knowledge in ways that mesh with strengths, and furthers educational and future workplace opportunities.

Another important capacity some learning technologies possess is to assist students with special learning needs or impairments. Instructional and assistive technologies can greatly benefit struggling readers and students with language difficulties, computational problems, and so on. For example, students who have difficulty reading could use an instructional technology to "erase" the area of weakness. This is significantly related to the goals of social justice by providing students with opportunities previously closed to them.

Reflection

An important aspect of adopting a framework of social justice when using technology in the classroom is for the educator to be reflective about how it is used in the classroom. Keeping a journal or making careful notes in lesson plans on the ways instructional technologies were used is a way to help examine the use in your classroom. As you monitor activities, consider whether the instructional strategies used in your lesson use technology for higher-order thinking, provide your students with meaningful interaction with the content, or allow students to use technology keyed to their learning style or impairment.

Another strategy is to survey your students on the experiences they have throughout the school day. This is particularly important if your students are with you for a portion of the day. Enabling every student to have engaging and powerful experiences with

Continued

Continued

> Enabling every student to have engaging and powerful experiences with multiple types of instructional technologies throughout his or her school experience can decrease the digital divide.

multiple types of instructional technologies throughout his or her school experience can decrease the digital divide. Lastly, you can find out discreetly which of your students do and do not have access to computers and the Internet at home and then point those who lack these resources to places in the community where they can turn to gain better access (e.g., public library, community technology center, Boys and Girls Club).

Conclusions

To date, decisions about if, when, and how to use technology in the classroom have been viewed as personal decisions by individual teachers. However, when teachers decide not to use technology in their teaching and learning environments, students are disadvantaged. Because the uses of instructional technologies in today's schools influence the opportunities for future educational and work experiences, instructional technology use in the classroom is a matter of social justice.

Teachers can influence the gap in the digital divide. If we as educators can infuse the use of instructional technology in classrooms as a component and catalyst for social justice, the educational experience for all students will change. Students can use instructional technologies to enable them to learn and demonstrate their learning in new ways, thus preparing them for an exciting and unlimited future. We hope these thoughts about and resources for social justice will assist you in your efforts to provide students with access to the critical technology tools that will define their future.

Acknowledgements

The authors would like to acknowledge the valuable contributions of Robert McLaughin, director of the National Institute for Community Innovations, and Rachel Vannatta, associate professor and chair at Bowling Green State University.

Resources

Access
CoSN K–12 Open Technologies: http://www.k12opentech.org
Digital Equity Portal and Toolkit: http://digitalequity.edreform.net
K12 Computers: http://www.k12computers.com
OpenCD: http://www.theopencd.org
Our Store: http://www.digitalequity.org
School Technology and Readiness (STaR) chart: http://www.iste.org/starchart.html

Assistive Technology
Kurzweil 3000: http://www.kurzweiledu.com
ReadPlease: http://www.readplease.com
WebMath: http://www.webmath.com

Instructional
Connecting Curriculum and Technology: http://www.iste.org/nets
MarcoPolo: http://www.marcopolo-education.org
Read, Write, Think: http://www.readwritethink.org
TeachersFirst.com: http://www.teachersfirst.com
Web Inquiry Projects: http://edweb.sdsu.edu/wip/examples.htm
Webquest Portal: http://webquest.org

Colleen Swain is an associate director and associate professor at the University of Florida. She works in the areas of curriculum and instruction with special emphasis on culturally responsive instruction and using technology in the classroom with a social justice perspective.

David Edyburn is an associate professor at the University of Wisconsin-Milwaukee. He teaches in the areas of mild disabilities related to learning and behavior. He investigates the use of technology to enhance teaching and learning.

authors' update

Colleen Swain and David Edyburn

When a teacher chooses to use technology in the classroom (or not) as a means of engaging students in a challenging curriculum, should the decision be considered simply a personal choice or are there deeper social justice issues at stake? In the year since our original article was published there have been a few interesting developments on the topic that warrant a brief update.

First, we have discovered few new articles published on this topic in the professional literature. However, issues of technology and social justice have caused periodic flareups in the blogosphere on sites such as Education and Class (Children Left Behind in a Profit Driven World, http://educationandclass.com/category/digital-divide/) and Dangerously Irrelevant (Social Justice, www.dangerouslyirrelevant.org/2007/03/many_of_my_educ.html).

Second, we are excited about evidence of a college course that focuses exclusively on the issues of technology and social justice (http://jus394spring2008.wordpress.com).

Third, we watch with interest as professional associations like the American Education Research Association adopt socially just mission statements (www.aera.net/AboutAERA/Default.aspx?menu_id=90&id=1960) and others, like the National Council for Accreditation of Teacher Education, struggle to define a commitment to social justice that allows principles to be implemented in practice (NCATE and Social Justice, www.ncate.org/public/0616_MessageAWise.asp?ch=150; "Social Justice" Removed from NCATE Standards, www.thefire.org/index.php/article/8541.html; A Spirited Disposition Debate, www.insidehighered.com/news/2006/06/06/disposition).

Finally, for all readers concerned enough to act on their conscience about the use of technology as a tool for social justice, we heartily recommend the tools and resources located at the Digital Equity Portal and Toolkit website (http://digitalequity.edreform.net).

December/January 2007–08

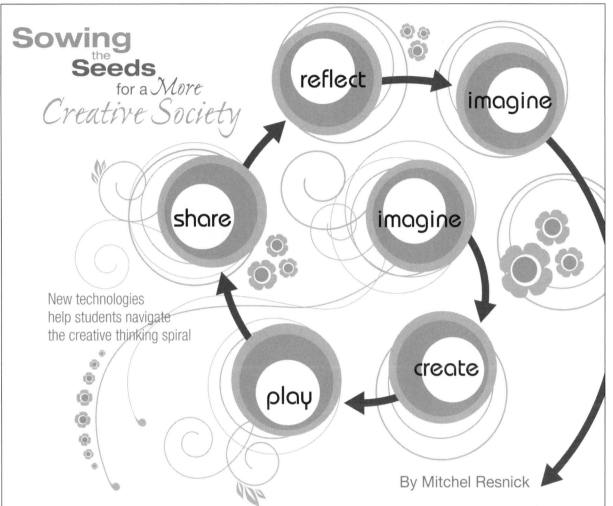

Sowing the Seeds for a More Creative Society

New technologies help students navigate the creative thinking spiral

By Mitchel Resnick

In the 1980s, there was much talk about the transition from the Industrial Society to the Information Society. Then in the 1990s people began to talk about the Knowledge Society, noting that information is useful only when it is transformed into knowledge.

But as I see it, knowledge alone is not enough. In today's rapidly changing world, people must continually come up with creative solutions to unexpected problems. Success is based not only on what you know or how much you know, but on your ability to think and act creatively. In short, we are now living in the Creative Society.

Unfortunately, few of today's classrooms focus on helping students develop as creative thinkers. Even students who perform well in school are often unprepared for the challenges that they encounter after graduation, in their work lives as well as their personal lives. Many students learn to solve specific types of problems, but they are unable to adapt and improvise in response to the unexpected situations that inevitably arise in today's fast-changing world.

New technologies play a dual role in the Creative Society. On one hand, the proliferation of new technologies is quickening the pace of change, accentuating the need for creative thinking in all aspects of people's lives. On the other hand, new technologies have the potential, if properly designed and used, to help people develop as creative thinkers, so that they are better prepared for life in the Creative Society.

In this article, I discuss two technologies developed by my research group at the MIT Media Lab with the explicit goal of helping people develop as creative thinkers. The two technologies, called Crickets and Scratch, are designed to support what I call the "creative thinking spiral." In this process, people *imagine* what they want to do, *create* a project based on their ideas, *play* with their creations, *share* their ideas and creations with others, and *reflect* on their experiences—all of which leads them to *imagine* new ideas and new projects. As students go through this process, over and over, they learn to develop their own ideas, try them out, test the boundaries, experiment with alternatives, get input from others, and generate new ideas based on their experiences.

Continued

Continued

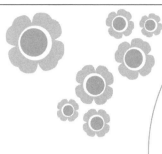

Crickets

Today's world is full of objects that sense and respond: doors that open automatically when you walk toward them, outdoor lights that turn on automatically when the sun goes down, stuffed animals that talk to you when you squeeze them. Children interact with these objects all of the time, but most have no idea how they work. And if children want to create their own interactive objects, most have no idea how to do it.

The Cricket is designed to change that. Children can connect lights, motors, and sensors to a Cricket, then program their creations to spin, light up, and play music. Children can use Crickets to create all types of interactive inventions: musical sculptures, interactive jewelry, dancing creatures. In the process, children learn important science and engineering concepts, and they develop a better understanding of the interactive objects in the world around them.

At a week-long workshop in Iceland, for example, Richard, an 11-year-old boy, decided to use a Cricket to create an automatic alarm clock to wake him in the morning. He connected a light sensor, a motor, and a sound box to a Cricket, and he attached a feather to the motor. Then Richard programmed the Cricket so that it would play a melody and gently twirl the feather against his face when the light sensor detected the sun shining through his bedroom window in the morning. Richard experimented with his new alarm clock, and it seemed to work well. But a friend pointed out a problem. Because Iceland is located so far to the north,

Cricket

Cricket Sensors:
Light sensor, touch sensor, sound sensor, resistance sensor.

Cricket Outputs:
Multi-colored light, sound box, numerical display, motor.

sunrise occurs at very different times over the course of the year, so the alarm clock wouldn't be very reliable. Richard thought about this problem, and when he created a poster about his project for the public exhibition at the end of the workshop, he included a warning at the bottom: "For Export Only."

As Richard worked on his alarm clock project, he actively engaged in all parts of the creative thinking spiral: he came up with an idea, created a prototype, experimented with it, shared his ideas with others, and revised his plans based on the feedback. By the end, Richard was full of ideas on how to improve his alarm clock—and he had refined his skills as a creative thinker.

In many ways, Crickets are similar to the Lego Mindstorms robot construction kits now used by millions of students around the world. But there are also important differences. While

Mindstorms kits are designed especially for making robots, Crickets are designed especially for making artistic creations with colored lights, sound, music, and motion. Crickets are now sold commercially as part of a kit, called the PicoCricket Kit, that includes not only Lego bricks and electronic parts, but also arts-and-craft materials such as pom-poms, pipe cleaners, and googly eyes. By providing a broader range of materials and supporting activities involving light and sound (in addition to motion), we hope to encourage a broader range of projects—and spark the imaginations of a broader range of children. We are especially interested in broadening participation among girls. Even with strong efforts to increase female participation, only 30% of the participants in Lego Mindstorms robotics competitions are girls. In Cricket

Continued

Continued

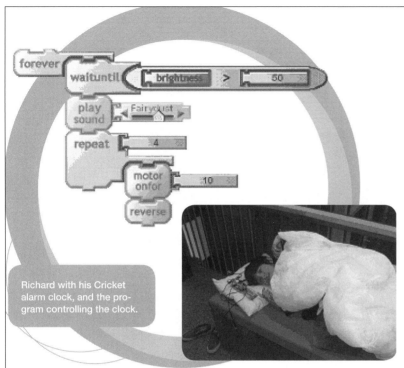

Richard with his Cricket alarm clock, and the program controlling the clock.

activities at museums and after-school centers, participation has been much more balanced among boys and girls.

Crickets have become especially popular in Hong Kong, where government and industry leaders are concerned about the outward migration of manufacturing jobs to other parts of China, and thus feel an urgent need to develop a more creative workforce. Cricket workshops in Hong Kong provide a glimpse into an alternative educational approach, where creative thinking is a top priority.

At one Hong Kong workshop, an 11-year-old girl named Julia was inspired by a pair of shoes that she had seen that contained embedded lights that flashed as the shoes moved. But Julia wasn't interested in buying shoes with pre-programmed lighting patterns; she wanted to create her own patterns. So she connected a Cricket and a series of lights to her boots, then installed a sensor near the bottom of the boot, where it could detect the up-and-down motion of her foot. She programmed the Cricket to change the colors of the lights, based on how fast she was walking.

At the same workshop, an entrepreneurial 12-year-old named Anthony came up with a business idea: a wearable jukebox. He cut a coin slot in the top of a cardboard box, then installed sensors on the underside of the slot to measure the size of the coin inserted. He then programmed the Cricket to play different songs based on what coin the customer put into the box.

For Julia and Anthony, the Cricket provided a way to create and personalize their own interactive inventions. As Julia explained, "With Crickets, you don't have to use what someone else made. You can make it yourself."

Scratch

Just as Crickets give students the power to create and control things in the physical world, Scratch gives them the power to create and control things in the online world.

For many students, the Web is primarily a place for browsing, clicking, and chatting. With Scratch, students shift from media consumers to media producers, creating their own interactive stories, games, and animations—then sharing their creations on the Web.

In classrooms, students have begun to use Scratch to create reports and presentations—replacing traditional PowerPoint presentations with content that is far more dynamic and interactive. At the Expo Elementary School in St. Paul, Minnesota, one student created a book report on Ben Franklin, including an interactive game inspired by Franklin's experiments with lightning. Another student created an animated documentary on the dangers of mercury in their school building. At another school, students created a penny-flipping simulation,

Workshop participants in Hong Kong engage their creative thinking to develop Cricket projects.

Continued

Continued

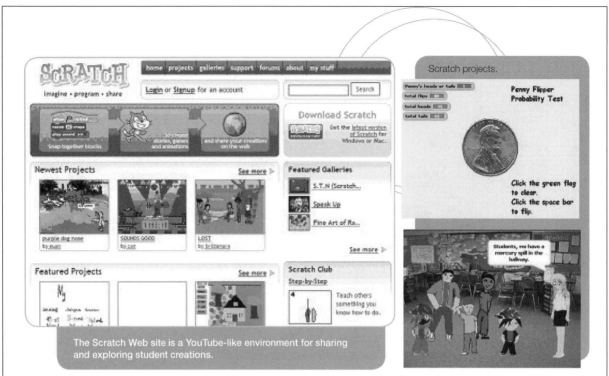

The Scratch Web site is a YouTube-like environment for sharing and exploring student creations.

then ran experiments to test theories in probability and statistics.

"There is a buzz in the room when the kids get going on Scratch projects," says Karen Randall, a teacher at the Expo Elementary School. "Students set design goals for their projects and problem-solve to fix program bugs. They collaborate, cooperate, co-teach. They appreciate the power that Scratch gives them to create their own versions of games and animations."

Students program their Scratch creations by snapping together graphical blocks, without any of the obscure punctuation and syntax of traditional programming languages. In this way, Scratch makes programming accessible to a much broader audience—at a younger age—than ever before.

In the process of programming their Scratch creations, students learn important mathematical concepts in a meaningful and motivating context. While visiting an after-school center, I met a student who was creating an interactive game in Scratch. He didn't know how to keep score in the game, and asked me for help. I showed him

how to create a variable in Scratch, and he immediately saw how he could use a variable for keeping score. He jumped up and shook my hand, saying "Thank you, thank you, thank you." I wondered how many eighth grade algebra teachers get thanked by their students for teaching them about variables?

Students can share their Scratch projects on the Scratch Web site (http://scratch.mit.edu), just as they share videos on YouTube. After the site was publicly launched in May 2007, more than 20,000 projects were uploaded to the site in the first three months. Students can browse the site for inspiration and ideas, and if they see a project that they like, they can download it, modify it, and then share the revised version with the rest of the community. The Web site has become a bustling online community. Members are constantly asking questions, giving advice, and modifying one another's projects. More than 15 percent of the projects on the site are extensions of previous work.

Collaboration on the Scratch Web site comes in many different forms. A

15-year-old girl from the UK with the screen name BeeBop created a project full of animated sprites, and encouraged others to use them in their projects. Another 10-year-old girl, using the name MusicalMoon, liked BeeBop's animations and asked if she'd be willing to create "a mountain background from a bird's-eye view" for use in one of her projects. MusicalMoon then asked BeeBop if she wanted to join Mesh Inc., a "miniature company" that MusicalMoon had created to produce "top quality games" in Scratch. A few days later, a 14-year-old boy from New Jersey who went by the moniker Hobbit discovered the Mesh Inc. gallery and offered his services: "I'm a fairly good programmer, and I could help with de-bugging and stuff." Later, an 11-year-old boy from Ireland calling himself Marty was added to the Mesh staff because of his expertise in "scrolling backgrounds."

The Scratch Web site is part of a broader trend toward a more participatory Web, in which people not only

Continued

Continued

point and click but also create and share. Many Web sites enable students to share text, graphics, photos, and videos. Scratch goes a step further, providing the tools for students to create and share *interactive* content, and thus become full participants in the online world.

Learning in the Creative Society

Today's students are growing up in a world that is very different from the world of their parents and grandparents. To succeed in today's Creative Society, students must learn to think creatively, plan systematically, analyze critically, work collaboratively, communicate clearly, design iteratively, and learn continuously. Unfortunately, most uses of technologies in schools today do not support these 21st-century learning skills. In many cases, new technologies are simply reinforcing old ways of teaching and learning.

Crickets and Scratch are part of a new generation of technologies designed to help prepare students for the Creative Society. But they are just the beginning. We need to continually rethink our approaches to education and rethink our uses of educational technologies. Just as students need to engage in the creative thinking spiral to prepare for the Creative Society, educators and designers must do the same. We must imagine and create new educational strategies and technologies, share them with one another, and iteratively refine and extend them.

Acknowledgements

Many people have contributed to the development of Crickets and Scratch—and to the educational ideas underlying them. The core design team for the latest version of Crickets included Brian Silverman, Paula Bonta, Natalie Rusk, Robbie Berg, and me. The core design team for the Scratch software and Web site included John Maloney, Natalie Rusk, Andres Monroy-Hernandez, Evelyn Eastmond, Tammy Stern, Amon Millner, Jay Silver, Eric Rosenbaum, Han Xu, Brian Silverman, and me at the MIT Media Lab, in collaboration with Yasmin Kafai's research team at UCLA. Many others have contributed to field-testing and development of activities. Our work on Crickets and Scratch was deeply influenced and inspired by other educational technologies, most notably Logo, Mindstorms, and Squeak Etoys. We greatly appreciate financial support from the Lego Company, Intel Foundation, the National Science Foundation (grants CDA-9616444, ESI-0087813, and ITR-0325828), and MIT Media Lab consortia. All children's names in this article are pseudonyms.

Resources

Cricket: http://www.picocricket.com
Lifelong Kindergarten: http://llk.media.mit.edu
Scratch: http://scratch.mit.edu.

Mitchel Resnick is a professor of learning research and director of the Lifelong Kindergarten research group at the MIT Media Lab. Resnick earned a BS in physics from Princeton and an MS and PhD in computer science from MIT. He is the author of the book Turtles, Termites, and Traffic Jams.

author's update   Mitchel Resnick

. . . .

I wrote this article just a few months after my MIT research group publicly launched our Scratch software and website. In the article, I reported that more than 20,000 projects had been uploaded to the Scratch website in the first three months after the May 2007 launch.

Now, more than a year after the launch, there are more than 125,000 projects on the Scratch website—and growing quickly. A new project now appears on the website every two minutes or so. But numbers tell just part of the story. What has been most impressive to us is the sophistication and diversity of the projects created by members of the Scratch community.

We had expected that students would create and share interactive stories and games with Scratch. But we hadn't expected that students would create entire new genres of projects. One student, for example, created a series of projects under the title SNN, for "Scratch News Network," modeled after CNN. In each SNN project, the news anchor reports on the most interesting projects that have been uploaded to the Scratch website in the past week. When I first saw one of the SNN projects, I thought: "That's nice. It's a simulation of a real newscast." But as I thought about it more, I realized that the SNN projects are providing useful information to an interested audience. They aren't just *like* newscasts, they *are* newscasts.

Another new genre is tutorial projects. Members of the Scratch community have created a large collection of projects to help other community members learn how to use Scratch, or how to create particular effects (like scrolling backgrounds) in Scratch. One tutorial project even provides advice on how to get your project featured on the home page of the Scratch website. As we all know, one of the best ways to learn is to teach, and many members of the Scratch community are learning through teaching.

When I see these projects, I am encouraged that Scratch has indeed helped students develop as creative thinkers. It is clear that many students are going through the Imagine-Create-Play-Share-Reflect-Imagine spiral as they work on their Scratch projects. But we are still in the early stages of the Scratch community. The current members of the community are "early adopters"—adventurous teachers and students who are willing to take risks and try something new. For the Scratch community to continue to grow, especially within schools, we need to provide better support for educators, to help them learn how to introduce Scratch effectively, and how to make connections to the important ideas and concepts underlying Scratch activities.

For example, my student Karen Brennan is developing a new community website, tentatively called ScratchEd, designed specifically to support ongoing professional development and community capacity-building among educators interested in Scratch. Through the website, educators will not only have access to new curricular materials developed by our MIT team, they will also have the opportunity to share their own stories and materials, as well as ways to coordinate in-person meetings with one another.

chapter 5

Learning
Connections

Learning Connections, the section of the magazine in which practitioners share their tips, tricks, and lesson plans, was known for years as "In the Curriculum." In the early days, the projects were often complete, stand-alone lesson plans that any reader could replicate line by line in their classrooms. As technology use became more commonplace, schools and districts began prescribing curriculum, so it became less useful for *L&L* to include technology-supported lesson plans. The section evolved to include descriptions of how a teacher or group of teachers used technology to support a learning activity. The articles were written in such a way that teachers could integrate the ideas into their own curriculum, in their own way, rather than simply using a predesigned lesson plan.

The name change coincided with a further change in the section. We began to include shorter tips and classroom ideas. We also began to solicit articles dealing with curriculum areas outside of the core, such as business education, health and physical education, and music. This broadening reflected the increased use of technology throughout the school day and even in extracurricular activities.

We begin with an article from outside the standard curriculum areas: business education ("Simulations as Action Learning Devices," Dan Smith, February 2008). Simulations are very powerful tools in the classroom, because they can provide experiences that are impossible to replicate under normal classroom conditions. They have been especially effective in science and math education, where they helped students visualize complicated ideas. Dan's company, Management Simulations Inc., creates simulations used in high schools, universities, and businesses to better prepare future executives. The simulations he describes in his article provide students with long-term projects that simulate up to eight years of company management so that they can develop skills and strategies that will help them throughout their careers. Dan points to IT skills, leadership skills, self-direction, work ethic, and social responsibility as direct benefits of the business simulations. His author's update provides some specific examples of the simulations in use.

Next, ed tech expert Kathy Shrock provides tips to help students evaluate a website ("Trash or Treasure: Evaluating a Web Site," December/January 2005–06). With the plethora of inaccurate and biased information available online, many articles over the years touched on the need to evaluate sites and ideas to help students do that. But this tool is a concise self-contained set of questions students can follow with each site they come across. By asking themselves the 5W questions—Who? What? When? Where? Why?—and using their current knowledge about the topic, students can tell whether a source is a valuable addition or something to be ignored. These tips are useful for all media, not just websites. And the critical analysis skills they learn by evaluating sites in this manner will help them throughout their lives, as they are presented with conflicting information and possibly unreliable sources in their work and personal lives and in the media. In her author's update, Kathy discusses new developments in technology and how her tools hold up when students need to evaluate them.

Next up is a really fun activity that acclimates young children to the inclusion of technology in their learning while also allowing the hands-on learning so essential at that age ("Digesting a Story," Stacy Bodin, May 2006). Stacy created activities around the holidays that incorporate video, word processing, and eating—how fun is that? Students take holiday treats (e.g., gingerbread houses at Christmas, chocolate bunnies at Easter) and write stories for them. They use their edible props to act out the stories, which the students videotape. Students then test each other on the concepts presented in their stories. Many teachers struggle with the need to use technology in early education. But Stacy proves here that not only are students ready for it, it can also prepare them for technology integration in later grades. In her author's update, Stacy talks about the challenges she faced after moving to a different school and trying to do the same types of activities with her students there.

We move on to a quick tip for foreign language learning that combines multiple modes of learning to help increase students' listening comprehension ("Improving Students' Language Learning," Lyn C. Howell and Robert Rose, March 2006). These authors saw improvements of, on average, 10 percentage points after their intervention. They combined the supplemental learning exercises in the Spanish textbook with an on-screen script to help students follow the conversations. This is the type of activity where technology shows its true power. With a quick retooling, pre-prepared activities become more relevant and usable. Technology allows multiple modes to be embedded in single activities, addressing the needs of all learners without having to assign separate activities. I remember how hard it was to learn conversational Spanish because the native speakers spoke too fast. This sort of tool would have helped me, as would the ability to listen at slower speeds to become more used to the cadence of native speech. Lyn and Robert provide the next steps in their authors' update, a description of the follow-up activities they used with students in Robert's Spanish classroom.

In our next Learning Connections piece, Ken Felker describes a tool that shows graphic and dynamic representations of human anatomy ("Dynamic Human Anatomy," March 2007). This tool provides a compelling simulation of dissecting a human body, which is not really feasible or desirable in the average high school health classroom. It provides the self-directed learning that allows students to learn at their own pace, following their own linkages between materials and ideas. It reminds me of the layered plastic anatomy diagrams from my old Encyclopædia Brittanica. Those were the most fascinating things I found in those dusty tomes, and I am excited that a similar, richer tool can provide an even higher level of exploration and interest in the inner workings of the human body—no cadavers required. Ken updates this article with an activity using Primal Pictures to enrich a high school health lesson.

The writing process is enriched when writers share their writing and get feedback on it. Rick Monroe created a judgment-free, technology-enriched method of incorporating critiques into his students' writing ("Electronic Read-Arounds," May 2007). His students use the classroom computers to post their writing, read their peers' writing, and comment on it. One of the hardest things to learn in writing is the concept of understanding your audience. Many teachers have asked their students to post their finished writing in public forums. This helps students put their best foot forward because they know that their work will be read by a broader audience than just the teacher. Even if they post their work anonymously, they don't want to be embarrassed by an inferior work. But how do these students learn what their final audience will want from their piece? Rick answers that question by adding the audience to the development phase, letting them ask the author for clarification and tell him or her what works or doesn't, and why. Can this activity be done without technology? Sure. In fact, Rick tells us in his author's update how he has continued this feedback loop without the access to technology he had when he wrote the article. And his students are still learning the fundamental lessons he needs them to learn. The addition of technology does not make or break this lesson, but is does make things more natural for the students. Students do a large portion of their research on the Internet, and they do their writing on the computer. Using the computer for gathering and responding to feedback is natural and appropriate. And, if Rick's students are anything like me, they can type a response a lot faster than they can hand-write it.

Long-time L&L contributor Margaret L. Niess provides our next article. In "Dynamic Visualizations" (December/January 2007–08), she discusses the tools provided in Microsoft Math and describes how they can bring math problems into a visual realm. The tools provided by the computer are more visually powerful and easily viewed than those provided by the typical graphic calculator. Teachers can lead lessons where they input variables and show the resulting graphs using a projector. Or small groups of students can work together to test solutions to homework problems. Many technology tools for teaching math have focused on drills and practice problems. They have made these rote learning tasks much more interesting, and they have had proven effects on student learning. But the tool Margaret describes allows students to use higher-order thinking skills in math and tap the real power of technology. The visual representations again bring multiple modes of learning into the classroom, helping strengthen student understanding. In her author's update, Margaret discusses the changes in math instruction and learning over the years.

Next up is a method to help students plan and conduct research projects ("Research, Deconstructed," Leslie Yoder, December/January 2007–08). Leslie describes an open-source software tool that breaks the research process into manageable steps and guides students through the process. The tool is based on a university-level tool and the Minnesota Educational Media Organization's Information and Technology Literacy Standards. The value of such a tool is in helping students plan their research and follow steps in a timely manner. This ability will help them greatly as they pursue higher education—following a process with benchmarks and steps can prevent the ever-popular all-nighters and hastily prepared papers that don't showcase actual learning or research skills. In addition, the teacher guide and lesson ideas ensure that the tool can be integrated into many different high school classrooms in a consistent manner. In the author's update she prepared with Jane Prestabek, Leslie describes what has happened with the tool since original publication and discuss some uses and coverage it has received.

We move to a simulated science problem that puts students in the role of environmental researchers ("Students as Environmental Consultants," Megan Roberts and Janet Mannheimer Zydney, September 2004). I described earlier the power of simulations in placing students into situations outside of the classroom that provide a greater context and show how classroom learning relates to the real world. This lack of connection to the real world is a real problem for many subjects, especially math and science. In the simulation presented in the article, students help a company deal with an environmental crisis. As green topics become more and more mainstream, this activity remains relevant. It bleeds into other subject areas, with a social studies element as students investigate the structure of government agencies and the rules and laws they oversee, a language arts element as they prepare persuasive writing on the topic, and a math component as students assess the economic consequences of the company's possible options. In the update, the authors discuss the use of the simulation with a different groups of students at a different level to assess the portability of the lesson.

We conclude our survey of the various curriculum areas with an example of students getting involved in the world around them ("Kids Galore Helping Kids in Darfur," Wendy Drexler, November 2007). We know that involving students in designing their learning activities is powerful. In this case, however, the power extended beyond the classroom, as students created a resource that helped bring attention to a human rights issue, connect them with other students and classrooms around the world, and provide a template for other classes to share their feelings about current events. The students created a website that was recognized by Congress, Amnesty International, and the Florida Holocaust Museum, among others. In addition, the student work on that website led to further collaborations between Wendy's students and older students, as she describes in her author's update. The take-away for teachers is the ease with which you can harness student excitement about a topic and direct it into positive, curriculum-based projects.

February 2008

Simulations as Action Learning Devices

In no subject is the effect of technology on the education process more apparent than in business education. Where textbooks and lectures fail to engage and teach business comprehensively to today's technology-oriented students, computer simulations provide logical and user-friendly platforms for learning.

Business simulations work by dividing high school business classes into teams that each manage a simulated company. The students, functioning as company managers, compete for market share and profits by making business decisions (from finance to marketing) that affect bottom lines.

In business simulations, students learn how to interpret financial statements and examine the competitive market. They devise business plans and make decisions in marketing. They hire and fire personnel and negotiate labor contracts. And they see how each choice affects the profitability of their simulated company. In short, they learn by doing—by far the best approach for young people.

"As an instructor of a college preparatory high school business management program, I use [business] simulations with students preparing for graduation to teach the big picture of how the separate functional areas, such as marketing and finance, fit together on a management team," says Wendi Howell, international business instructor for the satellite program of Eastland-Fairfield Career and Technical Schools located at Gahanna Lincoln High School in Ohio. "This knowledge helps students see how decisions affect other departments and how to run a business. The aver-age business person does not have the opportunity to understand these concepts until later in their careers."

Business simulations involve basic knowledge—including reading comprehension and mathematics—and applied skills such as critical thinking, problem solving, and teamwork and collaboration. Depending on related activities planned by educators, business simulations also can improve oral and written communications.

Other applied skills addressed by business simulations include:

- *Information Technology Application:* Business simulations are computerized and on the Internet—a good application of information technology.
- *Leadership:* Each management team has leaders. Students either are leaders or are associated with leaders. Either way, they experience how leadership works.
- *Lifelong Learning/Self Direction:* Defined as acquiring knowledge and learning from one's mistakes. Business simulations allow students to do both. In addition, assessment tools can help demonstrate mistakes, and through that, help students acquire knowledge.
- *Professionalism/Work Ethic:* Defined as personal accountability, punctuality, working productively with others, and time and workload management—all requirements of a successful team member.
- *Ethics/Social Responsibility:* Incorporating integrity and ethical behavior, simulations teach students to act responsibly with the interests of the larger community. A management team requires each member to act with the interests of the team.

By Dan Smith

Continued

Continued

The learning process for Management Simulations, Inc.'s Foundation Business Simulation is broken down into four phases:

- *Phase 1: Individual Assignments*—Climb the learning curve. All assignments are done on an individual basis. "You are only as strong as your weakest link." The more each person knows, the stronger the team will be.
- *Phase 2: Team Practice*—Next, students work in management teams, making decisions for their company, but in practice mode. It is about making mistakes and then learning the concepts.
- *Phase 3: Competition*—Student teams take over their company for a maximum of eight simulated years.
- *Phase 4: Boardroom*—At the end of their reign, the teams face their stockholders and the Board of Directors to explain how they managed their company. The real objective is having them explain what they did, why they did it, and what they learned from the experience.

See the sidebar of business simulations suitable for high school.

Business simulations arm students with enthusiasm, confidence in the decision-making abilities, and business acumen—powerful advantages they'll need in the real world. And they enjoy learning.

Dan Smith, president of Management Simulations, Inc. (http://www.capsim.com) and adjunct professor at DePaul University, is a leading expert in the field of simulation. With more than 20 years' experience in developing interactive business models, Dan condensed his broad business knowledge to create the specialized high school program Foundation Business Simulation.

Business Simulation Resources

The Association of Business Simulation and Experiential Learning (http://www.absel.org) is an organization dedicated to developing and promoting experiential techniques and simulations in business education. According to ABSEL's Web site, the group is "interested in the fields of business education and development, business gaming, experiential learning in higher education, online learning, distance learning, and professional training in national and international organizations."

Knowledge Matters' (http://www.knowledgematters.com) Virtual Business suite of simulations cover marketing, introduction to business, management, supervision, sports marketing and management, retailing, and entrepreneurship. In Virtual Business - Retailing 2.0, students manage a convenience store, with control over pricing, promotion, merchandising, and market research. Students get to pick from a list of 20 products to sell in their store. A Quiz Generator CD allows teachers to create customized quizzes based on selected lessons. The program is based on research funded by the U.S. Department of Education.

LavaMind (http://www.lavamind.com) offers a series of business simulations. In Gazillionaire, players run a trading company in outer space, and must make decisions about supply, demand, profit margins, overhead, account balances, and so on. The program offers a tutorial with adjustable complexity levels. Zapitalism is targeted at older students who are ready to explore more complex math, business and economics, and in Profitania, higher-level students manage and operate a factory using advanced structures and concepts.

Management Simulations, Inc.'s (http://www.capsim.com) Foundation Business Simulation teaches high school students the principles of business research and development, human resources, finance, marketing, production, strategy, tactics, leadership and teamwork. Student-run companies operate in "Low Tech" and "High tech" market segments. They begin the simulation with one product, but can develop a portfolio of up to five products. In team competition, four to six teams run companies and compete against each other, while in individual competition students each run a company, competing against five computer-generated companies.

Oak Tree Simulations' (http://oaktreesim.com) Micromatic is a medium to complex Web-based business sim targeted toward college undergraduate and graduate students in which players sell product through retail markets to the general public in three different sales regions. They decide the prices to charge for their products, the level of quality built into them, how to promote the products, and whether to sub-contract the manufacture of them to another company or produce the products themselves. In Team play, students are part of a group that manages a company competing with other companies in the same marketplace managed by other groups in the class. In the solo version of the game, students compete against companies managed by the computer.

—*Davis N. Smith, Managing Editor, L&L*

author's update
Dan Smith

Here are two examples of how simulation is successfully being used as an action learning device in semester and summer high school business programs.

First, Vicki Fuesz of Haxtun School in Yuma, Colorado, reports increased engagement after using the computer-based simulation with her students (she had used a non-technology simulation the year before). She saw her students using higher-order thinking skills, predicting sales, reading and analyzing data and graphs, solving problems and correcting mistakes, as well as learning to listen to each other and resolve conflicts.

Second, we hear about the use of simulations at the National Student Leadership Conference, an annual gathering of students that focuses on specific curriculum areas and allows the participants to earn college credit. The students in the program use the Capsim simulations. According to the NSLC website, "The competition is intense and student teams are given only a few hours to make annual decisions for their company. This condensed format forces students to work together and to rely on teammates. This simulated environment not only builds their knowledge and exposure to business areas (accounting, marketing, human resources, finance, strategy, etc.), but also exposes them to the difficulties of working with others and building leadership skills—skills that can only truly be learned from 'doing.'"

December/January 2005–06

Trash or Treasure? Evaluating a Web Site

Computer Science & ICT

Information found on the Web needs to be looked at with a critical eye. Anyone can easily publish a Web page or blog or change an entry in a wiki, and the information can appear valid. However, students must have a knowledge base in a topic before they conduct a Web search. If they know a little about a topic, it will be much easier for them to choose (and eliminate) some of the sites and information they find. In addition, if they are familiar with the topic, they are able to conduct more productive searches using related keywords and applicable phrases.

Here are some questions (based on the 5 W's) students can ask before they decide to use information they find online. You can post these by the computer(s) in your classroom or lab or hand out to students for home use.

Who?

Who wrote the pages, and are they an expert?
Is an author biography included?
How can you find out more about the author?

What?

What does the author say is the purpose of the site?
What else might the author have in mind for the site?
What makes the site easy to use?

When?

When was the site created?
When was the site last updated?

Where?

Where does the information come from?
Where can I look to find out more about the producer/sponsor?

Why?

Why is this information useful for my purpose?
Why should I use this information?
Why is this page better than another?

Standards: *NETS•S* 5 (http://www.iste.org/nets/)

Resources

Kathy Schrock's Guide for Educators: Critical Evaluation:
    http://discoveryschool.com/schrockguide/eval.html
The 5 W's of Critical Evaluation Handout:
    http://kathyschrock.net/abceval/5ws.pdf

—Kathy Schrock,
Administrator for Technology,
Nauset (Massachusetts) Public
Schools and ISTE board member

author's update
Kathy Schrock

I first developed these critical evaluation criteria in 1995, and they have withstood the test of time very nicely!

When web pages were the only type of online information students were evaluating, answering the posed critical evaluation questions was easy. Now that anyone can easily publish information on their own, and change it themselves (or have it changed by others), and with the proliferation of newer forms of web publishing, including podcasts and videos, there are additional aspects of critical evaluation to consider. Some of these other evaluation criteria are dependent on the format of the information being presented, including such things as RSS feeds and tags. The URL in the original article will lead you to lots of new resources and critical evaluation tools that I have developed including ones for teacher sites, virtual tours, blogs, and podcasts as well as updated student tools for the critical evaluation of websites.

Another thing that has changed since this article was originally published is the NETS•S standard that includes the aspects of information literacy. In the 2007 refreshed standards, critical evaluation falls under Standard 3, Research and Information Fluency.

May 2006

Digesting a Story

STILLS FROM VIDEOS SHOT BY STACY BODIN'S STUDENTS.

In this second-grade language arts unit, students help create edible props for a story setting, write an original group story, act out and film their story, create five original test questions that correlate with their story, and finally have a viewing party with the edible props as snacks. This project targeted a number of Louisiana grade level expectations and benchmarks.

Multimedia in the Classroom!
2nd Graders Digest a Story!

We developed our stories around holidays, but they could be organized around any topic with edible or non-edible props and scene elements. Our edible props for a Christmas story included gingerbread people, mini marshmallows and powdered sugar for the snow, brownies for trees, candy, and cake decorations. For Easter, we used chocolate bunnies, marshmallow candies, and other Easter candies.

Once the settings were built, I asked students to create a story with a setting, characters, a problem, and a solution. I gave each of the groups story maps with a block of space for each of the four parts to record their brainstorming session. The groups then typed the information in story form on the classroom computers. Using the writing process, the students proofread and edited their word processed work.

Once the stories were completed on the computers, copies were made and students mapped each other's stories by identifying the four parts (setting, characters, problem, solution). We used printed story mapping tools from Read Write Think (http://www.readwritethink. org). Finally each group typed five questions to test one another on each group story. Questions were factual in nature, such as, "Who was the main character?" or "When did the story take place?"

Students used their props and scripts to act out each story, which the kids videotaped using a digital video camera. I transferred the digital stories to a DVD that we shared with parents during Technology Week.

Find the complete lesson with story map, rubrics, and pictures at http://www.vrml.k12.la.us/dozier/EYE/EYE04-05/eyefeb05/tech/Digesting 201/digestinglessonplans.htm.

Stacy Bodin is a second grade teacher from Dozier Elementary in Erath, Louisiana. Born with a hearing disability, Bodin feels that just as her hearing aids are tools that have helped compensate for her hearing loss, computers are tools that help students meet individual academic needs and challenges.

By Stacy Bodin

author's update
Stacy Bodin

Without a doubt, the birth of my Digesting A Story technology lesson was a defining moment for me in terms of meshing multimedia tools, grade-level expectations, and higher-order thinking skills. Little did I realize how an epiphany during an early morning December shopping trip would embed a wonderful teaching experience in my heart.

After spotting gingerbread house kits on a nearby display table during my shopping trip, ideas stirred about a new technology idea using a video camera, computers, and food. Moments later, excited with the thoughts surrounding the project, I found myself literally running across the store grabbing edible Christmas treats to incorporate this new multimedia project into the curriculum.

In working with the actual project, I found myself impressed with the effectiveness of this technology-based lesson. Through an array of multimedia tools, I was able to productively target higher-order thinking skills in the students and have them excited about it.

On a personal level, I believe that writers place value in reading the final product of their creativity. With this project, technology helped bring it a step further. Eventually I realized what made this project more powerful, was a final visual and audio product that students took pride in. I thoroughly enjoyed the reactions of the students as they viewed their original stories brought to life on DVDs.

Not long after the birth of this project, my sleepy southern-Louisiana town was inundated with floodwaters in September 2005 from Hurricane Rita. Our school was lost to the floodwaters. However, I found that necessity really is the mother of invention. I worked with different ideas to implement the project despite the struggles of money, space, and different equipment.

Parents excitedly offered help by supplying us with the edible characters for the class. Due to lack of time, our first Digesting a Story that fall was an original group Halloween poem instead of the usual four or five group projects.

I also found that the use of a simple digital still camera, which produced MPEGs, extremely helpful at times when resources were limited. We also worked with still digital photographs in multimedia presentations. I think the beauty of the project for me, was that we could move forward even under different circumstances or given limited resources. Through my web page, I was able to post little segments to stream the segments.

Though health issues forced my retirement in September 2007, I had plans to try using this with podcasting and even student and parent blogging. I can see this type of technology-based project staying alive and productive in classrooms with emerging technologies at the fingertips of teachers.

March 2006

Improving Students' Language Learning

Our Spanish textbook, like yours we're sure, has supplemental listening exercises on CD. These disks are excellent, except that the native speakers are speaking at a normal conversational rate, which leaves most students unable to keep up with the discussion. So we converted the audio tracks into MP3s and used PowerPoint's "Custom Animation" feature to insert the files into a presentation in which we placed the text being spoken. As the speakers converse, the script appears, similar to a karaoke machine, allowing the students to follow the conversation visually as they listen to the tracks.

The visual representation combined with the audio improved students' grades dramatically. Before using this technique, grades were generally in the lower 80s even after students listened to the track three or four times. Afterwards, students consistently received grades of 90 or better after the first viewing/listening. The higher grades continued to be present on quizzes and exams when they did not have the benefit of the visual props. Those students who participated in both forms, with visual cues and without, insisted that this format is much easier to understand and to retain.

Standards: *NETS•T* III (http://www.iste.org/nets/). *FL* 1.2 (http://www.actfl.org/).

—*Lyn C. Howell, Assistant Professor of Education, Milligan College, Johnson City, Tennessee, and Robert Rose, Spanish Teacher, Andrew Jackson Elementary School, Kingsport, Tennessee*

Foreign Language

authors' update

Lyn C. Howell and Robert Rose

The next step is to help students develop a comfort level in speaking a new language. To facilitate this, students in groups of two or three write a dialogue and practice speaking to one another. To extend the lesson, they videotape their conversation. Using Movie Maker, they create their own "closed captioning." The teacher can then combine these clips so that students can watch and listen to themselves as well as their classmates.

The repetition as students create, practice, film, and caption their own conversation really helps ingrain those words and phrases in their minds and on their tongues. Listening to classmates perform gives students an opportunity to hear the words and phrases used in different ways, and the captions help reinforce the lesson for any students who need help.

March 2007

Dynamic Human Anatomy

Human anatomy is a commonly offered health course or unit in a high school curriculum. It can provide a foundation to students who wish to become emergency medical technicians, teach health and physical education, or pursue a career in the medical field. The evolution of instructional materials used to teach human anatomy has included anatomical models, charts, and flash cards. In addition, there have been several publications, such as *Gray's Anatomy* and the *Anatomy Coloring Book*, that have become discipline classics. Although few would classify these learning resources as inspirational, they have served a purpose because of the lack of a better alternative.

Dynamic human anatomy software developed by Primal Pictures (http://www.primalpictures.com) has provided teachers with unprecedented opportunities to create highly interactive lessons. Students may chart their own virtual tour through the layers of the human body with the use of realistic graphic models that have been created from MRI scan data. The software includes images, animation, clinical slides, text, MRIs, and quizzes to support and enhance the learning process. Fully interactive 3-D animations show both function and biomechanics, and all content can be copied for use in PowerPoint and Word. The figure above shows layer 11 of 24 of a knee joint, and can rotate 360 degrees to reveal all bones and soft tissue associated with the knee. In addition, selection of a bone, ligament, or tendon will reveal the name and definition in the right hand margin.

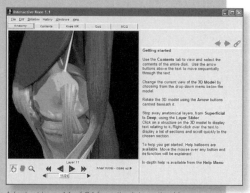

A look at layer 11 of 24 from the Interactive Knee. Various view options are described in the text located on the right side of the slide.

Various versions are available. The complete anatomy edition contains the interactive hand, head and neck, hip, knee, pelvis and perineum, shoulder, spine, and thorax and abdomen. Other available software includes interactive functional anatomy, and the sports injuries series, which includes the foot and ankle, the knee, and the shoulder. Primal Pictures software is available as interactive CD-ROMs, DVDs, and as a Web-based subscription service. So if you want to add some interactivity and multimedia spice to your anatomy lessons, Primal Pictures might be just what the doctor ordered.

—*Ken Felker, professor of health and physical education, Edinboro University, Edinboro, Pennsylvania*

Health

author's update   Ken Felker

Since publishing this article, Ken Felker has created more activities using Primal Pictures. The following activity can be used to enrich a high school health lesson.

Many students participate in some level of athletics and, as a result, have been injured or have a friend who has sustained an athletic injury. For this project, students select an athletic injury and, using Primal Pictures, develop a presentation that explains the nature of the injury, possible surgical repair options, and rehabilitation techniques.

Let's examine a knee injury. First, students enter Primal Pictures and capture a variety of screen shots that show a healthy knee. They can virtually dissect the knee to expose the muscles, tendons, ligaments, and bones and select from the most appropriate views as they rotate the knee joint 360 degrees. Next, they can browse the contents box for 3-D color slides of actual tissue, x-rays, and MRIs depicting such knee injuries as tears or ruptures of the meniscus, the anterior cruciate ligament (ACL), or patella dislocation. Also, they will find surgical repairs of the knee such as ACL reconstruction. The last step of researching the virtual knee is to examine the corresponding muscle groups, tendons, and ligaments that stabilize the knee in order to develop a greater understanding of the rehabilitation process, as well as the balance needed for corresponding muscle groups to work together. When this is complete, students combine all of the pieces (screen captures, MRIs, x-rays, text) and present them to the class.

This hands-on, active learning strategy addresses several of the standards from ISTE (NETS•S) and the National Association for Sport and Physical Education.

May 2007

Electronic Read-Arounds

I like to use this activity as students are developing their position about something we've read or viewed. Normally, students respond to a prompt in their learning logs and then we go to the computer lab, where they elaborate on these initial thoughts. After everyone has had a full class period to express what's on their minds, we return to the computer lab another day to conduct what I call the electronic read-around.

Here is how it works. Students retrieve their file and then depress the caps lock key or change the font. Then, everyone moves to a different computer. The reader follows the same procedure we use in class, reading the draft all the way through. The reader then reads the text again, this time responding to the content, inserting comments after the original. The student responding to the initial draft writes his or her initials after each reaction. Because the caps lock key is engaged or the font is different, the reader's comments stand out from the writer's text. We shift seats about every 10 minutes or so. A writer can receive as many as three honest and detailed responses in a normal class period.

Near the end of class, students return to their computer. The writer now has several choices: save the file with the comments included, rename the file and save it so the original file remains unblemished, or ignore the comments and log off without saving the document. Rarely do students ignore their peers' comments. Most of my students rename and save the file replete with comments. The benefits are obvious. Besides being fun, students get to read pieces from classmates not in their writing groups. When they retrieve the files later, writers get feedback that points to where or how they might revise. In addition, the integrity of the original file is retained, provided it was renamed. I firmly believe in delaying premature evaluation. Electronic read-arounds accomplish this, because students are focused on development.

A natural extension to the above activity is what Jamieson McKenzie calls accordian writing, a term he coined in "Accordian Writing—Expository Compostion with the Word Processor" (*English Journal*, September 1984). McKenzie talks about encouraging students to use the word processor to expand and compress text. Students arrange blocks of writing that seem related and then insert additional thoughts afterward. They delete ideas or comments made during the electronic read-around that are vague and develop what is more promising. Of course, the writer will have to decide which comments should be ignored and which should be expanded.

The point to the electronic read-around is to extend the conversation between the writer and the reader. This kind of feedback helps a writer test his intent against a reader's response. A mismatch reveals that the writer perhaps wasn't clear, the reader misread the piece, or some combination of both. Because comments are followed by a reader's initials, the writer can ask about any misunderstanding, again extending the conversation.

Students at all ages need to own their decisions if they mean to grow more sophisticated as writers and readers. This technique is only one way to encourage such growth. Of course, I don't abdicate my role, but I do believe it's important to shift the attention away from the teacher. Students are free to consult with me after they have reconsidered their piece. My intent is to get out of their way so they can take charge of their learning.

Rick Monroe began teaching English in 1978. Two years later he was using word processing with his students, and since then, has been an advocate for incorporating technology into the curriculum to help students articulate their thoughts.

By Rick Monroe

author's update
Rick Monroe

My original lesson was predicated on having access to technology and on my firm belief that whatever I did with technology should be transparent. That is, everything I do with technology should work (within limits) with readily accessible tools such as pen and paper. One of my maxims has been that no learning should depend on electricity, and thankfully, this has held me in good stead, especially because I have changed schools where I now have less access to technology than at any time in my career.

Because I no longer have access to a computer lab or a class set of laptops at least once a week, I've had to get more creative about engaging my students as they develop a piece of writing. I can still get students to conduct read-arounds, but in my situation today, we're using pencil and paper. In my new situation, I've been cast back to 1981, my pre-technology days.

So what am I doing now? How am I conducting this lesson? My students still respond to a prompt in their learning logs, but now students place their learning logs on their desk, and when asked, stand, and move around the room and read each others' handwritten entries, handwriting their responses and signing their name afterward. After three to four rotations where students move around the room reading and responding to learning log entries, the writer returns to his or her seat. Now students use a highlighter pen to mark responses from peers they think helped them elaborate on their thoughts. Now students take their learning logs home and draft their essays on their home computers. Individuals are still getting suggestions about how to elaborate on or revise their ideas, but now I no longer get to walk around the room and coach my students as they develop a piece.

Do my students still conduct multiple revisions? Yes. The biggest difference today is that, without access to a computer lab, it takes longer to develop and revise a piece of writing. What I miss most is talking with students while they develop their thoughts.

What I've noticed this year is that students are less enthusiastic about making changes to their writing, because handwritten suggestions tend to harden like quick drying cement. Students simply cannot capture the immediacy of the moment after they take their word-processed piece home. Students can't turn to me or a classmate and say, "What did you mean by…" In a lab students can make a change, have a peer or me read it, make adjustments, receive feedback again, and continue revising until the writer and reader are satisfied.

I'm still teaching writing and thinking, but without the consistent use of a computer lab or class set of laptops, the process takes longer, and unfortunately, my students are getting less timely feedback.

December/January 2007–08

LEARNINGconnections

Mathematics 29 • Multidisciplinary 32, 33 • Social Studies 36 • Geography 37

Dynamic Visualizations

By Margaret L. Niess

Mathematics

Microsoft Math is a mathematics tool that at first glance looks like a calculator with a scratchpad (called a *worksheet*) and a graphing space. The surprise is in the power that these features provide for a mathematics classroom for both teachers and students. Imagine being able to:

- dynamically manipulate graphs of both linear and nonlinear functions and equations. Microsoft Math provides the workspace for engaging in explorations of the effect of changes in the coefficients and constants for functions such as $y=ax^2+bx+c$ and equations such as $ax^2+by^2=c^2$.
- visualize systems of inequalities to identify regions for solutions to problems.
- conduct explorations in three dimensions. With Microsoft Math, teachers can guide students in developing spatial visualization skills as they investigate systems of three-dimensional (3D) equations, such as $\{x^2+y^2+z^2=4, x+y=-2, x+y=-2\}$.
- investigate data sets of ordered pairs. Students can enter multiple data sets and search for patterns from the visual graphics.

Teachers can use Microsoft Math as a tool for depicting visual images of many mathematical ideas, including linear relationships. They can guide students' analyses through active investigations of multiple graphical representations, connecting those representations with algebraic and tabular representations while also challenging their mathematical thinking and reasoning.

Figure 1. Animating the slope and y-intercept for the general linear equation.

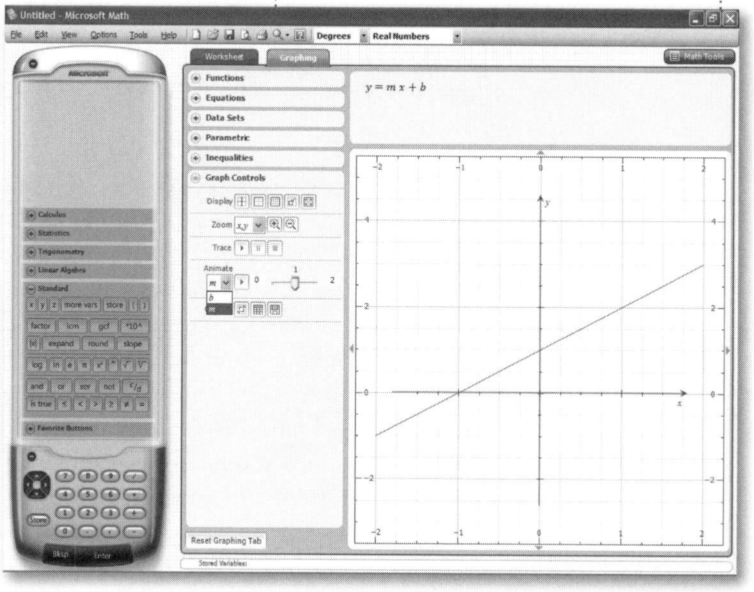

Initially, a teacher can invite the class in small groups to use their graphing calculators around an investigation of how the coefficient and constant values affect the function y1=3x-2. Their challenge is to propose a description of a general linear function. Once the groups have developed their conjectures, the challenge is for the class to share their ideas. This sharing does not have to be a series of stand-and-deliver reports. The teacher can facilitate the discussion using Microsoft Math as a demonstration tool to present visual graphs of the ideas that students propose.

With the graph of the function y=mx+b, the ideas can be demonstrated dynamically through an animation of the slider for *m* and *b* (See Figure 1). However, the students must identify the ranges for the slider. Retaining the default range of 0 to 2 for the slope (*m*) only presents increasing graphs; similarly, the y-intercept (*b*) would be bounded at the origin. Teachers can demonstrate the various proposals in conjunction with questions that challenge them to make, test, and even restructure their conjectures. Basically, the students instruct the teacher and the rest of the class as they demonstrate and explain their conjectures about the effects of the values on the

Continued

Continued

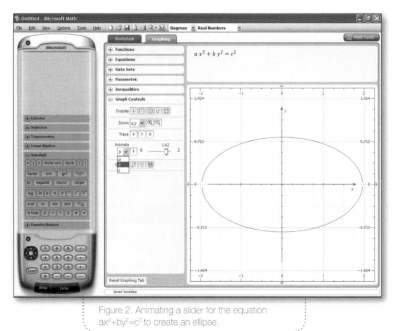

Figure 2. Animating a slider for the equation $ax^2+by^2=c^2$ to create an ellipse.

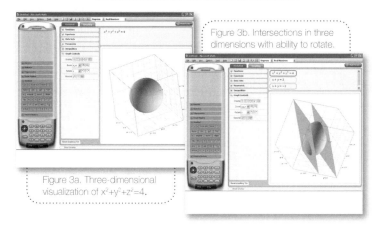

Figure 3b. Intersections in three dimensions with ability to rotate.

Figure 3a. Three-dimensional visualization of $x^2+y^2+z^2=4$.

visualize the graph of the equation $x^2+y^2+z^2=4$? If $x^2+y^2=4$ is a circle, then $x^2+y^2+z^2=4$ must be a circular sphere. True. (See Figure 3a.) Now what happens if you add the 3D graphical representations of the equations $x+y=2$ and $x+y=-2$? Can you visualize the graph rotating first about the z-axis, then the y-axis, and finally the x-axis (See Figure 3b)? Such visual thinking is rarely considered in secondary mathematics classes because of the difficulty of visually exploring 3D representations meaningfully. Yet, "students' skills in visualizing and reasoning about spatial relationship are fundamental in geometry" (NCTM, 2000, p. 237). The capabilities of Microsoft Math uniquely demonstrate 3D graphics and provide access that supports important experiences with spatial thinking and reasoning.

Microsoft Math is a learning tool for students to explore many problems graphically, but the program also supports them in looking at their representations in tabular form. For example, suppose students are asked to create as many ordered pairs in a data set table that fit this problem: *On most days Zoey works on both her math and science homework. Math takes twice as long as science. Describe visually the amount of time Zoey might be spending on her homework.* After students have developed an extensive data set of (minutes for science, minutes for math) and displayed the data visually in the graphing environment, their challenge is to propose an algebraic function to represent the relationship. Figure 4 shows students adding data points to the initial data set.

While mathematics is often filled with equalities, life is more aptly represented by inequalities. Thus, more realistically, suggest that the *math homework takes up to twice as long as science and Zoey spends no more than 2 hours a night on homework.* Students now can consider these inequalities

slope and the y-intercept of the linear function.

Similarly, students can be challenged to explore many quadratic relationships—both functions and equations. How do the coefficients and constant affect the function $y=ax^2+bx+c$? What coefficients make the equation $ax^2+by^2=c^2$ circular and what make it an ellipse? (See Figure 2.) What is the effect of the constant? What happens with inverse relation-ships in the form of $y=a/(bx+c)$? What happens if you graph the general linear form ($y=mx+b$) and its inverse ($y=1/(mx+b)$) on the same axis, activate the sliders for m and b, and use trace to find the points of the intersections? What about 3D functions and equations in which hand-graphical procedures are not only time-consuming but all too often significantly detract from the development of the mathematics concepts? Can you

Continued

Continued

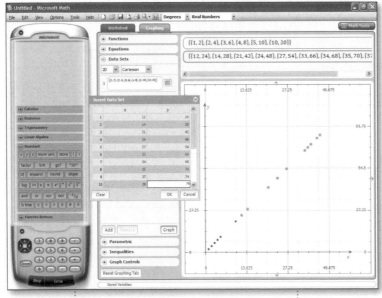

Figure 4. Addition of more data points that meet the condition for the problem.

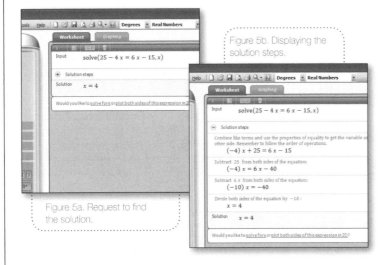

Figure 5a. Request to find the solution.

Figure 5b. Displaying the solution steps.

an explanation, shown in Figure 5b. This instructional tool capability frees up the teacher to work with individual students while other students check their work and try to answer their questions using the tool.

Microsoft Math provides additional benefits for teachers and students. As teachers and students work through the lessons, the Worksheet portion maintains a record of all input, output, and graphs created during the class activities that can be saved. The record provides valuable information for students who may have been absent or for those who were confused about certain portions of the lesson. In fact, teachers can prepare worksheets ahead of class to use to demonstrate other ideas.

A special note to teachers who are concerned that certain capabilities of Microsoft Math will detract from students learning mathematics is in order. In the 1960s I taught middle school 8th and 9th graders the square root algorithm. They dutifully found the square root of any positive rational number I asked. Today, I teach teachers to teach middle school students the concept of square root, how to estimate a square root, and how to use the appropriate tool to find more exact values as needed in their problem solving.

The challenge for today's mathematics teachers is in teaching estimation and graphical sketching for thinking through possible problem solutions. These skills are far more appropriate for developing students' abilities to think and reason mathematically in the construction of a more useful base of mathematical knowledge and skills.

Margaret L. Niess is a professor of mathematics education at Oregon State University in Corvallis, Oregon. She is the volunteer Curriculum Specialist for mathematics for L&L.

graphically to display the area about which other questions can be asked. Are there any other constraints on the situation? (Yes, the hours for both math and science are greater than or equal to zero [0].) Where is the region of possible solutions to this problem?

Microsoft Math provides many other capabilities in addition to these

visualization and dynamic capabilities that can be used in a variety of ways. Students can check their own solutions to warm-up problems where they find solutions to equations such as 25-4x=6x-15. Figure 5a shows a request for the solution, with the possibility for selecting the *plus* (+) icon to display the solution steps along with

author's update
Margaret L. Niess

I learned mathematics in the late 1950s. Perhaps the most vivid recollection of enjoying learning was a unit where we were asked to graph polynomial functions. The intent was to have us "discover" the effects of the variables in each of the functions and to give us graphing experience. For example, we were asked to propose a conjecture about parabolic functions in the form $f(x) = a(x–h)^2 + k$. Could we describe from the symbolic form how the graph would appear? We made many graphs that displayed multiple values for each of the variables a, h and k. The choice was ours such as beginning by comparing the graphical representations of $f(x) = x^2$, $f(x) = (x–4)^2$, and $f(x) = (x+2)^2$. Once we had mastered that idea we moved to creating graphs that varied a, h and k such as creating graphs of $f(x) = 2(x–2)^2 + 3$, $f(x) = 2(x–2)^2 + 6$, and $f(x) = 3(x–2)^2 – 3$? For two weeks, five days a week, one hour in class plus homework time each evening, our task was to create a notebook of different graphs. Imagine the tables of data (calculated by hand of course) and the mounds of graph paper over the two-week period. But, when we were finished, some of us had notebooks of graphs to support our conjectures.

Today, with the capabilities of computer-based, digital technologies, this same lesson can be accomplished in one class period in a very different manner. Technologies such as Microsoft Math provide for whole class collaborative exploration of the ideas with the possibility of students also working individually or in small groups. The slider capability in the graphical interface allows students to explore the transformations of the graphical representations dynamically, making multiple changes in the variable within seconds and visualizing the graphical representations almost instantly. The effect may perhaps best be described as an interactive video display of the changes where the student is the one directing the video. By the end of the class period, students are able to dynamically generate additional graphs to support their proposals.

The question is: What mathematical understanding have students lost and what have they gained using this technology? In both cases, the focus is on visualizing the mathematics. The dynamic capabilities of the newer technologies engage students more quickly into the idea of mathematical reasoning. The paper and pencil version takes lots of time, is often error-prone with many opportunities to lose student interest and engagement in the ideas. The dynamic version has the capability for multiple classroom organizations in the exploration. Of course it may progress too quickly for all students. And students may be losing the opportunities for graphing. Or will they? Maybe they are gaining a better sense of sketching the graphs as a result of the investigations. Rather than focusing on the concern of "ability to create graphs," these dynamic visualizations may be providing access for more students to the mathematical ideas. Perhaps the argument is similar to the one about the importance of long division. "Dad, why do I need to know how to do long division by hand?" As indicated in an edited version of the cartoon character Adam's response to his son: "I told you, in case some super strain of virus renders all technologies with dynamic capabilities, especially those in computers, watches, and cell phones, useless" (*Oregonian*, April 29, 2008).

December/January 2007–08

Research, Deconstructed

"If we knew what it was we were doing, it would not be called research, would it?"
—*Albert Einstein*

One of the greatest challenges in guiding students through a research project is helping them break the complex research process into manageable steps. This is even more challenging today when information overload can be daunting to even the most savvy researchers. Teachers struggle as well with how to create and manage good research projects. To the rescue comes the Research Project Calculator (RPC) and Teacher Guide (http://elm4you.org/research). Based on the research process outlined in the Minnesota Educational Media Organization (MEMO) Information and Technology Literacy Standards, the RPC breaks the research process into the following five logical steps:

1. Question
2. Gather
3. Conclude
4. Communicate
5. Evaluate.

Students choose the format of their research product (essay, slideshow, or video) and enter the assignment due date. The calculator estimates the dates by which each step of the process should be completed and, using a question-based approach, provides a script for the information-seeking process. A simple and concise guide for the complex process, the calculator walks students through the five steps, providing resources for each step. Students can print a one-page version of the research guide with due dates or e-mail the document to themselves. They can also elect to have e-mail reminders sent.

A Teacher Guide has recently been developed and added to the calculator. Intended to assist teachers in guiding students through the research process, the guide includes detailed instructions for teaching each of the five steps, "dribbling" exercises (for skill practice), and tip sheets. Special lesson ideas are included for overworked teachers. The RPC also includes a glossary, a rubric, and a link to the MEMO Information and Technology Literacy Standards. The tool is open source software and can be downloaded to individual district Web servers and customized to access local databases and/or files.

Intended for high-school-age students and their teachers, the RPC was adapted from the University of Minnesota libraries undergraduate Assignment Calculator and funded by MINITEX/MnLINK. Content for the calculator and the teacher guide were written by MEMO members Jane Prestebak and Leslie Yoder.

—Leslie Yoder is an information literacy specialist for Saint Paul Public Schools in Minnesota, and is President-elect of MEMO.

Multidisciplinary

author's update
Leslie Yoder

"Research is formalized curiosity. It is poking and prying with a purpose."

~ Zora Neale Hurston

In summer 2008, we updated and published the Teacher Guide, with lessons for media specialists and teachers to use in teaching the research process.

The Research Project Calculator (RPC) is being used extensively in Minnesota high schools and many college and university library websites link to it. One university website reports that the RPC was "designed to help you plan projects so that you get it done in bite-sized chunks over time instead of pulling an all-nighter." High school teachers appreciate the manner in which the tool helps prepare their students for college-level research. Though it is intended for high school-age students, Robbinsdale, Minnesota middle school library media specialist Dawn Nelson regularly introduces students to it as part of a collaborative process with teachers. She reports, "The value of the RPC to me is that it gives me a framework on which to build a common language and process of conducting research, regardless of the subject area."

Some states have downloaded the tool and adapted it to meet their own needs and standard sets. This development is very exciting to us, as it proves the universal value of teaching the steps of the research process and of the tool we created.

—*written with Jane Prestebak, past president of MEMO and media director for Robbinsdale Schools*

September 2004

Students as Environmental Consultants

Simulating Life Science Problems

By Megan Roberts and Janet Mannheimer Zydney

Subject: Biology, environmental science

Grades: 9–12 (Ages 13–18)

Technology: Video, Web

Standards: *NETS•S* 3–5; *NETS•T* II, III (http://www.iste.org/standards/). *NSES* Content Standards Grades 5–8 C (http://books.nap.edu/html/nses/html/).

PHOTOS BY MEGAN ROBERTS

As an eighth-grade earth science teacher, I (Megan) take every opportunity to incorporate the idea that Earth is a dynamic orb, constantly undergoing irreversible change. Of the myriad subjects that encourage students to contemplate environmental change, perhaps the most consistently thought-provoking topic is pollution. My students at East Side Middle School are amazed to find out that New York City, where we live, is home to one of the world's largest landfills or that U.S. drivers produce trillion of tons of carbon dioxide by driving SUVs.

I met Janet in fall 2001, when she was a doctoral student at New York University and was developing an interactive multimedia program called Pollution Solution. Her goal was to bring a real-world problem into the classroom that would challenge and motivate students. Janet came up with the idea for the program while reading the front page of the November 4, 1999, issue of the *New York Times*. She came across the article, "7 Utilities Sued By U.S. on Charges of Polluting the Air." She thought about how relevant this issue was to the topics students were studying in earth science. This article became the basis for the software, which presents students with a sticky environmental problem and challenges them to investigate the possible causes and probable effects and, ultimately, to recommend a viable solution. This problem seemed like a perfect fit for my students. We began our planning, and in spring 2002, we introduced my students to the project.

Assigning Students to Be Environmental Consultants

East Side was fortunate enough to have received a technology grant, and as a result, each of our students

Continued

Continued

had his or her own laptop computer to use each day in class. Pollution Solution puts students to work at a fictional environmental consulting company. The consultants are given a client, a utility company, which is being sued by the U.S. Justice Department on behalf of the Environmental Protection Agency (EPA) for violating the Clean Air Act. Students are asked to research what caused this problem and how best to fix it. After several weeks, they prepared their culminating project: a recommended, viable solution for the utility company. The various aspects of this environmental problem were presented to the students from multiple perspectives, thereby encouraging them to draw their own conclusions.

Introducing the Problem

The challenge was how to bring this problem to life for students. Janet cleverly decided to videotape her husband, who acted in the role of vice president of the utility company that was being sued. He addressed students directly, explaining the problem as if they were actually in his office.

In the middle of a phone conversation, the vice president of the company looks up from his desk and waves you and the other consultants into his office. As you take your seat, he abruptly ends his phone call, slamming down the receiver. He immediately launches into his explanation of the problem his company is facing. "I assume you've been reading the papers lately," he says. "My company is being sued by the Justice Department on behalf of the EPA for violating the Clean Air Act." He gives the details of the lawsuit and his reasons for needing consultants to advise him on

what to do. He then asks you to recommend a plan of action: Should the company fight the lawsuit and risk paying possible fines? Or should it make a settlement with the EPA and agree to find alternative solutions to reduce emissions?

Janet and I were excited by the students' enthusiasm for the project. The video clip of the vice president of the company is a powerful hook. To see if they understood their role and the nature of the problem, I asked students to tell us whom they would need to speak to first in order to give their client the best advice on how to fix its pollution problem. One student said she would like to visit a similar factory to see if it operates differently. Another added, "I want to speak to a scientist to find out how to prevent acid rain." Some students said they would need to speak with the EPA to hear its side of the case. Others felt that talking with engineers would help them to learn how the utility plant operates. Clearly, the class was beginning to get a sense of the complexity of the problem.

Developing a Research Plan

Over the next several classes, students researched the problem using the computer program and the Internet. Their virtual office included a filing cabinet with important documents about the company and reference manuals full of valuable information regarding environmental science issues, such as relevant technologies, environmental laws and policies, and basic economics. The information students needed was either embedded in the program or made available through links to the Web sites of various organizations, including the EPA, Department of Energy, National Park Service, and the Center for Renew-

able Energy and Sustainable Technology. To introduce students to these resources, I demonstrated a few of the sites. Using the LCD projector, I displayed a map of the United States from the U.S. Geological Survey that depicted the acid rain levels of various cities across the country. (*Editor's note:* Find this and other URLs under Resources on p. 25.) As a class, we hypothesized why the acid rain levels differed. One girl in the back of the class noted that the Northeast had higher levels of acid rain. The girl next to her noted that the wind might carry pollution from one part of the country to the other. To demonstrate this point, I showed an animation of the jet stream from the *Baltimore Sun's* Web site. This animation clearly shows how the pollution can travel across the country.

While students worked on their computers, Janet and I maneuvered our way through the consultant teams to address questions, offer ideas, or provide technical assistance. At one point during the first week of our project, Janet asked me to check out the problem statement that a student had typed. It said, in part: "The activists have protested that the company is burning massive amounts of fossil fuels and therefore creating more sulfur dioxide. Then, when the sulfur dioxide reacts with water, it forms sulfuric acid mist. Eventually this acid is rained out of the atmosphere and falls to the ground. This sulfuric acid destroys our environment by destroying trees and killing fish." Impressed, Janet whispered with a smile, "I couldn't have said that better myself."

Playing Roles

In the second phase of this work, students were challenged to become experts on one of four perspectives related to this problem: an environmen-

Continued

Continued

PROJECT TIME LINE

Week 1   The Problem

An electrical utility plant is out of compliance with the Clean Air Act and is being sued on behalf of the EPA because the plant is releasing dangerous amounts of emissions. The company needs to make decisions about how to handle this problem. Should it fight the lawsuit or settle? In the long run, would it be better for the company to convert to a different type of energy source? And if so, how do the company's executives decide what type of energy will be best for both the environment and their ability to make money? The company has hired you, an environmental consultant, to find a viable solution to the problem.

Students discussed and researched the causes and effects of acid rain, the details of the Clean Air Act, the government's economic policies, and similar legal cases.

Week 2   Developing a Research Plan

Using the Pollution Solution program and the Internet, students worked individually to develop their own problem statement, hypothesis, plan of research, and list of resources they planned to use in order to research their problem.

Week 3   Comparative Analysis

Each group of four students was assigned a type of alternative energy source to research from various perspectives.

Each student in the group chose to become an expert in one of the four categories: an environmental scientist, a lawyer, an economist, or an engineer.

Each student was challenged to research all the pros and cons of that energy source from his or her perspective.

The groups presented their analyses of their energy solutions to the class.

Week 4   Final Report

Based on their presented analyses, the students discussed which solution would be the most viable for the company.

The students wrote up their final recommendations for the company.

---

tal scientist, an economist, a lawyer, or an engineer. Each consultant team (made up of each of the four experts) was assigned an alternative energy source to research and then present to the class their analysis of that alternative from the four different perspectives. To do this, the team members needed to understand the economic, technical, legal, and environmental effects of one possible energy solution, so they could scientifically argue the pros and cons of it.

Each consultant team discussed the problem quietly. In one team, a girl leaned over, pulling her computer earphones away from her ear and asked the girl sitting across from her, "How much money can the company afford to pay?" Her partner, who had slid her earphone back, answered, "It says here that the company makes a profit of $6 million per year." Another student who was listening in pointed out, "But they spent $10 million last year to repair their plant." The first girl responded, "Well, if they spent $10 million to fix their plant, why couldn't they have installed something to reduce their emissions in the first place?" Students were clearly coming to their own conclusions

Continued

Continued

about how this problem began and, as budding scientists, were eagerly seeking solutions.

Reporting Their Findings

As their final project, the expert groups wrote up recommendations for the utility company based on their research. Afterwards, the class discussed which energy source was the most viable solution for the company to choose. As we watched them discuss and share their opinions, it was clear to Janet and me that students were not only becoming interested in the effects humans are having on the environment but also becoming vested in making a difference.

Looking at the Benefits of Problem-Based Learning

This type of learning atmosphere is student centered and allows each child to navigate through the Internet as he or she seeks to learn about a specific environmental problem. With regular benchmarks of student performance and individual and group assignments made clear at the beginning of the project, students were able to move at their own pace. Although all had the same end goal of finding an energy solution, each student was encouraged to be driven by his or her curiosity and self-interest as he or she sought to learn about how pollution affects the environment. In the end, we found that students learned a great deal about the scientific concepts, such as the cause and effects of acid rain, the cause and effects of the carbon and water cycle, and the effects different types of energy have on the environment. But possibly of the greatest importance, they also became more aware of how the way we live affects the natural world.

In talking with teachers of other disciplines, we realized that this type of project could be created for a variety of curricula. With relatively simple technologies such as video and the Internet, problems that we see in the newspaper can be brought to life in the classroom. Teachers could videotape their relatives or willing friends to introduce the problem or perhaps have their class create a newscast about the problem. This can provide a wonderful hook to motivate students and really bring the problem to life in the classroom. Teachers can also adapt the project that we did by using the Pollution Solution Web site, which provides information about the case as well as the necessary resources to research the problem. When given the opportunity to solve real issues, students rise to the challenge and clearly benefit from becoming personally involved with these issues and seeing the effects humans are having on the environment.

Resources

"7 Utilities Sued by U.S. on Charges of Polluting Air" By David Stout (Abstract): http://query.nytimes.com/gst/abstract.html?res=F10D11F73A5F0C778CDDA80994D1494D81

Baltimore Sun Weather Maps: http://weather.sunspot.net/maps.asp

East Side Middle School: http://www.eastsidemiddleschool.com

Pollution Solution: http://mypollutionsolution.com/

U.S Geological Survey: http://www.usgs.gov

Megan Roberts taught earth science at East Side Middle School in New York City, where she is now the regional instructional supervisor for science. She was a research fellow at both The Woodrow Wilson Foundation and the Fulbright Memorial Foundation. Currently, she is a doctoral candidate at Teacher's College, Columbia University.

Janet Mannheimer Zydney recently graduated with a PhD in educational communication and technology from New York University. This fall, she starts a post-doctoral fellowship with Dr. Ted Hasselbring at the University of Kentucky in special education technology. For more information on Janet's research on problem solving or the development of Pollution Solution, send a letter to the editor at letters@iste.org.

authors' update

Megan Roberts and
Janet Mannheimer Zydney

After using the Pollution Solution software in Megan's classroom, Janet decided to try it out in a high school setting. These 10th-grade students were using the software to prepare for the New York State Regents Exam on the Living Environment. The same benefits of the software in middle school could be seen in this high school setting. The real-world case within the software prompted students to use their scientific inquiry skills to come up with creative solutions to the problem. For example, one student thought the company could use a sulfur dioxide recovery system. She wrote: "This system removes sulfur dioxide as it is leaving the plant and converts it into usable (and sellable/profitable) byproduct, with no waste byproducts." This student's solution considered not only the environmental issue but also ways the company could financially benefit from the solution. This is a sophisticated solution to this complex problem and shows that environmental solutions can also be the most cost-effective solutions to companies in the long run.

One interesting anecdote during this high school pilot: several students didn't realize they were actually learning scientific facts during the project because the content was presented rather subtly within the legal case. In fact, a couple of students even complained to their teacher that they didn't feel the project was preparing them for the Regents exam. However, several weeks after project, the teacher excitedly e-mailed Janet about how well her students did on the Regents exam. Overall, 90% of her students passed. On the exam, there were a number of multiple-choice questions on air pollution and an essay question about acid rain. Almost all of the students received full points for their answers. The graders for the Regents exam were impressed with the students' complex solutions (e.g., scrubbers, low sulfur coal). Many of the students left the test saying that they felt confident about their answers and several mentioned how well the project prepared them for the Regents exam. Although they appeared unaware of their learning of factual knowledge during the project, it is clear that they later appreciated the knowledge they had gained. This type of instruction did not present content overtly in a manner in which these students were accustomed, but they did in fact learn scientific content along the way.

Pollution Solution continues to be used in high school and middle school settings. Since the project, the Pollution Solution website has also been moved and updated. Teachers can now visit http://homepages.uc.edu/~zydneyjm/PollutionSolution/ to try out the project in their classrooms.

November 2007

Kids Galore Helping Kids in Darfur
Third graders use technology to think and act globally

If you don't believe that young children can change the world, then read the persuasive reflections of third graders who are trying to inform others about genocide in the Darfur region of Sudan. "Kids Galore Helping Kids in Darfur" is a service-learning Web site complete with historical background, letters to Congress, a podcast interview, individual persuasive reflections, fundraising options, and a guestbook. It grew out of a brief class discussion about the United Nations and international situations in which the lives of children are threatened. At the end of that discussion one child asserted, "We have to do something!" Another chimed in, "Let's make a Web site!" That's all it took. The seed was planted. What started as a brief current events lesson evolved into something much more interactive and powerful, a movement owned by the children who conceived and created it.

The Darfur Web site gained recognition from members of Congress, the state legislature, Amnesty International, and the Florida Holocaust Museum. This recognition was the result of momentum that would not have been possible without the Internet. The class effort continues to achieve results even as they move on. Furthermore, the framework of the Kids Galore project can serve as a template for other service learning projects across all grade levels. Creative planning and diligent application of curriculum standards will help justify the time invested.

Finding the Time
The greatest challenge to this project was how to find the time to make it happen. The only solution was to integrate as many curricular areas as

By Wendy Drexler

possible and assemble collaborative groups that could work on different areas of the site concurrently.

At first, this task seemed daunting. However, viewing the project as an experiment and deciding not to set an aggressive deadline removed a considerable amount of pressure. The next step was to consider the educational goals for the year. The project spanned a number of curricular areas, including technology, reading, writing, language arts, and social studies.

Integrating the Curriculum
Covering required third grade content was easier than originally anticipated. An Internet scavenger hunt provided background knowledge and age-appropriate information about the situation in Darfur. The children recognized that they would not be able to complete this project without becoming well informed. They were intrinsically motivated to learn as much as possible because they were working on a meaningful, authentic problem. The class related deeply to the concept of losing home, school, and family members while being driven into the desert. The situation was especially real to them because it involved children their age.

Recording and sharing the research facilitated a lesson in expository writing. It built upon the students' prior knowledge of paragraphs. These concepts were extended further when each student wrote a persuasive paragraph to encourage site visitors to take the time to learn more or donate to UNICEF. As the class learned the parts of a formal business letter, these skills were practiced in letters written to Congress asking for attention from the U.S. government.

The children honed interviewing skills and questioning techniques via a podcast interview with a local volunteer for SaveDarfur.org. The process presented a perfect opportunity to differentiate between closed and open-ended questions and to discuss the value of who, what, where, when, and why in journalistic writing.

Basic technology skills improved as a result of the daily computer work. The technology instructor commented on the typing speed of this class in comparison to the other third grade classes. In addition, the children practiced guided Internet searches, online research, scanning, Web development, and audio recording.

Making It Happen
Bringing this all together effectively and efficiently came down to organization. Eighteen students were divided into teams of three, consisting of a researcher, writer, and illustrator. Students were assigned to these areas based on preference. Each team worked concurrently on one of the six main topic areas. All of the children had an opportunity to write a formal letter and include a persuasive paragraph.

Consider the following steps when contemplating a technology enhanced service-learning project.

1. Involve the students in selecting a cause.
2. Review your curriculum standards. Highlight those that can be addressed as part of your project.
3. Start with these topics. Add or change topics as necessary to meet the needs of your project:
   Learn More—Provide historical background and information.
   Write Letters—Most causes can be advanced through letters to local, national, or international officials.

Continued

Continued

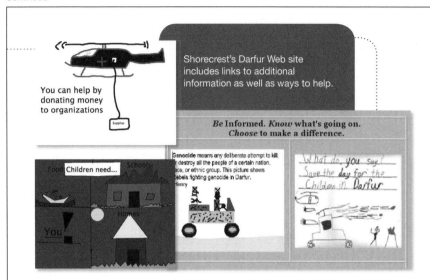

Give—Many nonprofit organizations are creating Web-based options for fundraising that will allow you to keep track of the funds collected by your class. Consider this option or use this section to give visitors instructions on how to give to your cause.

Listen to Our Podcast—Podcasts can be informational essays, interviews, skits, or news programs created by the students. Video is also an option.

Reflections—This section gives students the opportunity to explain why the cause is important. This is a great place for blogs, persuasive paragraphs, or editorials.

About Us—Take the opportunity to let site visitors get to know your class. Explain what motivated your hard work. Be sure to get parental permission before posting pictures of your students.

Guestbook—Students enjoy getting feedback from site visitors. There are numerous free guestbook options that will give you moderation rights. It also gives potential visitors a way to respond to your work other than donating money.

4. Share your site link with the world. Send it to your representatives in Congress, local officials, related non-profits, news organizations, stakeholders, parents, and other media.

5. Revisit the site often with your students.

6. Celebrate their success!

Resources

Amnesty International for Kids: http://www.amnestyusa.org/Individuals_at_Risk/AI_Kids/page.do?id=1101360&n1=3&n2=34&n3=67

Audacity: http://audacity.sourceforge.net/download/windows

Darfur Internet Scavenger Hunt: http://w3.shorecrest.org/%7Ethirdgrade/GR3/DrexlerclassWeb site/DarfurScavengerHunt.htm

Darfur Web site: http://www.shorecrest.org/Darfur.html

Free Guestbook: http://www.a-free-guestbook.com

SaveDarfur.org: http://www.savedarfur.org/content?splash=yes

—Wendy Drexler teaches third grade at Shorecrest Preparatory School in St. Petersburg, Florida. She holds an EdS in Educational Technology from the University of Florida and is working on a PhD. Her research interests include collaborative blogging, integrating technology with service learning, and effectively incorporating Web 2.0 resources into the curriculum.

www.iste.org/LL

author's update
Wendy Drexler

This project remains one of the most memorable of my teaching career. Former students and parents continue to talk about the educational impact of this experience. I believe this is because technology empowered the students and provided a foundation for learning as well as an authentic means to make a difference in the world. It's not easy to top that.

As a new school year began, I wondered if there was any way to maintain the momentum started the year before. I pondered this well into the second semester. Something very interesting happened when I least expected it. I owe that chance encounter to Twitter, a micro-blogging tool on which members post what they are doing in 140 characters or less. I had tried Twitter a few months earlier, but didn't give it the time needed to build an effective network. I didn't quite get it. For some reason, I decided to give it another try.

Within a few weeks came a "tweet" from teacher George Mayo. He posted, "Look what eighth graders are doing to change the world." To which I replied, "Look what third graders can do to change the world." George's students were blogging about Darfur. I sent him the link to the Kids Galore site. We were both impressed. Coincidentally, George and I ran into each other in person at the Educon Conference in Philadelphia a few weeks later. We started talking about Darfur and brainstorming ways to get our students involved.

We ultimately came up with the idea to create a 48-hour blog for Darfur. My students used the content from the Kids Galore site to learn more about the conflict. Mr. Mayo and I built a wiki on which anyone could post resources (http://stopgenocide.wikispaces.com). The Kids Galore link was included. We created three blog prompts to which students could respond over a specific 48-hour time frame. In order to promote the event, the third and eighth graders wrote press releases. They shared them on Skype. We posted invitations on Twitter for other teachers to participate. Soon George's and my students were Skyping with Bill Ferriter's students. More and more students and teachers posted content to the wiki.

On March 6, 2008, our classes launched the Many Voices for Darfur blog (http://manyvoicesdarfur.blogspot.com). There were 677 posts from K–12 students across the United States and beyond. The students were thoughtful, respectful, and genuinely concerned. There was not a single inappropriate comment.

chapter 6
As I See "IT"

As mentioned in Chapter 1, *L&L* has maintained a focus on serving technology coordinators and facilitators for many years. Because of that mission, the For Tech Leaders articles held special importance in the magazine. As the magazine grew and changed, many of the topics and ideas covered in For Tech Leaders were also being covered in the features. So, we morphed the For Tech Leaders articles into a monthly column, with alternating focuses. Four times a year, As I See "IT" was written by Don Hall and covered information systems and technologies. The other four issues covered technology facilitation and instructional issues, written first by Marilyn Brooks under the column title Hand in Hand, and later by Kimberley Ketterer under the As I See "IT" name.

In our first entry here, Kathleen Gora and Janice Hinson describe a mentoring project in which more experienced technology-using teachers worked with groups of less experienced teachers to improve technology use in all classrooms ("Teacher-to-Teacher Mentoring," December/January 2003–04). The building principal designed the program after attending technology training herself. All teachers participated in a skills assessment and then agreed to add extra time onto their days twice a month to help better their technology skills. The multi-year project not only improved schoolwide technology integration but also ensured that even the most technology-savvy teachers continued to learn through their continued mentorship of colleagues. We have learned through the years that students learn very effectively through teaching others—why not use that knowledge to help ourselves learn better? As Gora and Hinson said, "effective change is not static." Their authors' update covers the changes since they wrote their article.

Next up is "The Mature Family" by Marilyn Brooks (May 2006). Marilyn spent a year tracing the development of technology integration in her district, and the column included here reflected on the work done and the work they would need to do to continue to meet their students' needs. She likened the development of the district's technology plan to the development of a new marriage into a mature family unit. One thing that really came through in the entire series is the pride Marilyn felt about the work the district had done to ensure appropriate use of technology in the curriculum. Marilyn has since retired from the Plano (Texas) School District.

Our final For Tech Leaders article is Don Hall's "Herding Cats (April 2007). Through his years of experience in information systems management, Don learned much about managing technology and about managing staff. In the column included here, Don shared ideas for assessing staff and helping them achieve their fullest potential. Staff turnover is a large problem in education, and the tips Don offers may help technology managers retain their best and brightest. The important take-away applies to managers in all disciplines: the best way to manage and motivate staff is to allow them to grow while mentoring them as they fulfill their current responsibilities.

December/January 2003–04

Teacher-to-Teacher Mentoring

Kelley Faucheux, a faculty mentor seated on the right, assists teachers Mary Speranza (standing) and Julie Bourgoyne.

By Kathleen Gora and Janice Hinson

Subject: Professional development

Audience: Technology coordinators, library media specialists, administrators

Standards: *NETS•T* I–III; *NETS•A* I, II (http://www.iste.org/standards/)

Supplement: http://www.iste.org/LL/

PHOTOS BY CHARLOTTE PELLERIN.

Many principals want to provide effective professional development to assist teachers with technology integration, but they don't know where to begin. Sometimes teachers participate in professional development opportunities offered by local school districts, but these one-size-fits-all experiences seldom address teachers' specific needs or skill levels, resulting in uneven or infrequent implementation that rarely leads to instructional change. The Technology Study Group (TSG) Professional Development Model developed primarily by Maria Cloessner, the principal of Most Blessed Sacrament School, a K–8 Catholic school of 556 students, represents an effort to provide her teachers with comprehensive, in-house professional development to promote a positive change in instructional practice. The model can be adapted easily for use in a variety of public and private school settings.

As the technology facilitator at the school, I had an opportunity to be involved in the project and eventually submitted a description of the project as part of an assignment for a course titled Professional Development for K–12 Technology Integration. Janice Hinson, who taught the course, suggested we work together to prepare this article for publication.

Background
Three years ago, the Louisiana Department of Education created a professional development technology leadership initiative for school principals and district superintendents called Louisiana Educational Advancement and Development with

Continued

Continued

The Technology Study Group Professional Development Model

Technology (LEADTech). (*Editor's note:* Find this URL and others mentioned in this article under Resources on p. 40.) LEADTech, which began as a grant funded by the Bill and Melinda Gates Foundation, provides school and district leaders with a greater understanding of the role of instructional technology as it relates to total school improvement and student learning. As one of these leaders, Maria began to wonder, "What does it look like when technology is used well for teaching and learning? What needs to be done to have this happen at my school?"

Like many elementary principals, Maria is primarily responsible for the professional development of her teachers. One of her major goals is increasing the use of technology by teachers and students at her school. Under her direction, all classrooms have one to four networked computers, one of which is a multimedia teaching station with a TV for computer projection. Maria matched equipment with the needs of the school community, and parent volunteers stepped forward to provide technical support. Additionally, she formed a technology committee composed of faculty, parents, and technical advisors to assess the growing needs of the school. This committee met to assess the situation at Most Blessed Sacrament, looking at hardware and software needs now and for the future. It became obvious to us that a plan for maintenance was critical to keep the hardware and wiring infrastructure robust and to periodically evaluate for upgrades. We also identified the need for continuing education for the entire faculty.

Up to this point, professional development in educational technology at Most Blessed Sacrament had consisted of one-shot training workshops, guest speakers, and demonstrations by the computer lab teacher. Additional professional development opportunities were available to Maria's teachers through the local public school system and the local public broadcasting station, and Maria encouraged her faculty to attend. Even though technology integration was a "hot topic," these workshops were often generic and provided little instruction for more advanced computer users or ideas for relevant adaptation into curricula. Consequently, Maria noted little change in teaching practices and realized she needed another approach. While participating in LEADTech, she developed an in-house professional development model to increase the number of teachers at her school who could integrate technology into their teaching practices confidently and effectively.

The TSG Model
Maria recognized that professional development had to change if she wanted her teachers to make wide-scale leaps to tie technology to learning objectives and teaching strategies. She developed her own plan to provide her teachers with comprehensive, in-house professional development activities that were ongoing, relevant, and targeted to help faculty and

students meet specific teaching and learning goals. Her ideas reflected the intent of ISTE's National Educational Technology Standards for Administrators (NETS•A) in the areas of Leadership and Vision and Learning and Teaching. Her goals included developing a shared vision with stakeholders, crafting a cohesive long-term technology plan to achieve that vision, and cultivating a learning community that encourages responsible risk taking to improve student learning. Her objectives were to:

1. Increase teachers' comfort levels for using technology
2. Support technology integration through group membership
3. Identify and use expert teachers to provide training and mentoring for group members
4. Assess technology use often and modify plans to accommodate additional instructional needs

First Steps
The first step was to assess and increase the teachers' comfort levels for using technology. To do this, the entire staff completed the Bellingham Public Schools Staff Use of Technology Self-Evaluation Rubric and the Taking a Good Look at Instructional Strategies (TAGLIT) assessment tool. These assessments provided indicators of strengths and weaknesses, and targeted areas for technology staff development.

The Technology Study Group (TSG) Professional Development Model represents one principal's effort to provide her teachers with comprehensive, in-house professional development to promote positive change in instructional practice.

Continued

Continued

Patti Osterberger, Margaret Fortier, Deborah Watts, and Kem Sivils plan a lesson.

These assessments were followed with a survey of personal technology skills and experiences, which helped each teacher develop individual short-term personal goals. These goals are addressed by ISTE's NETS for Teachers (NETS•T). Specifically, teachers wanted to improve their knowledge, skills, and understanding of technology use in educational settings, stay abreast of current and emerging trends, and design appropriate technology-rich lessons that address content standards and student technology.

Lists of individuals' goals, skills, and experiences were then posted on a bulletin board in the library, and teachers formed groups based on commonalties and interests. Using the assessment tools, we identified an "Expert List" of teachers who were more experienced with particular programs and could offer individualized help.

Finding time for professional development is a problem at most schools, and Maria's school was no exception. To accommodate the TSGs, teachers agreed to meet from 7:30–8:20 a.m. twice a month from September to May. Once the groups were established, Maria outlined her expectations. Each group had to:

1. Identify 3–4 topics or concepts to explore, based on school goals, student achievement, or personal shared interests
2. Submit a work plan with specific goals
3. Meet before school every other Tuesday to develop ways to meet goals
4. Use expert teachers to learn new applications and techniques
5. Meet quarterly with Maria to discuss the group's progress
6. Provide feedback on progress through group member surveys and mid- and end-of-year evaluations

Model Implementation

For their first assignment, each group identified areas of interest and suggested strategies for classroom integration or schoolwide implementation. There was a wide disparity of skill levels, and this was reflected in each group's short-term goals. For example, some groups concentrated on becoming more proficient at software applications such as PowerPoint, while others concentrated on revising the school's technology plan. Teachers on the Expert List served as mentors to individual faculty members and assisted TSGs with specific software applications. Presentations were organized around topics of interest and delivered to individual groups.

The librarian, technology leader, and additional technology-practicing teachers prepared and presented various lessons. Even our middle school students conducted presentations to TSGs on specific software applications. In addition, guest speakers were invited to address topics of general interest. For example, a representative from the Gale Group made a presentation to the TSGs on Internet research skills. Once teachers and students learned to access the materials, most bookmarked the Gale Group on classroom computers and took home instructions for evening and weekend access.

In addition to asking teachers to meet specific group goals, Maria also asked them to become proficient users of specific software applications. For example, teachers needed to check e-mail twice daily for announcements or to communicate with parents.

Teachers were also expected by our administration to record grades using GradeQuick and to use SchoolNotes to post classroom announcements and Internet links that students could use at school or home. The TSGs offered training for these applications and provided mentoring.

Additional Classroom Support

To facilitate further technology integration, Maria reassigned a library paraprofessional to create a Tech Team of myself and Charlotte Pellerin. Weekly, the Tech Team visits each K–5 classroom to develop technology connections involving curricula, current areas of interest, and students' computer lab time.

Recently, while the third grade was studying the Peruvian town of

Continued

Continued

Paracas, Charlotte created a PowerPoint presentation with imbedded Internet links to supportive sites. One interesting site described petroglyphs so large they can only be seen completely through the use of satellite photography. During the next period in art, each student created his or her own petroglyph on a nature theme. Students later shared their petroglyphs and the information they had gathered from the Internet in their social studies class.

First-Year Results

As faculty members sharpen their skills, technology integration is spilling into classrooms. In the middle school, for example, students are participating in cross-curricular projects and using various technology tools to extend traditional research and reporting methods. Several ongoing middle school projects continue to be successful, such as producing a school newspaper, creating graphs and charts for science and social studies fair projects, generating a poetry book, investigating the legislative process for the Youth Legislature program, and developing PowerPoint presentations on the planets, oceans, plants, animals, and kindergarten graduation.

Teachers are finding that technology integration requires additional time to investigate computer programs and Internet sites and to discover positive ties to curriculum. Although a number of current textbooks incorporate technology links, even these must be previewed, as some are inactive, not on the children's reading level, or simply not useful. However, teachers reported that they enjoy working with the members of the TSGs to find or review suitable Internet sites.

Although no data were collected to assess the effects of this professional development model, the Tech Team and administration have observed an increase in the number of teachers who have been integrating technology into the curriculum. However, more needs to be done. Currently, teachers still rely heavily on the Tech Team for curricular support and rarely participate in computer lab activities with their students because this is a free period for them. To encourage more classroom technology integration, Maria plans to make schedule changes to help teachers collaborate with the Tech Team and participate in computer lab activities while still having a free period.

Second-Year Plans

Maria realizes that systemic change takes several years to implement. During the first year, teachers essentially concentrated on learning software applications. However, Maria wants her teachers to move beyond application comfort and focus on specific strategies to incorporate technology into the curriculum. She states:

> Having equipment and software is only a part of integration; the appropriate use of technology is a very necessary component of successful integration. Software should be acquired based on curriculum needs. Instructional goals should drive the use of technology.

During the second year, the TSGs concentrate on developing a technology-supported curriculum that shifts the focus of learning outcomes from, "What and how will I teach?" to "What do I want my students to learn, and how will I reach all students?" In support of this, teachers are using the TSG Technology Lesson Plan Profile (p. 40) to prepare two technology-rich lessons for classroom use. Teachers will present these lessons to their TSGs and then to the faculty. Collaboration is valued, and teachers are encouraged to share their skills, ideas, and expertise.

Continued

Continued

TECHNOLOGY LESSON PLAN PROFILE

Teacher's Name: _____   Grade: _____

Date: _____   Lesson Name: _____

Learning Objectives:

What will students be able to do after this lesson?

What are the steps to this lesson?

What software or Web sites do I plan to use?

What outcomes do I expect?

How will I measure student learning? If this doesn't work, then what? (Plan B)

Download this form for your teachers to use in the supplement at http://www.iste.org/LL/.

In addition to these changes, Maria hopes to develop an accounting system of software application classes taken by teachers. As more software is incorporated into schools, the need to stay current with technology and improve basic/advanced skills continues. During the last four years, teachers at Most Blessed Sacrament have participated in numerous workshops, inservice training sessions, and classes on applications and integration. Consequently, a tracking system to gauge present knowledge is necessary to project future professional development needs.

Summary

As principal, Maria realized that she needed to initiate changes to achieve desired outcomes. Therefore, she developed a model that enabled her staff, as stakeholders, to help each other meet individual and group goals for technology integration.

Results indicate that changes are occurring; however, Maria realizes that effective change is not static, and she continues to adjust the model to enable every teacher to exhibit stronger technology-integration skills. Through strong leadership, a vision, and a cohesive plan, any school can use or adapt the TSG Model to initiate cost-effective and meaningful professional development to improve teaching and learning.

Resources

Bellingham Public Schools Staff Use of Technology Self-Evaluation Rubric: http://www.bham.wednet.edu/technology/technology.htm

The Gale Group: http://www.gale.com/

GradeQuick: http://www.jacksonsoftware.com/

NETS: http://cnets.iste.org/

LEADTech (Louisiana Educational Advancement and Development with Technology): http://www.lcet.doe.state.la.us/leadtech/

SchoolNotes: http://www.schoolnotes.com/

TAGLIT assessment tool: http://www.taglit.org/taglit/Assessment/Preview Assessment.asp

Kathleen Gora has been the technology facilitator at Most Blessed Sacrament School in Baton Rouge, Louisiana, for 13 years. She holds a bachelor's degree in Spanish with a minor in elementary education from Mundelein College and a master's degree in educational technology from Louisiana State University.

Janice Hinson holds a doctorate from the University of Virginia in curriculum and instruction. Currently, she is on the faculty in the Department of Educational Leadership, Research, and Counseling at Louisiana State University, where she coordinates the Graduate Programs in Educational Technology.

Don Hall, L&L's For Tech Leaders editor, is the executive director for information Technology with the Kent School District, Kent, Washington. He also currently serves as vice president for ISTE's SIGTC. Don is a published author and veteran conference presenter.

authors' update

Kathleen Gora
and Janice Hinson

Five years ago, MBS principal Maria Cloessner took ownership for technology integration at her school and asked her teachers to do the same. She did this by asking them to visualize what they considered to be good teaching with technology. Her teachers then set personal goals for fulfilling their visions and formed teacher-mentoring teams to help them reach their goals. By establishing a teacher-mentoring model, Cloessner created a supportive environment where teachers felt comfortable experimenting with the most effective ways to use technology to meet grade-level learning expectations for their own students. Personalized mentoring also increased teachers' levels of confidence and expertise and paved the way for propelling forward technology use at her school.

Beginning in the second year, the Technology Study Groups (TSGs) became more specialized, focusing on specific software pieces and/or textbook supportive software. These efforts were aimed at greater technology integration into the curriculum. In math, for example, teachers are using technology resources from the publisher (Harcourt) to reinforce, intervene and quick check math skills in Grades K–5. The Glencoe Science series in middle school offers computer-generated labs in science lessons. Over time, the science teachers have voted "yea" or "nay" on particular lessons and incorporated other resources to support instruction. As their technology proficiencies increased, teachers developed WebQuests and scavenger hunts to stretch real-time science skills. An example is a life science lesson on nutrition that uses the national food pyramid to design and test healthy meals and spreadsheet software to track the healthiest fast food offerings.

Conversations in TSGs led to the establishment of an online grade database. Teachers were in-serviced on setting up lessons and generating reports. As a result of all of this, middle school students can now access their grades online, which required a "rethink" of grading procedures and prompt entry. The real-time data provides immediate opportunities for feedback, parental involvement, re-teaching and testing. As a result, students are becoming more responsible learners because they can track their own grades and adjust personal commitment and application. A decision is pending on whether to extend online grading to lower grades.

Additional professional development is being provided by the Diocese of Baton Rouge to each of its schools in three areas: differentiated instruction, curriculum mapping, and writing integration. During monthly sessions, the entire faculty and simultaneously several schools in our diocese are linked virtually to professionals in these fields. These sessions are delivered in virtual real-time, with discussion and feedback through a site monitor. Additional websites and technology extensions are available for practicing new skills. Teachers were also trained on the use of Thinking Maps, using technology to broaden the program's scope.

Our newest tech piece is the installation of SMART Boards in our elementary classrooms and StarBoards in the middle school. Although not all classrooms are yet set up, all teachers are involved in the in-service process. These tools will provide new opportunities for student engagement and curriculum integration.

Finally, Maria Cloessner is initiating an in-house learning management system by requiring each teacher to maintain a teacher web page crafted to the needs of each discipline. These pages, which are imbedded in the MBS website for easy access, inform parents of ongoing activities, long-term assignments, and pertinent web links. Teacher e-mail links also allow easy communication between parents and faculty. For students and teachers of this multimedia generation, new tools and ongoing training are necessary to achieve today's skills.

This coming year, we plan to return to a more structured TSG format. With several newer faculty members, it's time to revisit the basics and re-evaluate our core needs. Our goal is to propel our teachers forward in their use of technology and its successful integration in the classroom. The cycle continues, as we return to the basics.

May 2006

The Mature Family

I n the past three columns, I've described a major curriculum project that began in 1992 and continues today. I've compared the development process to a personal relationship beginning with an engagement, moving to a marriage, creating a family and, finally, maturing into a cohesive family unit.

We began by overhauling elementary curriculum and instruction before moving to middle school and, finally, to high school. Although curriculum content and instructional process is always evolving and improving, we will complete our major work this summer. What began in 1992 has kept our district focused on curriculum development the past 15 years. Along with the content and instructional strategies we've totally integrated technology for both students and teachers.

Following successful experiences with elementary and middle schools, beginning in 1992 and 1998 respectively, we began our high school project in 2002.

The high school project has used the same design model that we used for middle school (described in the December/January 2005–06 issue). Our working model includes teaching content through skills development, conceptual learning, enduring understandings, authentic learning, and assessment—all based on principles of Understanding by Design.

To ensure vertical and horizontal articulation, we put together core subject curriculum leadership teams that represent grades 5–12. Each team is composed of 15–20 teachers led by a subject area curriculum coordinator. The teams have become peer review groups to review the work of other teams that work on specific course

Just as a family is always changing and growing, school curriculum also changes and evolves to meet the needs of students.

curriculum within a subject area. For example, the biology writing team submits its work to the curriculum leadership team for science. This kind of teamwork—not unlike a family dynamic—must happen within a district to guarantee high quality writing and implementation.

Just as a family is always changing and growing, school curriculum also changes and evolves to meet the needs of students. As we know more about our state expectations for student achievement, we continue to adjust and modify specific parts of the curriculum. We continuously update the technology used by our students and our teachers. We constantly learn more about obtaining and using data to improve curriculum, assessment, and teaching strategies.

One major area that has our attention is writing continuous assessment into the daily curriculum. Many districts are using periodic assessments and stand-alone benchmarking, but we will use the model of continuous assessment embedded within the written curriculum to ensure progress as a student moves through the consistent, articulated curriculum during his or her school career in Plano ISD.

The work of the past 15 years and our future curriculum work will ensure that each student in our district experiences a consistent curriculum based on current research and best practices supported by updated technology. The school family must remain steadfast in our commitment to our students—we can do no less!

HAND IN HAND

By Marilyn Brooks

Marilyn Brooks is associate superintendent of curriculum and instruction for the Plano (Texas) Independent School District and a volunteer columnist for L&L.

April 2007

Herding Cats

By Don Hall

Don Hall is CEO of Mind Source Technology Group, Inc., an educational consulting firm serving the K–12 community. He has experience in teaching and administration and is a veteran presenter, author, and consultant. He serves as a volunteer columnist for L&L.

AS I SEE "IT"

I grew up in a household where the pets of choice—not mine—were cats and lots of them. At feeding time, my mother tried to organize them into groups so she could make sure each one got what it needed. It was the proverbial zoo. Sometimes it may seem that way when we try to lead a staff of IT professionals.

One key is understanding the composition of your staff. Each brings unique strengths, challenges, experiences, and personality. As the leader, you are responsible for each member of the team's growth, connectedness, and contribution.

As we draw near the close of another school year, many of you will begin preparing your annual staff evaluations. For far too many leaders, this ritual marks the highpoint or lowpoint in their professional development efforts.

Helping your staff achieve their fullest potential takes much more than a cursory examination at the end of the year, especially if we want to ensure they are contributing to the team, feel valued by the organization, and are growing professionally. I believe the annual benchmark approach is one of the reasons many employees leave organizations. Everyone wants to know their contributions matter and that someone is concerned about them.

One strategy that can significantly change the nature of the evaluation or assessment process for your department is to develop professional growth plans (PGPs). The goal of a PGP is to encourage personal and professional growth while mapping out a specific path to achieve it. A professional growth plan is an ongoing (formative) process. It also takes into account staff opinions, ideas, and personal vision for themselves.

The end results are much more productive staff members with higher levels of contribution and connectedness to your organization. A side benefit is that you may actually retain them longer as employees. Another benefit is that by the time you get to the annual evaluation, there are no surprises because both of you have monitored progress all year long.

Build or select a tool that will help you work through this process with your staff. There are several key fields that should be included in a PGP template. Among these are short- and long-term career goals, areas of interest, strengths and weaknesses, preferred learning style, and opportunities for such things as leadership, growth, and enrichment.

Although you have the responsibility, you may also realize the ability to initially implement this process is not within your core competence. Recognize you need help and secure the resources to do it. These resources may come from other departments within your organization or may be totally external.

Finally, you cannot let your staff needs go unfilled because "this is not your thing," as I have heard some CIOs say. This type of abdication of responsibility is the reason so many departments fail and employees bail. Step out of your comfort zone, grow, and just do it.

Providing human resource leadership is much more than conducting annual personnel evaluations. It is really about managing expectations, standards, and relationships. Once you begin to see your team as a collection of special individuals, rather than unruly cats, you can begin to address their needs. ∎

chapter 7

Research
Windows

The Research Windows column, like everything else in the magazine, has had an interesting history, especially in these past five years. It began as a review of recent research reports with an eye to how the conclusions could be applied in the classroom. As NCLB took the forefront, the column began to focus on how to read and understand research, allowing educators to take the research in front of them and make decisions themselves about how or if to apply it in the classroom. Then, as educators found they needed not only to understand research but also to be able to conduct it, we made the decision to focus on current terminology, procedures, and current issues in ed tech research. The beginnings of this focus actually showed up in the feature well, in Rob Kadel's "Statistics for Success," on pp. 29–32 in this collection.

We begin here with "Research into Practice" by John Collins (December/January 2004–05). John looked at a few of the most influential ed tech research reports, the important conclusions, and how those conclusions could be put into practice. This article was a sort of bridge between the older research reviews and the new Research Windows articles. John provided practical information that was grounded in research-based practices and he made it accessible to educators at all comfort levels. This is not an easy task, but one that has grown more and more important in the current educational climate.

In our next article, Rob Kadel discusses "Ethics in Ed Tech Research" (March 2006). I know that when I read research articles in ISTE's journals and elsewhere, I was struck by how hard it must have been to select which students would participate in the research. Students who were selected might have parents wondering why their child was being used as a guinea pig. And parents of students not selected might object that their children were not receiving the best instruction.

However, the bellwether of research designs must do just that—exclude a control group to test the intervention being researched. Rob points out the ethical dilemmas I had thought of, plus more. He also instructs readers on the different types of experimental design and why designs with a control group and experimental group are considered the best. Then, he invites further discussion on the ethical issues in research.

Finally, we look at an example of research in action ("Does Your District Need a Technology Audit?" Howard Pitler, April 2007). Howard suggests that, just as we perform curriculum and financial audits, we need to occasionally perform a holistic technology audit. In addition to a look at the hardware and the network, a critical element in a technology audit is how often and in what ways teachers use technology with students, how they feel about technology, how effective their professional development practices are, and other important issues related to actual use. Howard stresses the importance of bringing in an objective outsider to perform the audit. Not only will the auditor be familiar with what needs to be assessed and how, the auditor will also be able to provide unbiased recommendations based on the results. Once you have your results, you can plan the changes you need to take to increase the effectiveness of your district's technology program. This type of research, although maybe not what you traditionally think of when you think of research, is extremely important as we ensure that technology is used to its greatest effect in promoting student learning.

December/January 2004–05

Research into Practice

By John W. Collins

Subject: Research-based recommendations for Ed Tech

Standards: *NETS•T* II; *NETS•A* II
(http://www.iste.org/standards/)

Knowing about and understanding research can help each of us in our daily routines, although those same routines often keep us away from reading the research. There are, however, some landmark studies and books that compel us to investigate. If we fail to learn what works and what doesn't, we are destined to repeat and pass on poor practices to the students we teach. In educational technology, our efforts are especially imperative. We are preparing students for their futures, which will involve using technology tools in their lifelong learning, most vocational fields, and leisure-time activities.

Continued

Continued

The main reason most educational researchers do what they do is to inform practice—to produce action and improvement. Some call this establishing our knowledge base. Pragmatically, many of us refer to these concepts as *best practices*. You know from a daily perspective that barriers to using educational technology exist. Many people have documented those barriers and practices that work in overcoming them.

To that end, all educators should be aware of three major research-based contributions in the field of educational technology for K–12 settings and one recent observation-based book. The condensing of all of the research in the field does not imply these are the only resources. Myriad research studies allowed the authors to develop these documents.

1. *Educational Technology: A Review of the Research,* 2nd ed., by Ann Thompson, Michael Simonson, and Constance Hargrave, 1996. This work is a comprehensive compendium of research in the field.
2. *The Impact of Education Technology on Student Achievement: What the Most Current Research Has to Say,* by John Schacter, 1999. This analysis of seven major studies augments the work done by Thompson et al. It was published by the Milken Family Foundation. (***Editor's note:*** Find this report and other Resources on p. 64.)
3. *The Sustainability Challenge: Taking EdTech to the Next Level,* edited by Norris Dickard, 2003. This 10-year inquiry into educational technology in our schools highlights a lack of support in the current use of educational technology in many of our K–12 school districts. This report was published by the Benton Foundation.
4. *The Technology Fix: The Promise and Reality of Computers in Our Schools,* by William Pflaum, 2004. This book is a qualitative augmentation to Dickard's work.

It is important to note that Schacter's and Dickard's reports fill a void left because there is not yet a revised edition of the Thompson work.

Some may be critical of the research-based components in Schachter and Dickard, as certain conditions and situations in the cited research were less than ideal. Criticisms include small sample sizes, uneven adoption of educational technology, and untested variables. The list could go on for pages. The bottom line is that educational technology has yet to prove its effectiveness in improving student achievement.

We can learn lessons from all of these works, however. In particular, Dickard identified 10 critical issues needed in the United States to sustain school technology infrastructure and to advance to the next level:

1. Accelerate teacher professional development.
2. "Professionalize" technical support.
3. Implement authentic Ed Tech assignments.
4. Create a national digital trust for content development.
5. Ensure that all Americans have 21st-century skills.
6. Make it a national priority to bridge the home and community digital divides.
7. Focus on the emerging broadband divide.
8. Increase funding for the federal Ed Tech block grant.
9. Share what works.
10. Continue funding for Ed Tech research.

The list clearly illustrates that change is needed and difficult to implement. In particular, the recommendation to continue funding research is important.

Additional research is needed to have a valid and reliable knowledge base/best practices for our field. A few educators are convinced they have a near-perfect environment. Those conditions, variables, and settings need to be captured and shared with those who are less fortunate (research enables us in this endeavor). The observations captured by Pflaum can be considered a step in this direction.

Pflaum uses school and classroom observations from a one-year period of school visits to give readers insight into use of technology in a wide array of U.S. school environments (e.g., public, private, rural, urban). Like Dickard, Pflaum offers recommendations to help educators extend the value of technology in our schools, including:

• Focus computer use on students who will benefit most. Don't dilute the value of computers by insisting that all students have equal access.
• Use computers to support the alignment of standards, instruction, and assessment.
• Use computers for assessment. Their ability to correct tests automatically and provide results quickly can be very beneficial.
• Teach students to use productivity tools and the Internet, but wait until students are ready. Coordinate such teaching within and across grade levels.

Continued

Continued

The final recommendation includes the adoption of ISTE's National Educational Technology Standards (NETS) for Teachers and implies a need to adopt the NETS for Students and Administrators as well.

You may find that you agree or disagree to some extent with the lessons Pflaum points out. And this is to be expected; we each have our own experiences, opinions, and potential solutions. What is critical from a research perspective is that actionable information can be gleaned from observations that are informed by research on what is known to work, such as time on task (the more a student spends time on focused and teacher-directed tasks, the more they learn), student engagement (students who are active in their own learning do better than those who are passive), and class size (students in larger classes tend to receive less individualized attention from their teacher).

Incorporating technology into instruction can allow for increased time on task. Through direct instruction using computers or through individual and small-group work, students tend to be more attentive for longer periods of time when technology is involved. And, as you might expect, they also tend to be more engaged in their work, especially with programs that are heavily based in multimedia and are interactive. And finally, where class size is an issue, the use of computers to provide more individualized attention to each student can only have positive outcomes. Naturally, we don't want computers to become "babysitters" for our students; but as resources are limited and student-to-teacher ratios are high in almost every school in the country, technology can play a role in helping to give each student the attention he or she deserves.

For those of you who are interested in more detailed research covering our field, numerous professional journals are available for review, including ISTE's *Journal of Research on Technology in Education (JRTE)*.

The three compendiums of Ed Tech research discussed in this article should give you a fairly broad overview of where the field stands today. But, just as with technology, research is constantly moving forward. We are continually discovering new and exciting ways to use technology and valuable data to support different kinds of technology use. Therefore, don't feel as if this, the end of this column, is the end of the story—rather, I hope it will launch you to a new understanding of the role research plays in educational technology and in your own work. Happy learning!

Resources

The Impact of Education Technology on Student Achievement: What the Most Current Research Has to Say, by John Schacter: http://www.mff.org/pubterms.taf?file=http://www.mff.org/pubs/ME161.pdf

Journal of Research on Technology in Education: http://www.iste.org/jrte/

The Sustainability Challenge: Taking EdTech to the Next Level, edited by Norris Dickard: http://www.benton.org/publibrary/sustainability/sus_challenge.pdf

Dr. John W. Collins, Jr., is in the Department of Education Leadership, Management, and Policy in the College of Education and Human Services at Seton Hall University. His teaching and research interests are adult education, leadership, administration, educational technology, and distance learning.

L&L's Research Windows editor Robert Kadel is the founder and a general partner of Kadel Research Consulting, LLC, located in Columbia, Maryland. His firm focuses on the evaluation of educational programs in technology, school reform, and community involvement. With graduate degrees in sociology and his focus on educational research, evaluation of technology-supported education became a natural fit.

author's update
John W. Collins

. . . .

Since the publication of this article in late 2004, more research regarding technology has been completed that can be applied to practice. There has been an increase of publications on the topic, including dissertations, theses, peer-reviewed articles and books, among others. Trying to narrow down concise and comprehensive resources was next to impossible just three years since the original article appeared in *L&L*. However, there are a few important resources to look at, in addition to ISTE's publications.

First is the *Journal of Technology, Learning, and Assessment (JTLA)*, a peer-reviewed journal that addresses research on computer-based technology, learning, and assessment. The journal is housed at Boston College with current articles linked and readily available online (http://escholarship.bc.edu/jtla/).

The Internet itself is a viable resource for personal research and placing it into practice. To remain effective and efficient in using cyberspace, technologists need to stay abreast of ever-changing topics. Many of us have been self-taught and need to revisit our own web literacy. A book called *Web Literacy for Educators* (2008) by Alan November is a must-read, especially the chapters "The Empowered Researcher" and "Research Outside the Box: A Guide to Smart Searching."

Third, I have a new book coming out in 2009 that focuses on the pragmatic aspects of technology integration for education, government, and business. This book, *Technology Leadership, Management, and Policy: A Primer and Integrative Model for the 21st Century* will be published by Ithaca Press.

These recommendations are in addition to the ones cited in the original article. Note that the first focuses on new research that can be put into practice while the second addresses a void of information on proper research via the Internet. In the third source, the author offers additional guidance and pragmatic approaches for technology integration or mastery. The combination uniquely empowers readers to successfully put research into practice.

March 2006

RESEARCH WINDOWS

Ethics
in Ed Tech Research

By Robert Kadel

Robert Kadel is the founder and a general partner of Kadel Research Consulting, LLC, located in Hyde Park, Vermont. His firm focuses on the evaluation of educational programs in technology, school reform, and community involvement. Rob serves as a volunteer columnist for L&L.

This month, I want to tackle the ethical questions raised by experimental designs in educational research. If you're not familiar with this debate or not exactly sure what it's all about, this is your chance to learn from an expert. Or from me.

In all seriousness, a bit of a disclaimer here: I don't have all the answers. But I can tell you what I know and what I've heard in the hallways and read in journals and on discussion boards. My goal is to present you with some information that will help you make up your own mind.

We are told by the powers that be in the U.S. Department of Education (specifically from an office called the Institute of Education Sciences, http://www.ed.gov/ies) that we need experimental designs that allow the research to be replicated from school to school. Now, all politics aside, replication is a laudable goal. When a school wants to institute a new program or intervention, it sure would be nice to know if that program worked in similar schools.

To give you an idea of the amount of importance the IES has placed on experimental and quasi-experimental designs, they now have a Registry of Outcome Evaluators (http://whatworks.ed.gov/technicalassistance/overview.html). When an evaluator registers to be listed, after giving his or her contact info, the very next two questions are the number of years' experience the evaluator has in experimental and quasi-experimental designs. If you have experience in other areas, that's great, but they don't want to know.

I want to emphasize that experimental designs are often the most effective in determining whether a treatment is effective. Doctors and medical researchers, public health officials and psychologists have been using experimental designs for years. That's how we know, for example, that drugs such as ACE inhibitors and beta blockers can be effective in reducing hypertension (high blood pressure). Patients in a treatment group have been given ACE inhibitors while patients in a control group have been given placebos (sugar pills that have no effect on the body). The purpose would be to determine if patients receiving the real medication had significantly lower blood pressure over time than patients receiving the placebo—just the mere fact of taking *any* pill may cause some reduction in hypertension because patients feel like they're "doing something about it." (This is appropriately named the *placebo effect*.)

The question becomes whether this type of research design is appropriate in education. There are two ethical debates that revolve around experimental design. The first deals with whether it's ethical to withhold a potentially valuable treatment from a control group of students. It doesn't happen often, but in medical studies, the researchers can stop the experiment and begin distributing the medication being studied to the control group if it is found to be phenomenally effective in the treatment group. After all, potentially saving lives is more important than maintaining the original study design. The second debate is whether it is ethical to exclude all other valid research methods, but I'll get to that one later.

Part of the problem we have with educational interventions is that we don't know for sure if they will work, though we certainly can speculate and theorize about it. Suppose a school's goal is increasing math achievement. If using computers to learn math is instantly more engaging in schools than standard textbook-based methods, one could argue that the amount of student engagement is itself evidence enough that all students should be given the computer-based instruction (no more control group).

On the other hand, there are so many variables, so many factors that could contribute to increases in student math achievement that one

Continued

Continued

could argue that a computer-based math intervention is unlikely to be the only contributing factor. This person would make a case that the experiment would need to run its course to determine just how much of any increases in math achievement could be attributed to the computer intervention while also measuring other possible causes.

It is possible to take this argument even further by saying that educational environments are so complex and that so many factors contribute to math achievement that it is impossible to measure with any certainty the effects of a particular intervention. Comparing to the hypertension example, this is easy to understand. There are only a handful of known causes of hypertension: stress, obesity, too much salt in one's diet, smoking, certain genetic factors, and a few others. But it is possible to imagine dozens of causes of changes in math achievement, ranging from playing educational video games to parent involvement to music instruction. The list goes on.

To dismiss experimental design in education just because it is more difficult to pin down certain causes is, in my opinion, a cop-out. There is a wealth of research showing us how different factors can affect achievement. The challenge is simply to measure them and find appropriate research designs or methods of analysis to control for these other factors—to remove them, in effect, from the final results so that we know exactly how much the treatment caused math achievement to change.

Now back to the second ethical debate, which is more internal to the research/evaluation profession: is it ethical to rely on experimental designs at the exclusion of other valid research methods? This is where I take issue with the IES. When No Child Left Behind was first passed, we in the research community received a glut of information about how experimental designs will become the "gold standard" in educational research. Indeed, we were given the impression that we were to concentrate on experiments above all other research methods (e.g., surveys, observations, interviews). There was such a backlash in the research community that the IES stepped back from this position, saying instead that other methods were fine, but experiments are what we should be striving for. This is patronizing double-speak, as far as I'm concerned, because most grant announcements coming from the federal government now require that an experimental design be used in the evaluation of the grant's success. (See http://www.ed.gov/about/offices/list/ies/programs.html for a list of current grant competitions from the IES.) Without a major policy shift at the Department of Education, this is unlikely to change in the near future.

The problem is that not every solution to every problem facing education can be solved through an experiment. Have you ever been curious as to the effectiveness of sex education classes on promoting safe sex (including abstinence) among teens? I'm not even going to go there with an experimental design. What about the degree to which different pedagogies (e.g., constructivist versus traditional instruction) affect student engagement in subject matter? Someone might be able to make a case for an experimental design here, but classroom observations and surveys would be much more effective measurement tools.

The long-term effect of this emphasis on experimental designs is that the policy itself will have an effect on education, specifically in what problems we study (and what we fund) and thus what solutions we find. To use experimental designs, and to fund for the most part only programs that can be evaluated with them, is to try to solve educational problems with blinders on.

So there you have it—the ethics of experiments in a nutshell. Again, this is certainly not all that can be said on the subject, and I invite you to read more for yourself, post to a discussion board, or just strike up a conversation on the topic sometime. Put in your two cents, and perhaps someday we can come up with a balance that fits everyone's needs.

Experimental versus Quasi-experimental Design

The difference between experimental and quasi-experimental design is pretty simple. In an experimental design, subjects (e.g., students) are randomly assigned to a treatment group or a control group. (Sometimes there are multiple treatment groups for slightly different kinds of treatments within the same study.) Treatment groups receive an intervention (a stimulus), such as a new instructional program in reading or a computer-based math tutorial. Control subjects do not receive the intervention, but—at least in theory—everything else about the two groups remains about equal. That is, both receive the same instruction in other subjects, both have presumably equally qualified teachers, both have about the same amount of parent involvement on average, and so on.

Quasi-experimental design has one major difference in that subjects are not randomly assigned. That means they select themselves into the treatment or not (volunteering for a program) or are selected to receive the treatment because they fall below some minimum requirement, like below a certain proficiency level (while those that meet the requirement are considered the control group). Statistical methods make up for the difference in randomness.

author's update
Robert Kadel

ISTE published this column originally in March 2006, and in the three-plus years since, not too much has changed.

The ethical questions still remain. Today, the issue has evolved into, "How do we address ethical questions?" Researchers at the Institute of Education Sciences and around the country are recognizing the difficulty in establishing randomized control trials (RCT) for testing educational interventions. And although RCTs will remain the standard to which the educational community should be held, alternative methods will almost always be accepted when RCTs do not meet ethical standards of equity for all students. In other words, let's be fair to students: ed tech, properly implemented, has an effect on student outcomes in terms of achievement and/or modern skills. Research is overwhelmingly supportive of this conclusion. If an RCT were to deny such benefits to a control group of students, then the methodology shouldn't be used. My understanding is that now that the uproar over RCTs has died down—and cooler heads have prevailed—the research community, from academia to government to private organizations, is now accepting the utility of methodologies that are perhaps less rigorous, but also more ethical.

April 2007

RESEARCH WINDOWS

Does Your District Need a Technology Audit?

The tech audit is a prime example of data-driven decision making and how appropriate research and evaluation tools can be used to provide useful information for district planning.

By Howard Pitler

Howard Pitler, EdD, is the Senior Director of Educational Technology at Mid-continent Research for Education and Learning. McREL, headquartered in Denver, Colorado, provides educators, school leaders, and policymakers with research-based, practical guidance on how to improve student achievement. Robert Kadel will return next month.

Most districts are required by law to conduct a yearly financial audit, during which an independent third party examines the district's financial statements and writes an opinion on whether those financial statements are relevant, accurate, complete, and fairly presented. Similarly, some schools engage independent firms to conduct curriculum audits to determine if what they are teaching in their classrooms is aligned to their published curriculum documents, and whether their published curriculum is aligned to what is tested on state and national accountability measures. However, although technology is a major line item in most districts' budgets, few districts engage independent organizations to conduct technology audits.

What are the advantages of a technology audit? A comprehensive tech audit provides a district with broad, objective information about the efficiency of its existing network. Primarily, it provides a view of:

- How teachers feel about using technology
- How teachers and students actually use technology in the classrooms
- Barriers that might prevent effective use of technology
- The effectiveness of existing technology-related professional development
- The effect of technology-related district policies on the integration of technology, and
- The perceived effect of building and district leadership on technology integration in the classroom

A good auditor is free of local bias or ownership of the existing situation. He or she does not "sell" anything; rather, an auditor's job is to provide an analysis of data. A tech audit for a medium-sized school district will likely cost between $20,000 and $50,000, depending on the number of schools and scope of the audit. For example, a district might only want an analysis of the network server topology, or they might want a more detailed look at each school's subnet and a security analysis. Once presented with these data, a district can begin the process of developing a technology plan that measures more than the "wires and pliers" aspects of technology. The district can develop a tech plan that is integrated with and supports the school improvement plan—a technology plan that is focused on student outcomes rather than district inputs.

Collecting the Data

Several data collection tools are available to auditors, beginning with a thorough analysis of the physical structure of the district's network. The first step is for the district to *provide documentation* of its network and a copy of its current technology plan. The auditor examines this documentation and verifies its accuracy with an onsite visit. Some of the questions an auditor asks include:

- Does the design of the network provide sufficient connectivity capacity for the users it supports?
- Have processes been implemented to safeguard the future viability of the system and the data residing on the system in the event of a malicious or catastrophic event?
- Can users of the network complete the work necessary in support of the district's mission?

Continued

Continued

- Are the computers sufficiently configured to support the various work activities of users?
- Is the technical support group satisfactorily staffed to effectively support the systems and end users?
- What processes have been implemented to allow for efficient management of the district's deployed software and hardware?
- What planning processes exist for the upgrade of hardware and software assets to stay technologically current?
- Is a process in place for the technology support group and teachers to communicate about the district's future direction in education technology and any challenges they might encounter?

In addition to this comprehensive look at the physical network, a quality technology audit includes the perspective of the users—staff and students. One way to begin this process is to *survey every teacher* in the district using an online tool. This online survey should include questions about teachers' comfort with technology, their perceived level of technology expertise, how students use technology, and any barriers they perceive as keeping them from fully using technology as a teaching tool.

Following the online survey, auditors should *conduct interviews* with a few individuals from every building. This sample usually includes the building principal, technology teacher, and at least two other classroom teachers. Interviews also should be conducted at the district office and include representatives of the IT department, curriculum and instruction, assessment, and other groups that the district identifies. Interviews are particularly rich resources for data about professional development, real or perceived barriers to implementing technology, perception of the leadership's support of and knowledge about technology, and specifics about how students use technology.

Another strong data collection tool is the *focus group*. Focus groups should be composed of staff members, parents, students, and business leaders, and allow the auditor to clarify concerns that arise in the survey or during the interviews. They also allow for a more robust data set from which to draw conclusions.

A final data collection tool is a *building walkthrough*. There are two primary reasons to visit each classroom in a district. First, it is important to see firsthand how technology is deployed and how it actually is used by students and teachers in the classroom. The second goal of a walkthrough is to verify statements made during interviews and focus groups. For example, if the principal states that students use technology in every classroom on a regular basis, and the auditor only sees unused technology stations and labs, that disparity needs to be addressed.

Data Analysis

After all data is collected, the auditor combines it and looks for common themes to emerge. These themes become the primary sections of a written report. It may be necessary during this process to talk with district staff to verify or clarify statements or observations. It is typical for an auditor to enlist the assistance of a peer reviewer, someone knowledgeable in both technology and school improvement.

Final Report

After a period of time, usually two to four weeks, the auditor will present a final report to the district. This presentation often is limited to the district's executive cabinet or a similar group. At the superintendent's discretion, the audience might also include building principals, curriculum specialists, and even board members. It is important to remember that the purpose of this audit is to shed the clear light of day on the district's current state of technology implementation. The wider the audience, the more likely that action steps will result.

Follow-up

A technology audit will only be of benefit if the district uses the data from the report in a constructive manner. Some organizations that offer tech audits also provide additional assistance. A good tech audit will be an objective and independent tool that will suggest a process rather than a product. Be leery of an audit that implies that the auditor's organization can and should serve as a one-stop solution.

Most audits will suggest types of professional development that will help a district move forward. Remember, what worked in one district may or may not work in another. Insist on seeing the research behind all professional development. Professional development that is built on a solid research base will have a higher likelihood of success. Ask for a list of clients, and make some phone calls.

Conclusion

A comprehensive technology audit as described in this article is not an inexpensive process, but the money spent will be worth the investment. Unless you are able to say with assurance that your technology dollars are being maximized, your technology instruction aligned to your curriculum in a coherent manner, your staff well-trained and knowledgeable on how to use technology within the curriculum, and your student achievement enhanced by technology, you should consider investing in a tech audit. The money invested in this process will reap benefits in the long term. ■

author's update
Howard Pitler

When it comes to our health, most of us willingly invest the time and money for a second or even a third opinion. But a district's "technology health" seems to be quite another matter. Although technology is a major line item in most districts' budgets, few districts engage independent organizations to conduct technology audits, despite its advantages. When well chosen, a technology audit provides broad, objective information about the efficiency of a district's network. With a comprehensive third-party analysis in hand, a district can develop a technology plan that integrates with and supports its school improvement plan.

An On-Site Visit Starts the Process

An auditor's work begins with a thorough analysis of the physical network. During an on-site visit, an auditor can verify the district's documentation and current technology plan against the actual existing network. Some of the questions an auditor seeks to answer during an on-site visit include these:

- Is there sufficient connectivity capacity for users to complete work supporting the district's mission?

- Are there processes to safeguard the future viability of the system and the data residing on it?

- Are computers sufficiently configured to support the various work activities of users?

- Is the technical support group satisfactorily staffed to support the systems and end users?

- What processes are in place for efficient management of the district's deployed software and hardware?

- What planning processes exist for the upgrade of hardware and software assets?

- Is a process in place for the technology support group and teachers to communicate about the district's future direction?

Surveys and Interviews Complete the Picture

A high-quality technology audit must include the perspective of staff and students. Using an online tool, it's possible to survey all teachers in the district as to their comfort with technology, their perceived level of technology expertise, how students use technology, and any barriers they view as keeping them from fully using technology as a teaching tool. Auditors should conduct face-to-face interviews with individuals from every building on campus, including the principal, technology teacher, and at least two other classroom teachers. District office interviews should include representatives of the IT department, curriculum and instruction, assessment, and other groups that the district identifies. Interviews are particularly rich resources for data about professional development and teachers' perceptions of the leadership's support of and knowledge about technology. Similarly, focus groups composed of staff members, parents, students, and business leaders clarify concerns that arise during the survey or interviews.

An invaluable data-collection tool is the building walkthrough. There are two reasons to visit each classroom in a district. First, an auditor can see firsthand how technology is deployed and used by students and teachers. Second, walkthroughs verify statements made during interviews and focus groups. For example, if the principal states that students use technology in every classroom on a regular basis, and the auditor only sees unused technology stations and labs, there is an important disparity to address.

Data Analysis Reveals the True State of Technology Implementation

After all data is collected, the auditor looks for common themes, and, if necessary, talks more with district staff to verify or clarify statements or observations. After a few weeks, the auditor presents a final written report to the district's executive cabinet or a similar group. At the superintendent's discretion, the audience might also include building principals, curriculum specialists, and even board members. The wider the audience, the more likely that action steps will result.

Final Thoughts

A good technology audit is an objective and independent tool that suggests a process rather than a product, but any technology audit is only as good as its follow-through. Some organizations that offer audits also provide assistance with using the data constructively, but you should be leery of an audit that implies that the auditor's organization is a one-stop solution. Ask auditors for a list of clients to contact and, because most audits suggest types of professional development that will help a district move forward, insist on seeing the research behind the recommendations. Remember, too, that what worked in one district may or may not work in your district.

A technology plan should focus on student outcomes and measures, not "wires and pliers." Unless you are able to say with assurance that your technology dollars are being maximized, your technology instruction is aligned to your curriculum, your staff is well trained and knowledgeable on how to use technology within the curriculum, and your student achievement is enhanced by technology, you should consider investing in a technology audit. The money you invest will reap benefits in the long term.

chapter 8

Media Matters

As the number of media specialists among the ISTE membership grew, ISTE began to find new ways to serve that segment of our membership. In addition to forming a special interest group for media specialists and publishing books for them, ISTE backed this constituency by supporting *L&L* when it created Media Matters, a column by media specialists, for media specialists. This column deals with a variety of issues, from instructional techniques to professional reading.

We were very lucky to have a solid editor for the column in Doug Johnson and great contributors. Later in the evolution of the column, Doug began writing for every other issue.

We start our collection with "Substantive Searching" by Joyce Valenza (November 2004). Joyce provides specific activities to use to help students perform effective searches that lead them to rich resources appropriate for their needs. She sees many students perform sloppy searches and thus fail to find what they need to do their projects or papers. It is easy to just type a few keywords into Google and take what you get on the first page. But as a media specialist, you know so many more effective tools and techniques, and with a little coaching, your students can adopt those same techniques. This, when combined with the information Joyce provided in a feature article she wrote in 2001 ("What's Not on the Web," September 2001), certainly helped me create more effective web searches. If students use just a fraction of the techniques she presents, they will find that they get the information they need in a much shorter time.

Next, we go to our series on blogging ("Blogging and the Media Specialist," parts 1 and 2, March and May 2006). In the first article, Doug Johnson lists the blogs he reads and finds useful professionally. He gives tips for finding blogs that you enjoy as well as keeping up with them once you find them. In the second part, Frances Jacobson Harris describes the joys of blogging about your own experiences. She helps readers get started and gives ideas for what to focus on and how to keep it going. One of the really exciting things about blogs is that you can get nearly instant feedback on issues you need help with, and you can quickly share new techniques. Also, you have complete control over the finished product. Now I love writing for print, books, magazines, and the like. But I know that I must give up some level of control to the publisher and that it will take a while to appear in print. With blogging, I have all the control, and I can get published immediately. That definitely appeals to the control freak in me. But the benefit for a professional blog is that, as long as you have regular readers, you can get quick feedback when you post questions. Say you need advice on to handle a particular issue with a student. You can post that on your blog and have advice from your readers within a day or two.

Speaking of user control and instantaneous publishing, we close this section with a discussion of Wikipedia ("Wikipedia: Ban It or Boost It?" Doug Johnson, October 2006). The lack of editorial control over Wikipedia entries can be scary to those of us who value authority in our reference sources. But that same lack of control allows Wikipedia to be more current than most printed resources. And users can and will fix errors when they occur. Because of these interesting features, there is much controversy over how useful Wikipedia is in student research. And that controversy is what Doug addresses and defuses. Doug believes strongly that Wikipedia and other web 2.0 tools are useful for students and educators. He is drawn to the currency and the egalitarian nature of the tool. Personally, I find Wikipedia useful for finding obscure information that most printed resources simply wouldn't waste space on. It also helps me get some early background information to help me craft the effective searches Joyce described in her article.

November 2004

Media Matters

Substantive Searching
Thinking and Behaving
Info-Fluently

By Joyce Valenza

Subject: Information literacy

Grades: 5–12 (Ages 10–18)

Standards: *NETS•S* 3; *NETS•T* II; *NETS•A* II (http://www.iste.org/standards/)

In my position as a teacher-librarian, I watch students search. Over the past several years, I have grown less satisfied with the results and products of student research, and so have my colleagues. One reason is students' difficulty finding and discerning the best sources to support their research. Settling for what they can find easily, students often have little real idea of what is out there to find.

On a daily basis, in formal and informal ways, I teach students to search. As the online landscape evolved, my own notion of essential searching skills has evolved, too.

I no longer expect students to embrace searching as a science. As a science, it is flawed. The precise searching logic I learned in graduate school—complex search statements resembling mathematical equations with synonyms grouped in parentheses connected by Boolean operators—did not stand the test of time. It did not hold up across emerging search interfaces with their friendly pull-down menus and tabs. And I certainly don't expect students to memorize the many shifting interfaces they are likely to face in a lifetime of information seeking.

Because locating, recognizing, and effectively using information are critical life skills, I expect students to exhibit and embrace several key understandings and larger concepts. I expect them to adopt certain attitudes and behaviors that will serve them their lifetime as information users. These understandings and behaviors resonate across all content areas and across our technology and information literacy standards. They are as useful for creating formal papers as they are for creating thoughtful, interactive media. But in a larger sense, these understandings and behaviors have legs. They give students the power to be better learners for the rest of their lives.

Continued

Continued

Smart Students Are Not Always the Best Searchers

Why is it that a student who masters such challenges as calculus may not excel at finding information? I've got a few theories.

A know-it-all sense of self-efficacy may present barriers to learning and to seeking the best stuff. The turf on which we ask students to perform academically is the very same turf our students use as their playgrounds and entertainment venues. Though we celebrate student familiarity with the landscape, their transfer of entertainment habits to more serious academic enterprises can present problems.

The Internet has transformed research into a largely independent pursuit. Gone may be the chat a parent would conduct on the car ride to the library or what librarians call the in-person "reference interview," where an information professional intervenes to help a student assess a problem, focus a topic, suggest keywords, suggest a critical book, or recommend the best index or database in which to begin a search. Student independence is something we promote and can celebrate at many points in the research process, but adult intervention is critical. Even the brightest of our 17-year-olds don't know what they don't know (e.g., the keywords associated with a specialized field the historical context for an event, the seminal works or classics in an area of knowledge).

Finally, although teacher-librarians learn searching skills in preservice programs, most classroom teachers do not. As well intentioned as they might be, a large number of educators approach searching without refined knowledge of how to help their students move the best results up to the top of the list, evaluate a works-cited page, guide learners to their search tool options, or gain an awareness of the developmentally appropriate databases available to help students prepare for the research tasks they are

likely to face. And classroom teachers may also not be aware that they have knowledgeable partners, teacher-librarians, who will, every step of the way, help them plan, implement, and assess information-based activities for learners.

Good Searchers Have Common Abilities and Behaviors

Good researchers not only have specific skills, but also a set of attitudes and behaviors that promote success. In terms of cognitive abilities, the information-fluent student:

- Knows what he or she is looking for
- Realizes he or she has search choices
- Recognizes research holes
- Knows basic strategies for evaluating sources
- Recognizes that searching on the Internet is an interactive, recursive process
- Knows that advanced search screens exist and offer greater searching power
- Knows that there are three main types of searching: keyword, subject/topic, and field searching
- Knows how to think about a query
- Knows when quality matters

Prior Information. It may take some messing around at first, but the info-fluent student has at least some information about the area he or she is researching. This may mean doing some background reading before

Because locating, recognizing, and effectively using information are critical life skills, I expect students to exhibit and embrace several key understandings and larger concepts.

conducting any serious searching. Any thesis-based project requires significant reading and refining before a student can move from topic to question to thesis. The info-fluent student learns to disregard material that does not further his or her question or support his or her thesis.

Search Choices. Once the student has done some background research, he or she must choose where to search for more information. Google rocks, but it is not the only band in town, and it is not always the best place to start. Although it is not likely that a student will recognize the names of more than two or three search tools, the info-fluent student knows that search tools can be organized into clusters or genres, and that different

Continued

Continued

tools are more effective for different tasks. You may create a search tool page like mine or link to Debbie Abilock's Choose the Best Search for Your Information Need or Laura Cohen's How to Choose a Search Engine or Directory. (*Editor's note:* Find these and other resources on p. 43.)

Among the clusters are:

- Search tools that organize results in helpful ways, such as concept clusters (e.g., Vivisimo) or mind maps (e.g., KartOO)
- Metasearch tools, which search across many search tools at one time (e.g., Ixquick)
- News tools (e.g., Headline Spot, Yahoo! Full Coverage, World News Network)
- Image and media tools (e.g., AP Photo Archive, the Library of Congress's American Memory Collections, Pics4Learning)
- Reference tools such as online dictionaries, quotation databases, encyclopedias, and Today in History sites (e.g., Merriam-Webster Online, World Book, This Day in History)
- Subscription services (e.g., EBSCO-host, GaleNet, WilsonWeb, Facts on File, SIRS, bigchalk)
- Subject-specific search tools (e.g., Scirus, Artchive)
- Portals (e.g., Kathy Schrock's Guide for Educators, Multnomah Homework Center, FirstGov, Internet Public Library)
- Subject directories (e.g., Librarians' Index to the Internet, About.com, Infomine)
- Special tools for children (e.g., Ithaki, Yahooligans!, Searchasaurus, SIRS Discoverer, FirstGov for Kids)

Research Holes. The info-fluent student who is immersed in a topic begins to note the experts and the important books that people cite repeatedly. He or she examines others' bibliographies. Overlooking important people, sources, and concepts would constitute holes in research.

Strategies. The info-fluent student knows that authors' credentials are important, that any cited source ought to be defendable in terms of relevance, timeliness, bias, credibility, accuracy, and reliability. This student knows that free hosting services are likely to raise red flags on works-cited pages. Reliable authors don't usually rely on free services with their ubiquitous advertising. Instead, these authors are typically hosted by museums, universities, and other respected institutions.

The Process. When things don't go well, info-fluent students consider the cause and refine their search strategies. They know a tip or help sheet is readily available within most search tools. They examine and mine their result lists for alternate ideas, words, phrases.

Advanced Searches. The info-fluent student knows that advanced search pages, unlike the general opening search box, allow him or her to limit results by date, by field, for media format, or file format; to more easily use Boolean operators; and to filter problem words, for example, returning only pages that do not contain the word *football* in a search for eagles.

Three Types of Searches. The info-fluent student knows he or she can search in one of three ways (keyword, subject/topic, or field).

Keyword searching allows searchers to combine terms strategically, for instance enclosing phrases in quotation marks to ensure those words stay together (e.g., "vitamin A") or including *and* between words that absolutely need to be included in results.

Topic or subject searching is generally the best strategy when a student is searching one broad concept. Based on a database's controlled vocabulary, searchers can browse through a standardized set of subject terms and subheadings to focus their

Google rocks, but it is not the only band in town, and it is not always the best place to start.

Continued

Continued

search as suggested by the structure of the database.

In some cases, keywords may be searched within designated fields of a database. For instance, looking for a keyword in a title or abstract, might be more meaningful than looking for that same keyword in an article's full text. Prompts for using keywords and fields successfully are often located in advanced search screens in both subscription databases and on the free Web.

Thinking about Queries. Natural language searching (entering questions as if you were engaging in natural communication) does not give a searcher much power. When a student learns how to construct a query, he or she knows how to formally pose a question to a search box, making use of its syntax, or special language. For instance, "Romeo and Juliet" AND criticism AND Mercutio will return more targeted results than a search for Romeo and Juliet.

Quality. Do I ever do sloppy Google searches? Sure I do, when I am checking on spelling or getting a broad idea of what's out there. But when I know it matters, I create thoughtful queries. I visit specialized databases. I figure out who wrote the documents I find and where they were originally published.

Cognitive abilities won't stick unless they are supported by attitudes and behaviors, habits of mind. The info-fluent student:

• Has a sense of inquiry
• Has a plan
• Has mind tools for organizing materials he or she gathers as well as tools for designing the product
• Is persistent and fussy
• Recognizes when he or she might benefit from consulting an information professional

A Sense of Inquiry. The info-fluent student is curious and develops

exploratory questions out of that curiosity.

A Plan. This student thinks about words. He or she is able to envision a dream document and what words and phrases that document might contain. Time management is key in student planning. Info-fluent students do not back themselves into a time crisis, understanding that good research takes time, and that the process is recursive; it is all about refining, organizing, analyzing, drafting, concluding— about going back.

Mind Tools. The info-fluent student continually looks for information patterns. What buckets does this information fit into? Does it look like a comparison? A chronology? A thesis? A debate? What type of presentation is most likely to be effective?

Persistence and Fussiness. The info-fluent student does not settle for good-enough information, recognizing that the first page of a result list may not contain the best stuff out there. He or she is willing to think about how a search may be improved, refine strategies, and try other search tools. At times, this may mean seeking full text when it is not easily available. If all that appears in a database is an abstract and that abstract is "killer," the info-fluent student will seek the full text, even if it means going to a library, checking another database,

The info-fluent student does not settle for good-enough information.

initiating an interlibrary loan transaction, going to a bookstore, or locating a collection of e-books.

Consulting a Professional. The info-fluent student can put aside any sense of technological arrogance to ask for help. His or her question might have nothing to do with technology. It might, perhaps, involve asking for help brainstorming alternate keywords. It may be asking about potential sources beyond the free Web, the particular experts in a specialized field, or the unique vocabulary of a new area of knowledge.

Teachers Can Encourage Better Searching

What can you do to encourage better information use?

Create Research Challenges. Eliminate reports that merely ask for recall and comprehension. That work—a report on a state or president or planet—is far too easily copied and printed. Ask students instead to explore provocative questions—to compare, analyze,

Continued

Continued

evaluate, and invent, rather than simply paraphrase.

Evaluate Students' Works-Cited Lists. If you are not comfortable with this task, you can have your school librarian evaluate the list with you. On the high school level, reward the use of scholarly sources. On other levels, reward the use of high-quality sources from reliable databases and journals.

Learn to recognize suspicious URLs. Free hosting services, such as AOL Members or Geocities, and personal sites should raise red flags and inspire questions. "K12" in a URL may tell you that the source may be the product of someone else's sixth grade class.

Examine the "bread crumbs" you find in student citations. Did the student track down the source of the material? If it was found on a database, what was the original source type—a magazine article, encyclopedia, or scholarly journal? With your librarian, decide to what depth you require those bread crumbs to be

documented. If you want students to evaluate their sources, then these crumbs are important in determining the quality of the original source.

Any mention of Google, Yahoo, AltaVista, or other general search engines should send a message that the student is referencing the index, not the original source, and has likely avoided energetic research.

What types of sources does the student list? Are they all from popular quick news sources, such as CNN? Was any attempt made to balance resources among books, journals, or general Web sites? Did the student attempt to balance points of view? Did the student use popular, trade, or scholarly journals? Be aware that when you look for balance, a book is a book, whether it appears as an e-book or as a physical volume. An article from *National Geographic* is a magazine article, whether it comes from the shelves or an online database.

Scaffold. Help your students develop organizers for data collection and

restructuring. A Venn diagram or a matrix will help students collect data for comparing and contrasting. A time line or flowchart may aid in the analysis of an historic event. A concept map will aid students as they brainstorm subheadings or arguments supporting a thesis.

Create Online Pathfinders with Your Librarian. Pathfinders are blueprints for student research. Focused on a specific project or a particular curriculum, they create a kind of self-service intervention, respecting students' independence while guiding them through the process. Pathfinders may suggest keywords, databases, special search engines, directories, call numbers, and multimedia resources—any special advice necessary for success on a specific project. Project rubrics should heavily value the suggestions of the pathfinder.

Create an Appropriate Search Tool Page for General Student Research on Your Web Site. Do you want students to start with Google? EBSCOhost? Literature Resource Center? ProQuest Historical Newspapers? KidsClick!? Facts.com? World Book? Let them know, and make these tools no more than a mouse click away. On this page, link students to the more powerful advanced search screens of the search engines you'd like them to use.

Ask Students to Annotate Their Works-Cited Lists. Annotations are metacognitive activities that force and value critical thinking and careful selection. In an annotation, the student should consider authors' credentials, relevance of the source to the project, how it compared to other sources, and how it informed his or her knowledge. Include criteria for evaluating annotations in your rubrics.

Use Formative Assessments to Check Student Progress. Collect organizers, outlines, source cards, note cards, tentative thesis statements, and pre-

Examine the "bread crumbs" you find in student citations. Did the student track down the source of the material?

Continued

Continued

liminary works-consulted pages. It's too late to assess only at the end. Assessing the process throughout the project has the greatest learning value.

This knowledge may have longer legs than calculus.

Resources

Search Tools

Artchive: http://www.artchive.com

Debbie Abilock's Choose the Best Search for Your Information Need: http://www.noodletools.com/debbie/literacies/information/5locate/adviceengine.html

Ixquick: http://www.ixquick.com

Joyce Kasman Valenza's Search Tools Page: http://mciu.org/~spjvweb/searchtip.html

KartOO: http://www.kartoo.com

Laura Cohen's How to Choose a Search Engine or Directory: http://library.albany.edu/internet/choose.html

Scirus: http://www.scirus.com

Vivisimo: http://www.vivisimo.com

News

Headline Spot: http://www.headlinespot.com

World News Network: http://www.worldnews.com

Yahoo! Full Coverage: http://news.yahoo.com/fc/

Image and Media Tools

AP Photo Archive: http://photoarchive.ap.orgLibrary of Congress' American Memory

Collections: http://memory.loc.gov

Pics4Learning: http://www.pics4learning.com

Reference Tools

Merriam-Webster Online: http://www.m-w.com/dictionary.htm

This Day in History: http://www.historychannel.com/today/

World Book: http://www.worldbook.com

Subscription Services

bigchalk: http://www.proquestk12.com

EBSCOhost: http://search.epnet.com/

Facts on File: http://www.facts.com

GaleNet: http://infotrac.galenet.com/

Literature Resource Center: http://www.gale.com/pdf/facts/lrc.pdf

ProQuest Historical Newspapers: http://www.proquest.com/proquest/histdemo/default.shtml

SIRS: http://www.proquestk12.com/

WilsonWeb: http://vnweb.hwwilsonweb.com/hww/login.jhtml

Portals

FirstGov: http://www.firstgov.gov/

Internet Public Library: http://www.ipl.org/

Kathy Schrock's Guide for Educators: http://school.discovery.com/schrockguide/

Multnomah Homework Center: http://www.multnomah.lib.or.us/lib/homework/

Subject Directories

About.com: http://www.about.com

Infomine: http://infomine.ucr.edu/

Librarians' Index to the Internet: http://lii.org/

Tools Especially for Children

Facts for Learning: http://factsforlearning.2facts.com/

FirstGov for Kids: http://www.kids.gov/

Ithaki: http://www.ithaki.net/

KidsClick!: http://kidsclick.org/

Yahooligans!: http://yahooligans.yahoo.com/

Searchasaurus: http://www.epnet.com/school/k12search3.asp

SIRS Discoverer: http://proquest.com/products/pt-product-SIRS-Discoverer.shtml

Searching Tips

21st Century Information Fluency Project Portal: http://21cif.imsa.edu/

Big6 Web Site: http://big6.com/

CyberBee: http://www.cyberbee.com

CyberSmart! Curriculum: http://www.cybersmartcurriculum.org/

Four NETS for Better Searching: http://webquest.sdsu.edu/searching/fournets.htm

Joyce Valenza's Information Literacy Lessons: http://mciu.org/~spjvweb/infolitles.html

KidsClick! Worlds of Web Searching: http://www.rcls.org/wows/

Landmark Project: http://www.landmark-project.com/citation_machine/

Noodle Tools: http://www.noodletools.com

Research 101: http://www.lib.washington.edu/uwill/research101/

University of Albany's Internet Tutorials: http://library.albany.edu/internet/

University of California, Berkeley, Teaching Library Internet Workshops: http://www.lib.berkeley.edu/TeachingLib/Guides/Internet/FindInfo.html

Yahooligans! Teachers' Guide: http://yahooligans.yahoo.com/tg/

Joyce Valenza is librarian at Springfield Township (Pennsylvania) High School, techlife@school *columnist for the* Philadelphia Inquirer, *a doctoral student at the University of North Texas, and a founding member of ISTE's SIG for media specialists (SIGMS). Publications include* Power Tools Recharged *(American Library Association, 2002),* Super Searchers Go to School *(Information Today, in press), and the video series* Library Skills for Children *(Schlesinger Media, 2003) and* Research Skills for Students *(Schlesinger Media, 2004).*

Doug Johnson edits L&L's Media Matters column on behalf of ISTE's SIGMS. He has been director of media and technology for the Mankato (Minnesota) Public Schools since 1991. Doug is a veteran author whose works have appeared in books, journals, and magazines and serves on ISTE's board of directors.

author's update
Joyce Valenza

The search landscape shifted profoundly since this piece first appeared in November 2004, but the need for information fluency—those critical habits, dispositions, and skills—remains.

In 2009, we need to add a few tools to our students' toolkits. Searching was once a one-way street—the student searched across several search tools for information. Traffic patterns have changed. In the web 2.0 world, savvy researchers know they can organize the web so that the information they need most is automatically and regularly pushed to them as it is published. Students who know how to set up RSS feeds, iGoogle or Page-Flakes pages, or e-mail alerts from search engines and databases work smarter than those who do not. Push is a new strategy worth teaching.

Web 2.0 is newly media rich and inclusive. Search tools now gather a wealth of shared images, video, audio, blogs, and other content from around the world. Some of these search tools display results in new visual ways that allow searchers to explore relationships among the resulting documents.

The notion of audience has shifted, as have notions of ownership of intellectual property. My learners publish the results of their research in multiple media. Because they publish on the web, they need to know about searching for copyright-friendly content. Web-based pathfinders, such as the STHS Virtual Library wiki (http://copyrightfriendly.wikispaces.com), lead them beyond Google Images to portals that direct them to content with Creative Commons (http://creativecommons.org) licensing, which is shared with the larger community.

And speaking of pathfinders, librarians and classroom teachers, with new abilities to easily publish and collaborate online, can guide learners through the search process. Like many of my colleagues, I create wiki pathfinders (www.sdst.org/shs/library/pathmenu.html) to help students navigate a far bigger web, a far greater number of information choices. Many of us also share our suggested resources through social bookmarking sites such as http://del.icio.us/. We encourage young searchers to share as well.

March 2006

Blogging and the Media Specialist

By Doug Johnson

Doug Johnson has been director of media and technology for the Mankato (Minnesota) Public Schools since 1991. He is a veteran author whose works have appeared in books, journals, and magazines. Johnson serves on ISTE's board of directors and as a volunteer columnist for L&L.

MEDIA MATTERS

Have you noticed that the Web is undergoing a transformation? Are terms like blogs, wikis, podcasts, and RSS feeds now a part of your and your students' vocabularies? If they aren't, they should be. These forms of communication and information management are part of what Tim O'Reilly describes as a shift from Web 1.0 to Web 2.0: a movement from the Web being a static means of one-way, mass communication to an interactive, personal communication medium. (***Editor's note:*** Find O'Reilly's and other articles listed under Resources at the end of this column.)

The next two Media Matters columns will focus on a single aspect of the Web 2.0 movement: Web logs, or blogs as they are more commonly called. In this issue, I look at the definition of a blog, show you how to find blogs to read, give ideas to help you keep up with them, and present a short list of professional library media and technology-related blogs. In the May 2006 issue, Frances Jacobson Harris, library media specialist at University Laboratory High School, University of Illinois at Urbana-Champaign, will describe how she and others use blogs as a means of communication in the library media program and will share her observations about how students use blogs.

So What's a Blog?

A blog in its most generic sense is a Web site that is updated on a regular basis, displays the content in reverse chronological order (newest entries first), and allows, even invites, reader response. See "Writing with Weblogs" by Glen Bull, Gina Bull, and Sara Kajder (*L&L,* September 2003) and EDUCAUSE's *Seven Things You Should Know About Blogs* for good overviews. Although text remains the primary means bloggers use to communicate, these sites increasingly include text, audio (podcasts), and video clips. Anything found on a Web page can be found on a blog. For example, Will Richardson at Weblogg-ed (http://www.weblogg-ed.com) makes some interesting observations about using blogs for "connective writing," pushing the envelope about the definition of a blog.

A blog requires little, if any, knowledge of HTML coding. Many no-cost sites allow the creation and hosting of a blog. Popular blog sites include Blogger (http://www.blogger.com), Livejournal (http://www.livejournal.com) and Xanga (http://www.xanga.com). Edublogs (http://edublogs.org) and Blog Meister (http://epnweb.org/blogmeister) are specifically designed to support use by educators.

Blogs got their start as personal journals, often with highly political overtones. But increasingly, blogs are replacing e-zines and static Web sites as a means for organizations to communicate with members and customers on a more formal basis. Some K–12 schools have replaced their regular Web sites with blogs that are easy for multiple authors to update.

Finding Blogs of Personal Interest

There are two basic ways of locating blogs of interest (among the 20+ million existing!): using a search engine or finding links to other blogs on blogs themselves.

Continued

Continued

Three popular specialized blog search tools are Technorati (http://www.technorati.com), Google Blog Search (http://blogsearch.google.com), and Bloglines (http://www.bloglines.com). In their current forms, I've found these tools to be rather inefficient.

Another means of finding blogs of interest is to examine the "blogs I read" or "blogroll" section that is a common part of many blogs. If you find a particular blog interesting, there is a good chance you will like the blogs the writer of that blog reads.

Keeping Up with Blogs

It's easy to find a large number of blogs that have interesting and useful content. But it's time consuming to bookmark and check each blog on a daily basis for updates, especially when updates to most blogs are made irregularly. An RSS (Rich Site Summary or Really Simple Syndication) feed aggregator (e.g., Bloglines) can help.

RSS is programming code in a Web page that allows readers to "subscribe" to the site, and be alerted when additions have been made.

Most blogs include an RSS feed that aggregators recognize. Bloglines, a simple, free, online RSS aggregator becomes a blog reader's one-stop shop for organizing blogs and checking for blog updates. After adding the URL for a blog to your "feeds," a single glance at this Web site will show whether a blog has been updated. The new entry can either be read in Bloglines itself, or the reader can click through to the actual blog site itself. A very good tutorial is available.

Recommended Blogs

Although blogs tend to come and go, some are updated more regularly than others, I've found the following to have interesting and current content.

Increasingly, blogs are replacing e-zines and static Web sites as a means for organizations to communicate with members and customers on a more formal basis.

School Library Media
Alice in Infoland (Alice Yucht): http://aliceinfo.squarespace.com/blog/

The Blue Skunk Blog (Doug Johnson): http://doug-johnson.squarespace.com/blue-skunk-blog

Deep Thinking (Diane Chen): http://deepthinking.blogsome.com

The Free Range Librarian (Karen Schneider): http://freerangelibrarian.com

Infomancy (Chris Harris): http://www.schoolof.info/infomancy

Infosearcher (Pam Berger): http://www.infosearcher.com/

Librarian in the Middle (Robert Eiffert): http://www.beiffert.net/wordpress/

The Neverending Search (Joyce Valenza): http://joycevalenza.edublogs.org

School Library Journal Blog (Amy Bowllan): http://www.schoollibraryjournal.com/blog

Ed Tech
The Committed Sardine (Ian Jukes): http://homepage.mac.com/iajukes/blogwavestudio

Education/Technology (Tim Lauer): http://tim.lauer.name/

Kaffeeklatsch (Kathy Schrock): http://kathyschrock.blogspot.com

Neat New Stuff (Marylaine Block): http://www.marylaine.com/neatnew.html

Pedersondesigns (John Pederson): http://pedersondesigns.com

The Savvy Technologist (Tim Wilson): http://technosavvy.org

Teach and Learn Online (Leigh Blackall): http://teachandlearnonline.blogspot.com/

2 Cents Worth (David Warlick): http://davidwarlick.com/2cents

Weblogg-ed (Will Richardson): http://www.weblogg-ed.com

For an interesting view of librarian bloggers worldwide, look at the Frapper Web site (http://www.frappr.com/blogginglibrarians). And add yourself if you are a library blogger.

In the role of "information expert," school library media specialists should know about blogs and use them professionally. They are an increasingly popular source of information and a popular communication tool for students and adults. They can be a powerful tool for media specialists to communicate with staff and students. And they bring with them their own special set of safe, ethical, and appropriate use issues.

Acknowledgements

Thanks to John Pederson's wiki Web 2.0 Tutorials for Educators (http://www.pedersondesigns.com/wiki) for several of these resources. Also thanks to Graham Wegner, Donna Baumbach, Josh Thomas, and Sue Tanner for the improvements they made to this article when it was posted as a wiki.

Resources

O'Reilly, T. (2005). *What is Web 2.0: Design patterns and business models for the next generation of software.* Available: http://www.oreillynet.com/pub/a/oreilly/tim/news/2005/09/30/what-is-web-20.html

Bull, G., Bull, G., & Kajder, S. (2003). Writing with Weblogs. *Learning & Leading with Technology, 31*(1), pp. 32–35. Available: http://www.iste.org/ll/ (Scroll to the bottom of the page and use the Search *L&L* feature.)

EDUCAUSE (2005). *Seven things you should know about blogs.* Available: http://www.educause.edu/LibraryDetailPage/666?ID=ELI7006

May 2006

Blogging and the Media Specialist, Part 2

MEDIA MATTERS

By Frances Jacobson Harris

Guest columnist Frances Jacobson Harris is the librarian at University Laboratory High School at the University of Illinois at Urbana-Champaign. Harris wrote I Found It On the Internet: Coming of Age Online *(American Library Association, 2005). Author photo by student Isaac Chambers.*

Does it seem as if all your students are either blogging or commenting on their friends' blogs? Web logs, or blogs, are one of the most popular tools of what has become known as Web 2.0, the Web as an interactive, personal communication medium rather than a static means of one-way, mass communication.

In the March 2006 Media Matters column, regular columnist Doug Johnson gave an overview of blogging and described how school library media specialists can find blogs and use them for professional development. This issue, he asked me to write about how students use blogs and how library media specialists and teachers can use blogging in their programs.

The Teen Blogger Versus the Adult Blogger

Teenagers blog very differently than adult bloggers. Their focus is primarily on self-expression and community, and only secondarily on information. Teen blogs are typically diary-like, decorated and customized, and often feature interactive or multimedia elements such as polls and sound clips. Teen bloggers take maximum advantage of social functions that allow them to link to like-minded souls. For example, a LiveJournal (http://www.livejournal.com) profile typically links to friends lists, friend of lists, group blog memberships, interests, and even maps of friends' locations.

Like other technologies, blogging has spawned its share of unanticipated consequences. Many teen bloggers have a skewed sense of privacy, forgetting that their posts can be read by the world at large. When I talk to my students about privacy they think I mean withholding basic factual information about themselves, such as their home addresses and telephone numbers. They don't understand how much they reveal about themselves in the course of routine postings. Although unknown predators may take advantage of this information, teens are probably more likely to be hurt by those they know. The result is, at best, gossip and teenage drama and at worst, serious bullying. Oddly, teens often feel violated when their "private" thoughts are read by parents, teachers, or school administrators.

The adult professional blogger is a different creature altogether, usually focused primarily on information and information networking and, secondly, on self-expression. This blogger embeds links within posts, values archived posts, provides permalinks (permanent URLs) to individual entries, and often includes a blogroll (a list of favorite blogs).

Taking the Plunge

Why should media specialists create their own blogs? Blogs provide a natural environment for active learning, as well as an opportunity to connect teens to the media center.

So how do you get started? In March, Johnson described the mechanics of the process and provided a list of resources. You can host a blog yourself or you can use a hosting service such as blogger.com or edublogs.org. School climate will influence how blogging is managed. What is the level of administrative and technical support? How open is the culture of the school? For example, will commenting be allowed on a

Continued

Continued

school blog? What are the potential consequences one way or the other? Look at the blogs of other library media centers and schools to find models and develop ideas that suit your own setting. Media center blogs should also provide RSS feeds so readers are always alerted to new content. If readers have to keep checking your site, you may drop from their radar.

Ways to Blog in the Media Center

Official Face Blogs. A good way to start blogging is to create a blog that serves as an "official face" of the media center—the spot for news, updates, and communication with students, staff, and parents. Blogs of this sort focus on current information and are generally not highly interactive. Some media center Web sites are created with blog software, which makes it easy for the site to be maintained and updated by multiple staff members. The Huntingtown High School Library Media Center (http://www.hhsmedia.blogspot.com) is one such example. Library news takes center stage, and links to databases, class research projects, and other information appear in the right column. At Mabry Middle School (http://mabryonline.org/blogs) every teacher, including the media specialist, has a blog, and the principal is the Webmaster!

Single-Purpose Blogs. Blogs can also be highly focused, dedicated to a single function rather than acting as a global resource. For example, the blogging environment is a natural one for hosting book discussions such as the book club blog at Hawley Library Media Center at Winnacunnet High School in Hampton, New Hampshire (http://bibliotalk.blogspot.com). Blogs are also effective platforms for posting information about class assignments and projects. The teacher blogs at Mabry Middle School are good examples of this type of use. The students (and their parents) in Renee Kaplan's

language arts classes can check her blog (http://mabryonline.org/blogs/kaplan/) for daily homework assignments, class notes, and student work. In contrast, my blog (http://www.uni.uiuc.edu/library/blog) is a "single-purpose" blog in that it fulfills a public relations function for my library. I think of it as the virtual personality of our Web site, a way of extending a human voice and presence beyond the walls of the school building.

Active Learning Blogs. Blogs can be used very effectively for active learning (as can wikis, but that's for another column!). Two critical features of blogging promote active learning: built-in access to a wider audience than the traditional student-teacher relationship provides and the potential for collaboration and feedback from others. Classroom teachers have been the leaders in using blogs for active learning, but there is no reason why media specialists cannot jump into this arena with equal fervor. On his blog (http://www.weblogg-ed.com/best_practices), Will Richardson maintains a running list of blogs that demonstrate the potential for active learning using this medium. Among others, he links to Canadian math teacher Darren Kuropatwa's class blogs (see http://pc20s.blogspot.com/ for one of his current offerings). Kuropatwa has students serve as scribes for each day's activities, posting notes from the day as well as relevant formulas, activities, and visuals. He also requires students to post a reflection about where they are in their learning at least once before each test. One student recently posted the following insightful commentary:

And to Mr. K, I'd just like to say something upon my behalf and it is the complete truth. When we first started this thing I thought it was a complete waste of time, especially since I dont have a computer at home and I would

have to spend extra time finding a computer that I could use. But at the end of the year I realize that the blog is for every student that has ever looked down at their paper and said "what the heck (i know how dumb it sounds) am i doing." The blog is something you can resort to when you need help, or need someone to explain something to you.

Media specialists and teachers who create active learning blogs must build in mechanisms that protect the privacy of student contributors and the integrity of the blog. Blog commenting (and even reading) can be made "members only" and confidential information such as grades can be shared in other ways.

Closing Thoughts

One of the unique attributes of blogging is that it can transmit a sense of voice. Do not miss the opportunity to share more than the (potentially boring) facts about your services. One excellent example of how voice and personality are transmitted, yet a sense of professionalism is maintained, is the Northfield Mount Hermon School Library's "Reading Room" blog (http://nmhlibrary.typepad.com). My favorite feature is their periodic "Library Lounge Lizard of the Week," a candid photo of students at work (or play) in the library. The link in the sidebar to the photo-tale "Hoggers Visit the Library" is not to be missed. My guess is that this library is a very welcoming place in person as well as online.

Blogging and other social networking services such as MySpace.com and Facebook.com serve as important vehicles of self-expression, communication, and information exchange for teens. This is our chance to join the party and put our own spin on things. The blogosphere is big enough for everyone.

October 2006

Wikipedia: Ban It or Boost It?

"Wikipedia Celebrates 750 Years of American Independence"

—headline from *The Onion,* July 26, 2006

MEDIA MATTERS

By Doug Johnson

Doug Johnson has been director of media and technology for the Mankato (Minnesota) Public Schools since 1991. He is a veteran author whose works have appeared in books, journals, and magazines. Johnson serves on ISTE's board of directors and as a volunteer columnist for L&L.

A collective gasp and shudder went palpably through the entire room of library media specialists when I first heard a conference presenter describe how Wikipedia (http://wikipedia.org) entries are written—by anyone, at any time, on nearly any topic. No editors or editorial process. Instantaneous changes. Faith that the "lay" viewer of the entry will correct any inaccurate information found. Wikipedia flaunts every rule our library schools taught us about the authority of a reference source.

Wikipedia, that growing, user-created online encyclopedia, is the poster child for Web 2.0 and is fostering a sea change in ideas about the credibility and value of information, products, and services. The philosopher Arthur Schopenhauer wrote: "All truth passes through three stages. First, it is ridiculed. Second, it is violently opposed. Third, it is accepted as being self-evident." Since it has emerged on the scene in 2001, Wikipedia seems to have already gone through Schopenhauer's "stages of truth" in the general public's mind. More than a million people a day visit the site.

The thought of a reference source that anyone can edit seems ridiculous on its face to those of us who have been taught to identify the reliability of a resource using traditional criteria. And indeed there have been highly publicized cases of deliberately false, even malicious, content placed in Wikipedia entries. But when *Nature* magazine reported a study late in 2005 that

showed *Encyclopedia Britannica* and Wikipedia were comparatively accurate in their respective science entries, the theory of "self-correcting" information seemed to be validated. Historian Roy Rosensweig defends the accuracy of Wikipedia entries as well: "Wikipedia is surprisingly accurate in reporting names, dates, and events in U.S. history. In the 25 biographies I read closely, I found clear-cut factual errors in only four. Most were small and inconsequential." And on May 8, 2006, respected *New York Times* columnist Paul Krugman quoted from Wikipedia to define "conspiracy theory."

Ridicule, opposition, self-evidence. Where are you? How many of you already turn to Wikipedia for a quick understanding of a topic? How many of your students do? And how do you counsel them when asked about accuracy? Should Wikipedia be an accepted source for a research assignment?

Although it is difficult to give Wikipedia a blanket endorsement, it can be a valuable resource for students and staff alike. Why would you turn to Wikipedia instead of the *Encyclopedia Britannica*?

It has a wider scope. As of August 2006, Wikipedia contained more than a million articles in its English-language version; *Encyclopedia Britannica* had 65,000 articles in its 2005 print edition and 120,000 in the online edition. In her delightful *New Yorker* article, Stacy Schiff writes:

Continued

Continued

"Apparently, no traditional encyclopedia has ever suspected that someone might wonder about Sudoku or about prostitution in China. Or, for that matter, about Capgras delusion (the unnerving sensation that an impostor is sitting in for a close relative), the Boston molasses disaster, the Rhinoceros Party of Canada, Bill Gates' house, the forty-five-minute Anglo-Zanzibar War, or Islam in Iceland. Wikipedia includes fine entries on Kafka and the War of Spanish Succession, and also a complete guide to the ships of the U.S. Navy, a definition of Philadelphia cheesesteak, a masterly page on Scrabble, a list of historical cats (celebrity cats, a cat millionaire, the first feline to circumnavigate Australia), a survey of invented expletives in fiction ("bippie," "cakesniffer," "furgle"), instructions for curing hiccups, and an article that describes, with schematic diagrams, how to build a stove from a discarded soda can."

It has up-to-date information on timely topics. Wikipedia may be one's only reference source on recent technologies and events. For current popular social concepts such as "the long tail," technology terms such as "GNU," or up-to-date information on political groups such as Hezbollah, print or traditionally edited sources can't keep up. (As I write this, dozens of updates have been made to the Hezbollah entry already today.)

Web 2.0 sources may state values closer to that of the reader. The voice of the common man, vox populi, is being heard and heeded as a source of authentic, reliable information. My own view of the reliability of informa-

tion has changed. In selecting hotels, I now use TripAdvisor.com, with its multiple, recent, and personal reviews of lodging rather than Fodors or Frommers. Why? It's more accurate, timely, and allows me to read a variety of opinions. This has become my habit with almost any consumer-type purchase. What do "real" people have to say?

Controversial/undocumented information is noted as such. David Weinberger writes, "There's one more sign of credibility of a Wikipedia page: If it contains a warning about the reliability of the page, we'll trust it more. This is only superficially contradictory." Wikipedia entries are flagged with readily visible warnings such as "The neutrality and factual accuracy of this article are disputed. See the relevant discussion on the talk page." The user who reads the "talk page" will glean an understanding of the controversies about the topic.

Hey, it's only an encyclopedia! Basic references sources—whether Wikipedia or *World Book*—should be used to get a general overview of a topic or put a topic in context, not be used as a sole and final authoritative source.

We also need to teach our students strategies for evaluating Wikipedia entries—indeed, any information source online or in print. Even very young students can and should be learning to consider the accuracy and potential bias of information sources. Because junior high students can make Web sites that look better than those of college professors, appearance is no guarantee of authority. We need to teach students to look:

- For the same information from multiple sources
- At the age of the page
- At the credentials and affiliation of the author
- For both stated and unstated biases by the page author or sponsor.

Kathy Schrock has a useful and comprehensive approach to Web site evaluation at http://schrockguide.org/abceval, listing 13 questions students might ask to determine the reliability of a resource.

As students use research to solve problems about controversial social and ethical issues, the ability to evaluate and defend one's choice of information source becomes as important as finding an answer to the research itself. As the Internet (and especially Web 2.0) allows a cacophony of voices to rise, expressing an increasing range of views, a conclusion without defensible sources in its support will not be of value.

Look that up in your *Funk and Wagnalls*…er, Wikipedia.

Resources
Rosenzweig, R. (2006). Can history be open source? Wikipedia and the future of the past. *Journal of American History, 93*(1). Available: http://chnm.gmu.edu/resources/essays/d/42

Schiff, S. (2006). Know it all: Can Wikipedia conquer expertise? *New Yorker,* July 31. Available: http://www.newyorker.com/fact/content/articles/060731fa_fact

Schrock, K. (n.d.). *The ABC's of Website Evaluation.* Available: http://schrockguide.org/abceval

Weinberger, D. (2006). Why believe Wikipedia? *JOHO: Journal of Hyperlinked Organization,* July 23. Available: http://www.hyperorg.com/backissues/joho-jul23-06.html#wikipedia

chapter 9

Project-Based Learning

This is an interesting column. Its entire lifespan, under the steward-ship of Diane McGrath, lasted just a couple years. It began in April 2003, and it ended as a separate column in March 2005. What makes it interesting, though, is that it didn't end because project-based learning fell out of favor. It ended because project-based learning (PBL) was so much a part of all of our articles and, in fact, all of education that it didn't make sense to separate it any longer.

We kick off with a description of what makes a good project and how to ensure that your projects contain those elements ("Building Better Projects," Diane McGrath, Mark Viner, and Allen Sylvester, November 2003). Diane interviewed researcher Mark and classroom teacher Allen about their experiences working together on a classroom integration project using STELLA and HyperStudio. Eighth graders used STELLA, a college-level research tool, to simulate events such as biodiversity on an island or the effects of damming a river. They then used HyperStudio to present their results to the class. Mark and Allen were excited at the results, but their suggestions for future improvement were telling. They believed they needed to better model PBL for students and provide more pre-learning activities to prepare them. They also believed they needed to introduce authentic audi-ences earlier in the intervention to help students focus and create better work from the get-go. In the author's update, Mark discusses the changes he has seen in preparing teachers to use PBL in their classrooms.

We move to a look at how a district committed to a five-year plan for technology-infused PBL ("Taking the Plunge," Diane McGrath and Nancy Sands, April 2004). The district was inspired by leader-ship from the state, which created its own technology plan with a heavy emphasis on project-based learning. The initiative was also supported financially through a federal grant. The plan included the most important element: professional development. They trained a cadre of teacher teams and all of the instructional technology specialists and media specialists to ensure that all teachers in the district were supported adequately. Teachers competed to be on the teams trained and to receive the high-level equipment. At the time of the article, they were about halfway through the five-year plan, and they were seeing successes as well as areas for further work. They had enough experience to offer guidance to other educational systems that wanted to follow their path. In the years since the article was published, Nancy retired from the district.

We conclude with tips to ensure that your projects activate students' higher-order thinking skills ("Visualize, Visualize, Visualize: Designing Projects for Higher-Order Thinking," Pearl Chen and Diane McGrath, December/January 2004–05). They deal specifically with methods to help students who have difficulty reconciling concepts taught with their own intuitions, difficulty understanding multiple points of view, difficulty applying knowledge to new situations, and difficulty controlling their own learning process. Pearl and Diane provide not only instructional strategies but also specific technologies and techniques to use to help students move beyond these difficulties. In the author's update, Pearl describes new technology developments and research that can inform project design.

November 2003

Building Better Projects

By Diane McGrath with Mark Viner and Allen Sylvester

Subject: Mathematics, action research, applying research in the classroom

Audience: Teachers, teacher educators, educational researchers

Grade Level: 8–10 (Ages 13–15)

Technology: STELLA, HyperStudio

Standards: *NETS•S* 3–6; *NETS•T* II–IV (http://www.iste.org/standards). *Kansas Eighth Grade Mathematical Standards* 2, 4 (http://www.ksbe.state.ks.us/assessment/#math).

A classroom teacher and a researcher involve students in rich, meaningful projects while conducting action research.

H aven't there been times when you wished you could have someone tell you whether something was really working, someone who had the time to interview, observe, and analyze what was happening when you tried out a classroom innovation?

Here I report on a year-long series of five technology-based projects teacher Allen Sylvester and researcher Mark Viner carried out, and studied, in Allen's eighth-grade mathematics classroom. Through interviews with the teacher and researcher, we can look specifically into what they learned about these questions:

- When youngsters do a series of projects, what do they get better at and what does that progress look like?
- When a teacher designs a series of projects, what does the teacher get better at?

Student Progress during a Project Series

Mark's research (for his dissertation) was a case study of one classroom of 22 eighth graders over a series of five projects, the first two of which were practice projects designed for learning specific software and mathematical concepts. (See Project Descriptions on p. 34.) The three later projects each had a mathematics learning component and a teacher-presented problem that provided students with a driving question. Then the students had to do sustained, collaborative research to answer the question, produce an informative, technology-based artifact with the other members of their group, and present that artifact to an audience, although there was only one

Continued

Continued

project in which the audience were students from another classroom. They used STELLA, powerful simulation software with an intuitive interface, and HyperStudio, a software package that allowed students to insert their graphs and write about the mathematical ideas. Over the series of projects, Mark and Allen hoped that a community of inquiry would develop in that classroom. Mark and Allen shared in both the design of the projects and the teaching and technical assistance duties.

The student population of the middle school was racially mixed, and 57% were categorized as disadvantaged. The mathematics involved is generally considered very difficult for the average eighth grader; typically eighth grade mathematics focuses almost exclusively on linear relationships, and this series of projects asked them to grapple with nonlinear relationships such as overshoot-and-recover graphs, periodicity, and feedback loops. STELLA itself is a college-level research tool, but with some scaffolding, Allen was able to get his eighth graders to use it productively. By the second project, students were regularly helping each other with STELLA and having some success in creating models. Students also went "many steps beyond" what they had been told in their HyperStudio instructions.

In the final project (Project 5: City of the Future), students were much more confident about both the mathematics and the writing because they knew what they were doing. Though it seems obvious that students need to buy into this kind of learning, as well as learn to manage their time, resources, and tasks, what has been less obvious is that teach-

ers need the same buy-in, practice, time to change, and skill to manage complex projects. I thought it might be useful to reflect on the changes teachers go through over a series of projects.

Both Mark and Allen came to this year of projects with a solid understanding of why it would be a good thing to try. Though Allen had a few years of experience doing projects in his classrooms, Mark was newer to the practice.

Q&A

L&L: Do you think you got better at designing projects as you went along?

Mark Viner (researcher): The first thing I learned was that these projects require continual adjustment based on feedback from the students. By the third project (Easter Island), I could just tell if the students were getting it or not. So, what I got better at was adjusting to the students' needs: what they were having trouble with, putting the content into a presentation mode for an audience, and using the hardware and software.

Allen Sylvester (teacher): Definitely. We had to make adjustments for three main factors: time, interpersonal relationships, and student engagement.

L&L: What did you do to deal with the time limitations?

Allen: The project was important enough that it deserved to have the

full time needed to allow students to complete it. For my students to develop the skills needed to move from the graphical representation of data using simulation software to a verbal description of their own was more important than anything else I might have planned. I think it depends on what you want out of the project as to how much you cut it short. One can do two kinds of projects—ones that reinforce some learning or ones that are the learning. In this case, the learning couldn't have happened without the project.

Mark: Often when the students were stuck on the math models we would move them to the HyperStudio part of the project. This helped students visualize the models. They would then go back to the math models and complete them.

L&L: How did you group students?

Allen: In the Easter Island project, we used a sociogram to match students who were willing to work with each other (and not pairing those who were unwilling to work together). Unfortunately, when partners chose each other this way, tempers still flared, and we ended up with one student angrily not participating. Often in this situation one student would end up doing most of the work. So, we did a purposeful pairing on Project 4 (the dam project). Those who were strong-willed got to work with other strong-willed students. Passive students got to work with other pas-

A teacher has to learn to be comfortable letting go of some aspects of control and management. If the project is engaging, the students manage themselves. If the project isn't engaging, then change the project or change your expectations.

Continued

Continued

Now I'm sure that an integral part of PBL must be a set of pre-learning activities, not only to teach how to do projects (deal with rubrics, peer evaluation, teamwork, etc.), but how to think metacognitively.

PROJECT DESCRIPTIONS

1. Practice Using HyperStudio: The Interactive Adventure Story. Students created their own interactive adventure story in HyperStudio.

2. Practice Introduction to STELLA: Students created a model of a population of animals, complete with disease, predators, and overconsumption of resources, and a model of a factory with production, sales, and inventory.

3. Easter Island: Students used the STELLA model to understand birth and death rates to determine what happened to the Rapa Nui people and created a HyperStudio stack telling how they would avoid that catastrophe.

4. Dam: Students used STELLA to manipulate water levels above and below a dam. They then played various roles in order to create and justify perspectives on dam water level uses and practices. Next, students presented their point of view in a HyperStudio stack.

5. City of the Future: Students designed an energy efficient city using alternative energies and calculated the energy costs for that city. They then produced an advertisement for that city using HyperStudio.

sive students, and a couple of loners got to work as singletons.

Mark: Initially, we placed students in the debating groups for later projects based on similar opinions. However, students on their own initiative met and formed groups with fellow students who had different opinions. They started debating among themselves without our prompting. This led to students forming new groups and working together to find information on the Internet to back up their points of view.

L&L: How did student engagement issues affect your strategies for designing projects?

Allen: The first practice project was a hit. Students loved creating their own stories, and embellishing them. But when the task involved real mathematics and students were asked to do analysis and summarization of data in Project 2, students began to balk. To counter this, we moved to make Project 3 even more of a simulation than it had been by making Mark the chief of the Rapa Nui tribe the students were studying, and had them interact with him through their HyperStudio stacks. We also added a "sci-fi" flavor by making them into Time Travellers examining a lost tribe from the standpoint of knowing the end result and trying to avert the impending disaster. In terms of engagement with the task,

this worked well, but then the problem shifted to an issue with their writing.

We enlisted the language arts teacher to help us with the writing issue, and that ended up being disastrous. We thought we had engagement problems before! Students felt that the projects were not theirs once the language arts teacher imposed structure on them. They felt they had lost ownership of the project, and began to believe that all their stacks had to look the same (from a writing point of view). "Why did you bring her in here, we liked what we had written—now we have to rewrite it!" was the comment we got most often.

For the dam project, we did not try a language arts intervention. We used a videotape of the 1993 flood that affected most of the Midwest and had a great impact to area residents, and also had a guest speaker. The students shared stories of remembering the flood after they viewed the video. They liked the guest speaker, but wanted to debate with her. Time and scheduling did not allow this, but we did allow students to debate with each other, and their engagement went up. Putting the gist of the debate into HyperStudio was easier this time, as they had already solidified their positions through debating. It was in this project that we saw students becoming more autonomous when searching for points of view, facts, and perspectives. Students would debate issues, ask each others' points of view, and then research their own perspectives. It was at this point that our hopes for the development of a community of learners began to be realized.

There is this "lag" that happens as you pull a student out of traditional learning environments, where they are uncomfortable with the idea that there is no "right" answer, just right thinking. They need to be taught to realize that the process is more important than the product, the path more important than the destination.

Continued

Continued

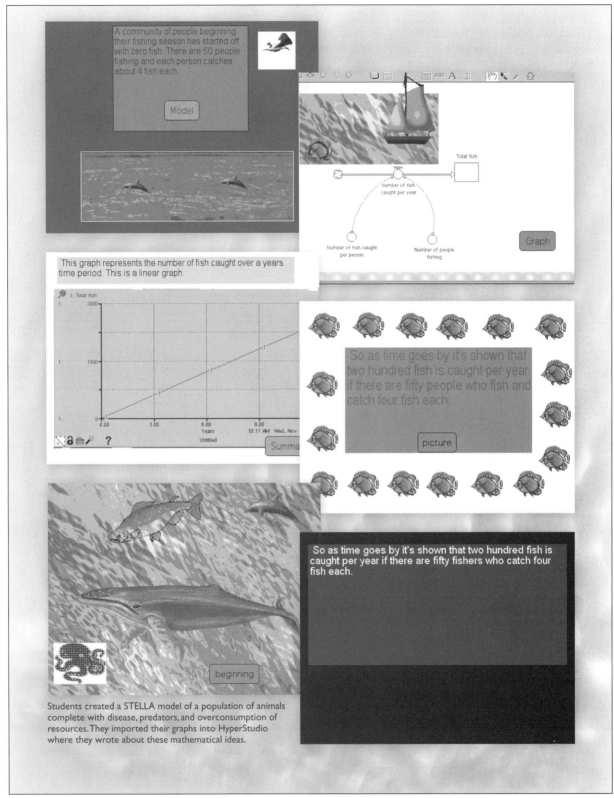

A community of people beginning their fishing season has started off with zero fish. There are 50 people fishing and each person catches about 4 fish each.

Model

Total fish

number of fish
caught per year

Number of fish caught
per person

Number of people
fishing

Graph

This graph represents the number of fish caught over a years time period. This is a linear graph.

1: Total fish

1:     3000

1:     1500

1:        0
        0.00   3.00   6.00   9.00
                        Years
                        Untitled   10:11 AM Wed, Nov

Summa

So as time goes by it's shown that two hundred fish is caught per year if there are fifty people who fish and catch four fish each.

picture

So as time goes by it's shown that two hundred fish is caught per year if there are fifty fishers who catch four fish each.

beginning

Students created a STELLA model of a population of animals complete with disease, predators, and overconsumption of resources. They imported their graphs into HyperStudio where they wrote about these mathematical ideas.

Continued

Continued

The last project was the most successful of all. They loved simulating a future city, although they didn't so much like the math and calculating for energy costs, but they can do persuasive writing quite easily. They were not short on imagination.

The longer we did PBL, the easier it was for students to stay engaged in their projects. I think this is due in equal parts to the students' comfort with that mode of learning and to our ability to adapt to their reactions to PBL. A teacher has to learn to be comfortable letting go of some aspects of control and management. If the project is engaging, the students manage themselves. If the project isn't engaging, then change the project or change your expectations.

Mark: When we moved from the individual ownership of the practice story to the STELLA models, students were made to follow a prescribed set of rules and guidelines. They lost ownership of the project. Students' engagement level also dropped as they began struggling with the math concepts and the STELLA models. When we went back to HyperStudio and the kids could create something, the engagement level picked up again.

By the time we got to the dam project, we designed roles (e.g., farmer, conservationist, etc.) that students could choose from. Students actually suggested this approach in the student interviews. This was a big hit. Students were passionate about their positions and could build a stack from their own points of view. Thus the engagement level went way up. Students also made the suggestion that they build their own individual stack and then connect them as a group.

In the City of the Future project, we gave students a few simple guidelines about what they had to have in their stacks (they still had to do the math content and concepts). They

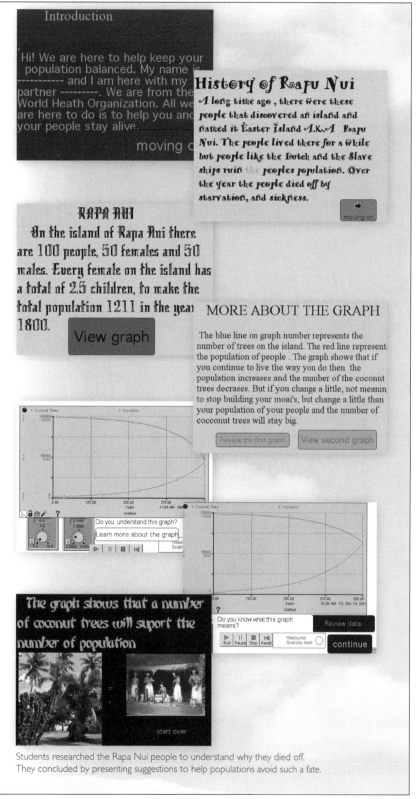

Students researched the Rapa Nui people to understand why they died off. They concluded by presenting suggestions to help populations avoid such a fate.

Continued

Continued

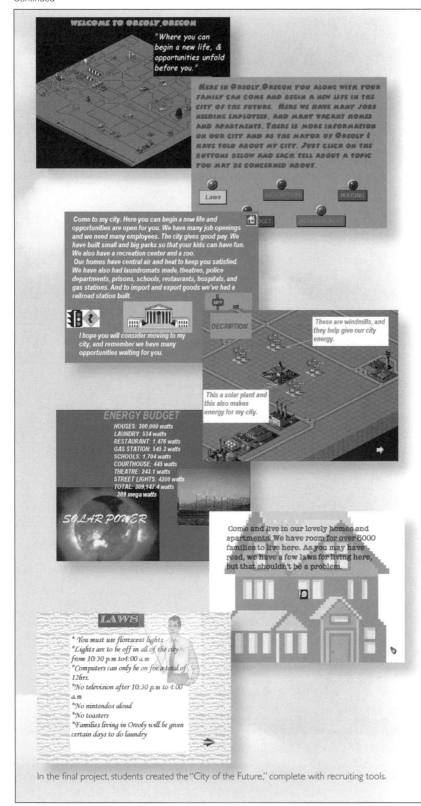

In the final project, students created the "City of the Future," complete with recruiting tools.

created their own city using SimCity and had control (within limits) over the type of energy that ran their city. Student engagement level was best summed up by one student who said, "This project was the best. We get to build our own city. We get to be our own mayor, the boss, the big guy."

We also noticed that the students wanted contemporary issues. After the interviews with the students, it became clear that students didn't feel the Easter Island project was relevant to their lives because it was situated in the past. Making the dam project and the City of the Future project deal with contemporary issues increased the students' engagement level.

L&L: What would you change the next time you try a project?

Allen: I've become a very firm believer in scaffolding and modeling of expectations. We were very reluctant to model what we expected (or were hoping for) in terms of a finished product. We believed that if we modeled something, we'd get copies with minor modifications because we had "poisoned the well" of creativity. Similarly, we were reluctant to provide pre-learning scaffolding because we wanted to see what they could come up with based on what they already knew.

Now I'm sure that an integral part of PBL must be a set of pre-learning activities, not only to teach how to do projects (deal with rubrics, peer evaluation, teamwork, etc.), but how to think metacognitively. There is this "lag" that happens as you pull a student out of traditional learning environments, where they are uncomfortable with the idea that there is no "right" answer, just right thinking. They need to be taught to realize that the process is more important than the product, the path more important than the destination. By the time we got to the last project, I was comfort-

Continued

Continued

> We don't give kids enough credit—we think that
> if they can't solve any equation we give them, they
> can't handle the higher levels of mathematical
> concepts. The work that these students did
> ought to be some sort of proof, if only anecdotal,
> that the *concept* can truly be learned absent the *skill.*

able enough with their ability to deal with "examples" that I gave them a very brief, very sketchy HyperStudio stack of "Sylvesterland", which was more of an anti-example. We all had a good chuckle over the silliness of it, but they did get the hint about what a "bad" example looks like, and how to avoid those mistakes.

Mark: Maybe next time we would have told them up front that their designs are okay if they are different.

Also, we should have had a better system in place to work with the kids on their writing. If you are going to have kids develop multimedia documents, they need to learn how to incorporate their ideas into story form, and to write about their research.

I would also use peer or authentic audiences earlier. We used the outside audience only once (Project 4, the dam). It was a seventh-grade class at another middle school. Our students responded well (they fixed their grammar and spelling) once they knew it was going to be graded by an audience. Students felt that an outside evaluation was more valuable than in-house evaluations because the outside audience didn't know the authors of the stack and gave a more honest score than people who knew the stack authors. Several students suggested

that if someone doesn't like you, they were going to give you a bad grade, no matter what.

We didn't create a tutorial or help list for the students in using the software. We just let them play (discovery learning). Next time I would create a simple list of commands and help sheets students could use as a reference. This would have saved some time and frustration.

L&L: What recommendations would you make to someone starting one or more technology-related projects in a classroom?

Allen: Resources—if you want multimedia, one set of clip-art (or sound or movie) CDs is not enough. Nor are 15 computers for 30 kids. If you're not concerned with multimedia, then yes, students in pairs will work just fine.

Get to know your kids first! Trying to form workable pairs is a nightmare until you know the dynamics of your group.

Change groups frequently: friends one week are enemies next week. Although learning to work together no matter what is a valuable life skill, save it for a project based on interpersonal skills. Rivalries and animosities will kill a project. How frequently?

> By allowing the computer to do the computation
> that was clearly beyond their skill level, we found
> that the students jumped a huge intellectual gap
> into understanding the mathematical relationships—
> how the variables they manipulated changed the
> simulation, and ultimately the graph of the simulation.
> Wow! Powerful stuff!

Continued

Continued

Weekly/biweekly/no longer than three weeks, if at all possible. It depends on the group of students, of course.

Always overplan—the project will take more time than you think. To overcome this, provide intermediate drop-dead dates so smaller chunks of the project are due prior to the finished item.

And remember, they're pretty smart about technology—they've seen what's cool, listen to them.

Mark: Patience. This type of learning initially takes longer than traditional learning approaches. Teachers need to be clear about their expectations of students. Students need to learn how to plan, research, present their findings, and collaborate in groups in addition to learning how to use the hardware and software. That's a lot to ask of a teacher in one or two projects, but it does pay off in the later projects. Our students eventually became self-sufficient in creating a hypermedia/multimedia document. They learned the process of designing.

A teacher has to be able to constantly monitor the students, to learn when the students are "getting it or not." Allen was very good at this. I would suggest that this is because he has previous experience doing PBL in the classroom. Allen would occasionally stop the class and return to direct instruction when he knew the kids were lost or having trouble.

Also, the projects should be "real-world" and contemporary. The students need to have ownership over both the design process and subject matter. They need to know their designs can be different, yet still meet good standards for writing, for mathematics, and for design. Students need to be responsible for researching and representing their own perspective. Students need to be involved in a series of design projects. As students' experiences evolve, so does their engagement level.

I've become a very firm believer in scaffolding and modeling of expectations.

In addition, students need to "buy into" the grading process. We had the students come up with a list of criteria on which they wanted to be graded, what they thought was important. Based on this list, we created a grading rubric for the peer evaluations. The grading rubric gave students an understanding of how their projects could be "different" than their fellow classmates' yet still correct.

L&L: Allen, can you sum up your observations of what your students learned through this series of projects?

Allen: For one brief moment, these students had the opportunity to see how math really works in the real world. We don't give kids enough credit—we think that if they can't solve any equation we give them, they can't handle the higher levels of mathematical concepts. The work that these students did ought to be some sort of proof, if only anecdotal, that the *concept* can truly be learned absent the *skill*. By allowing the computer to do the computation that was clearly beyond their skill level, we found that the students jumped a huge intellectual gap into understanding the mathematical relationships—how the variables they manipulated changed the simulation, and ultimately the graph of the simulation. Wow! Powerful stuff! I'm willing to bet many college graduates don't have the conceptual framework our students had by the end of the project.

Resources

In addition to Diane McGrath's PBL Web site (http://coe.ksu.edu/pbl/), which expands on resources mentioned in the PBL columns, with annotations and further links, you may also find the following resources useful.

Center for Highly Interactive Computing in Education: http://www.hi-ce.org
Creative Learning Exchange: http://www.clexchange.org
High Performance System: http://www.hps-inc.com
HyperStudio: http://www.hyperstudio.com
Illuminations: http://illuminations.nctm.org
National Council for Teachers of Mathematics: http://www.nctm.org

Diane McGrath is an associate professor of educational computing, design, and online learning at Kansas State University. She is former editor of the Journal of Computer Science Education *(now published on ISTE's SIGCS Web site as JCSE Online) and the* Journal for Research on Computing in Education *(now the* Journal of Research on Technology in Education*), and she has written a number of articles related to technology and higher-order thinking for ISTE periodicals.*

Mark Viner is manager of professional development in educational technology at St. Vincent's College in Chicago.

Allen Sylvester is an eighth-grade mathematics teacher in Junction City, Kansas, and a doctoral candidate in curriculum & instruction, specializing in educational computing, design, and online learning at Kansas State University.

author's update
Mark Viner

Currently, Allen and I co-teach a project-based learning (PBL) online course for the Office of Catholic Schools in Chicago. I have noticed a difference in the last five years with respect to teachers' attitudes towards PBL. Based on their journal entries, teachers taking the online course in the last year seemed to be more receptive to the PBL process than teachers three to five years ago. At the start of the course, I always ask the teachers to journal their personal points of view as it relates to engaged learning/PBL. Three to five years ago, the majority of the responses were negative. For example, responses include phrases such as: fuzzy thinking; too time-consuming; we need to teach the basics.

In contrast, in the last year I have had teachers who are actively seeking me out to take the online course and (in general) excited to be able to do projects in the classroom. I have also noticed that it is not just the young teachers right out of college but it is also the older teachers looking for new ways to reach their students. Find sample lesson plans that teachers submitted as their final projects at http://edlearn.net/ocstech/Main/PBL.htm.

April 2004

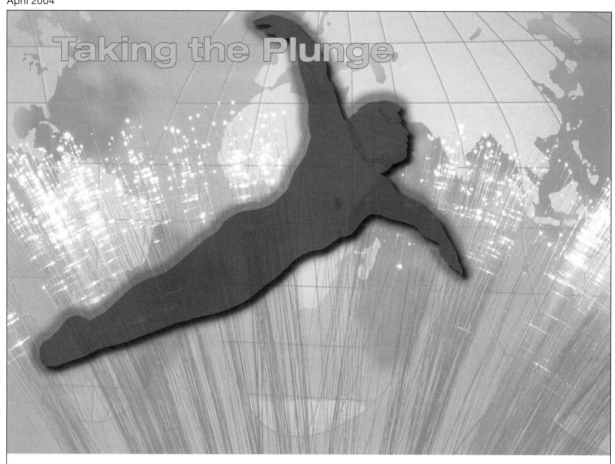

Taking the Plunge

A School District Commits to a Five-Year Plan for Technology-Infused PBL

By Diane McGrath and Nancy Sands

Subject: Implementation of district-wide initiatives

Audience: Technology coordinators, technology facilitators, technology integration specialists, district and school administrators

Standards: *NETS•T* II; *NETS•A* I, II (http://www.iste.org/standards/)

The Davidson County School District in Lexington, North Carolina, has jumped into project-based learning with both feet: they have committed to using PBL in all their schools and classrooms by 2006, and they have received a U.S. federal government Enhancing Education Through Technology grant to help provide the staff development and equipment needed to succeed. In this month's column, I work with Nancy Sands, the district's technology coordinator, to tell you about the district's experiences, successes, and challenges after nearly four years of commitment to PBL and during their second year of professional development provided by the grant. Next month, we focus in on one example of PBL at the high school level in that district.

The District's Story
The initial inspiration for Davidson County's commitment to PBL came from the North Carolina Department of Public Instruction (DPI). The DPI

Continued

Continued

developed a state technology plan for 2000–05, and then each district used that plan as a model for their own technology plans. PBL was an important part of the state's vision. In drafting their plan, Davidson County noted that it had a 4:1 student to computer ratio, so it was time to go to the next level: expanding the "teacher's role in creating an effective, technology-based learning environment." They focused on how technology fit into their lofty goals of:

- high student achievement
- safe and orderly schools
- quality teachers, administrators, and staff
- effective, efficient operations
- community and family.

Part of the vision was for 50%–75% of the teachers to integrate PBL into their teaching. PBL was new to most of the teachers. One idea they had to work to change among their teachers was that constructivism (a guiding principle of PBL) is only for young students. The district used the following ideas to guide staff development in and implementation of PBL:

- Even older students learn when they collaborate and build on what they already know.
- Students should be encouraged to engage in dialogue.
- The role of the teacher may be viewed as a project manager rather than the dispenser of information.
- Students actively solve problems rather than passively receive information.

Davidson County began implementing its new plan in the 2000–01 academic year. The biggest success was the high school–level class Project-Based Web Authoring. The projects coming out of this class were excellent. In fact, one on Roman Architecture won the 2002 ISTE HyperSIG Multimedia Mania award

for the upper grades. This course was the brainchild of the district superintendent, Dr. Fred Mock. Fred believed high-level integration of technology was a key component in solving long-term problems of unemployment in the local community by improving students' skills before they graduated high school and chose whether to enter college.

The overall plan, however, needed some improvement. Davidson County saw quickly that it had been a little too ambitious in its planning. They had introduced WebQuests as a great way to organize units of study. They offered 10 hours of training in how to develop a project-based lesson and post it on the Web. Most of the teachers, however, were not ready to develop a high-quality WebQuest after just 10 hours. They simply needed more instruction to grasp the concepts of the methodology.

The district saw that they needed a different approach to professional development. Staff development involved two areas. The first was PBL methodology, which included constructivist philosophy, PBL strategies, developing teacher expertise using PBL, access to resources to develop instructional materials, cross-curricular integration, using rubrics and authentic assessment. They looked to the Buck Institute for Education, the George Lucas Educational Foundation (GLEF), and the U.S. government for help and funding. (*Editor's note:* Find these and other URLs under Resources on p. 36.) The second area of staff development involved learning to use advanced technologies, such as Internet publishing, Web page design, presentation software, digital cameras, camcorders, and scanners.

In the 2002–03 academic year, the district selected teams of three teachers using a competitive application process. A committee reviewed the

applications to decide who would be most open to change and who would be able to work in collaborative groups. The teacher teams received a high-end computer with DVD burner, digital video camera, digital still camera, data projector, and a cart that can move the equipment among the three teachers. Eeva Reeder came from GLEF to train the teachers in the basic tenets of PBL. The district also ensured that its instructional technology personnel were trained in the use of the equipment given to the teachers. The teams then came together during the summer to organize their PBL units and post them on the Web. The training was completed at the end of the 2002–03 school year, so this is their first year using PBL with students. The district is continuing the professional development using Intel's Teach to the Future program during the 2003–04 school year.

Teachers who were not in these teams receive training in PBL and mentoring from the district instructional technology specialists.

Davidson County also provided in-depth training to its school media coordinators, who then work to help classroom teachers have successful PBL experiences by making resources available, organizing teams to work collaboratively, and providing leadership. In Davidson County schools, school media coordinators are envisioned as instructional leaders. By helping teachers use PBL, media coordinators realize an important aspect of that vision.

What Other Districts Need to Know
Three critical factors for success have emerged from Davidson County's experiences:

- Evaluation
- Support at all levels
- Funding

Continued

Continued

Evaluation. Davidson County focused their evaluation on teacher advancement of technology skills. But they made sure never to separate technology skills from PBL. They received permission from Dr. Sheila Cory from the North Carolina Principal's Program to use the Taking a Good Look at Student Learning (TAGLIT) instrument to assess teachers' use of technology. They found from a pretraining assessment that teachers needed training in using multimedia tools. So they taught teachers to use digital cameras, with a focus on using them "to increase student learning by providing real-world, hands-on instruction," a goal in their tech plan.

Support. Davidson County found that it was important to have support for this new initiative from district staff, principals, and teachers. The district serves 19,000 students, and the district's instructional technology employees were simply not enough to implement the entire technology plan. So, they decided to enlist the support of the principals.

The district began by inviting presenters to its biennial technology leadership conference in 2002. Gerry Smith, founding principal of River Oaks Elementary School in Canada, shared real-life stories of PBL's positive effects on student learning as the keynote speaker at the conference. They also invited presenters throughout North Carolina to share their PBL success stories. Then, the district offered training sessions during curriculum meetings attended by school and district administrators. Finally, the district has asked its school administrators to share their success stories at statewide conferences.

The district has found that these experiences have really helped them get the support of the school administrators they need. In fact, their success is exemplified by Kevin Firquin, the principal of Central Davidson Senior High School. He is one of those people whom lots of people like. He is funny, witty, genuinely loves kids, and is in love with education. When he is excited about something, he shares it. He gave a big presentation to his staff about how easy this was going to be and how great it was going to be for the students. Because everyone was doing a little bit, when added together, it would be a huge accomplishment. This is exactly the type of top-down excitement and sharing of information that the district believed would convince teachers to step outside their comfort zones and embrace PBL.

Funding. Finally, school districts need financial support to engage any major change in instruction. Davidson County's Enhancing Education Through Technology grant is not a huge amount of money, but it is dedicated to staff development and it is promised for five years of funding. The grant provides teacher stipends or substitute pay, it offsets the cost of equipment that is used as an incentive, and it helped pay for the GLEF consultant during the 2002–03 school year.

The district was also able to use state technology funds to help support their plan.

Tell Us Your School's Success Story
We have looked at a school system's large commitment to professional development for teachers using PBL methods that also integrate technology. Next month, we will look at one successful high school interdisciplinary project that resulted from this commitment to use PBL in all of their schools.

Consider sharing with us, by e-mailing Diane or writing a letter to the editor, successes you have had in professional development using PBL and technology or school- or district-wide commitments to PBL and technology.

Resources
Diane McGrath's PBL Web site (http://coe.ksu.edu/PBL/) will take you directly to the Web resources discussed in this column, as well as resources that have been mentioned in other columns. So check in early, and check in often.

Buck Institute for Education: http://bie.org/
Davidson County Schools: http://www.davidson.k12.nc.us
Education World Administrators Center: The Grants Center: http://www.educationworld.com/a_admin/grants/
Enhancing Education Through Technology Grant—Projects and Lessons created by Davidson County Teachers: http://www.davidson.k12.nc.us/pbl/eett/eett.htm
Enhancing Education Through Technology State Program: http://www.ed.gov/programs/edtech/
The Foundation Center: http://fdncenter.org/
GLEF: http://www.glef.org
Grants & Contracts—ED.gov: http://www.ed.gov/fund/landing.jhtml?src=rt
Intel's Teach to the Future: http://www.intel.com/education/sections/section1/
Multimedia Mania: http://www.ncsu.edu/mmania/
Project-Based Learning in Davidson County Schools: http://www.davidson.k12.nc.us/pbl/pbl.htm
TAGLIT: http://www.taglit.org/
Web Authoring Across the Curriculum— A Course for High School Students in Davidson County Schools, North Carolina: http://techcenter.davidson.k12.nc.us/web.htm

Diane McGrath is an associate professor of educational computing, design, and on-line learning at Kansas State University. She is former editor of the Journal of Computer Science Education *(now published on ISTE's SIGCS Web site as* JCSE Online*) and the* Journal for Research on Computing in Education *(now the* Journal of Research on Technology in Education*), and she has written a number of articles related to technology and higher-order thinking for ISTE periodicals.*

Nancy Sands is director of media and instructional technology for the Davidson County Schools in Lexington, North Carolina. She is president of the North Carolina Association for Educational Communications and Technology, an ISTE Affiliate.

December/January 2004–05

Visualize, Visualize, Visualize

Designing Projects for Higher-Order Thinking

Project-based learning provides a way of learning that seems to be particularly attractive to students who are struggling with conventional school assignments. In the study we described in our 2002 *Journal of Research on Technology in Education* article, Moments of Joy, we found that at-risk students became active learners willing to engage in cognitively challenging tasks when presented with a PBL opportunity.

Like many other educators, we believe PBL offers positive effects in cognitive, metacognitive, affective,

By Pearl Chen and Diane McGrath

Subject: Cognitive PBL

Standards: *NETS•T* II; *NETS•A* II
(http://www.iste.org/standards)

and social domains. Good outcomes seem to occur almost without special effort: increased student involvement, persistence, and motivation; opening up a new conceptual space for students who begin to see themselves as learners; and benefits in understanding.

However, the extent and nature of these effects vary greatly depending on the types of projects you create for your students. After engaging students in simple projects (hands-on learning projects), well suited for learning in the affective and social domains, you may want to increase the complexity of the projects to include specific cognitive and metacognitive learning goals. We will use the term *cognitive PBL* to describe projects that specifically aim to support these goals of higher-order thinking.

As teachers, we have all observed with a sense of frustration that stu-

dents will successfully complete a learning process, but they do not seem to be able to use that knowledge effectively. Typical difficulties in the learning process are:

- *Conceptual difficulty:* students have difficulty when their naïve intuitions come into play
- *Foreign knowledge:* students have difficulty understanding multiple points of view
- *Knowledge transfer:* application of learning to new problems or situations
- *Self-regulation:* students have trouble taking charge of their own learning processes

We propose that with the use of cognitive PBL and appropriate technologies, we can move learners toward greater understanding and ability to apply that understanding.

Continued

Continued

Cognitive PBL, Knowledge Strategies, and Technology

In cognitive PBL, students not only process knowledge content in a deeper and more mindful manner, but also learn valuable thinking skills, something about their learning processes, and about how to learn. The goal in cognitive PBL is to move students from simple knowledge-telling to complex knowledge-transforming by deliberately using explicit cognitive strategies. In contrast to simple projects that may be more transparent and regulated by teachers, cognitive PBL involves students in complex tasks that require considerable effort and exercise of self-regulatory and judgment skills with appropriate teacher guidance.

We believe that constructivist and creative use of technology can be very effective in helping students escape from their passive and habitual learning patterns—the first step necessary toward developing mature cognitive strategies.

Several strategies and technologies exist for each of the four problem areas we described. To help you choose appropriate tools, we use examples based on the categories proposed by Bruce and Levin: tools for inquiry, communication, construction, and expression. (*Editor's note:* See this and other resources on p. 57.)

The strategies we suggest in Table 1. (p. 56) are based on two important concepts that emphasize making thinking visible: cognitive apprenticeships and computer-supported intentional learning environments (CSILEs). The idea behind cognitive apprenticeships is to take the scaffolding and authentic participation portions of a traditional apprenticeship and bring those stategies into the school setting. Teaching methods involved in cognitive apprenticeships can include modeling, coaching, scaffolding, articulation, reflection, and more.

In CSILEs, the learning environment becomes knowledge centered—everyone contributes to the growing knowledge of the entire classroom. Much more in-depth information on these ideas is in a supplement available on McGrath's PBL Web site.

The focus of cognitive PBL should be on guiding learners to go beyond information given. This strategy helps learners develop more complex, higher-level cognitive processes and experience cognitive emotions that develop into intellectual passions. One common thread that runs through the research on higher-order thinking is the idea of helping learners gain conscious access to their own minds. As long-time Harvard educational researcher D. N. Perkins, in his book *The Mind's Best Work*, has reminded us, "We have more access to our minds than we might have thought. With that greater access might come greater opportunity to tinker." This is why it is so important to make thinking visible—you are able to talk about it, think about your understanding, and fine-tune or reorganize your thinking. It is important to make both the learner's thinking process observable to him/herself and to the teacher or expert, and to help the learner to observe a teacher's or an expert's thinking process.

There are many strategies for making thinking visible.

Asking students to speak their minds or write down their thinking process, and then identifying patterns in their thoughts and gaps in their understandings. A program such as Inspiration with an accompanying note for each symbol can be used to explain reasoning and thinking steps. Both concept mapping and hypermedia authoring tools can be used to help students easily reorganize and fine-tune their representations. Figure 1 is an example of such a concept map on the topic of water.

Using technology constructively in a way that pays special attention to cognitive principles. This strategy can provide greater flexibility for students to confront the discrepancies of their understanding for conceptually difficult knowledge and for defending alternative points of view for foreign knowledge.

Encouraging learners to deliberately practice effective thinking strategies. Some general principles might be enough to do the trick. For example, to promote inventive thinking, Perkins says that principles given to the students should be "as easy as a recipe for boiling water" to alert them to certain methods and re-shape their

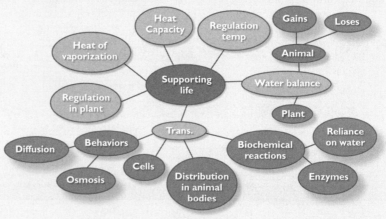

Figure 1. An example of using a concept map to fine-tune concepts during knowledge construction.

Continued

Continued

Table 1. Knowledge Strategies and Appropriate Technologies for Designing Cognitive PBL Projects

Knowledge Strategies, Scaffolding Techniques	Examples of Appropriate Technologies
Learner Difficulty: *Conceptually Difficult*	
• Modeling: given a model, ask learners to "rediscover" and interpret in an active and exploratory way. • Scaffolding: find out misconceptions and look for internal patterns. • Articulation and reflection: organize knowledge actively, make knowledge-construction activities overt, use presentation and peer critiquing.	Tools for inquiry (theory building): • Model exploration and simulation toolkits • Visualization software • Virtual reality environments • Data modeling—defining categories, relations, representations (e.g., Stella) • Procedural models, mathematical models • Knowledge representation: semantic network, outline tools (e.g., Inspiration)
Learner Difficulty: *Foreign*	
• Design learning tasks that require identifying and explaining or defending alternative points of view. • Encourage examination of existing knowledge. • Encourage multiple passes through information. • Treat gaps in knowledge in a positive way. • Support varied ways for students to organize their knowledge.	Tools for communication: • Asynchronous and synchronous computer conferencing (e.g., e-mail, iSight/iChat, conferencing on the Web [see Resources]) • Student-created hypertext environments Tools for inquiry: • Knowledge representation: semantic network, outline tools (e.g., Inspiration) • Internet for research Tools for expression: • Multimedia composition
Learner Difficulty: *Knowledge Transfer and Application*	
• Design projects to build cognitive and metacognitive capabilities. • Explicitly demonstrate and discuss how the knowledge gained in this project may be applied in other projects and domains. • Facilitate transfer of knowledge across contexts by applying knowledge across disciplines.	Tools for communication (collaboration): • Collaborative data environments • Group decision support systems • Shared document preparation. Tools for inquiry: • Knowledge integration (e.g., hypermedia authoring) • Knowledge representation: semantic network, outline tools (e.g., Inspiration) • Internet for research
Learner Difficulty: *Self-Regulatory Learning*	
• Teach students to think like experts and encourage learning strategies other than rehearsal. • Make thinking visible and maintain attention to cognitive goals rather than task goals. • Make learning processes visible and provide relevant feedback on the procesess. • Give learners legitimate role in the community of learners. Give students more responsibility for contributing to each other's learning. • Use a real audience to evaluate their work. • Provide opportunities for reflection and individual learning styles.	Tools for inquiry: • Knowledge representation: semantic network, outline tools (e.g., Inspiration) • Online inquiry tools (e.g., WISE [see Resources]) • Internet for research Tools for construction: • Robotics kits Tools for expression: • Hypermedia authoring • Multimedia composition

Continued

Continued

behaviors to meet the demands of the task. His examples of good principles include such things as practicing in context, and when confused, employing concrete representations.

Modeling, coaching, and scaffolding to enable learners to observe a teacher's or an expert's thinking process. Learners can refine their understanding through articulation and compare their strategies to those used by the teacher/expert through reflection. Eventually, learners are pushed to the stage of exploration in which they independently use the expert strategies in framing and solving the problem. Technology can be used for modeling, scaffolding, reflection, promoting intentional and exploratory use of thinking strategies, and restructuring.

For example, in our study of a project that used hypermedia for high school students to represent their understanding of water concepts, modeling was provided through a hypermedia document we created to teach hypermedia concepts (links, nodes, paths, and so on). This allowed students to explore the hypermedia environment while learning the concepts that made such an environment possible. Coaching was provided through discussion of hypermedia concepts and demonstration of examples and techniques for designing hypermedia. The teacher coached students in taking notes as well as summarizing and synthesizing information by modeling his own "brain net" on an overhead projector while reading a passage from the textbook. At the same time, he also helped students in developing associative ways of thinking by demonstrating the techniques of concept mapping on an overhead projector. Scaffolding was provided through a designer's notebook to support students' linking of ideas and organization of the knowledge content. Finally, articulation and reflection were provided through a continuous process of peer critiquing and a public presentation of student project.

Using technology to provide a trace of students' tuning, organizing, and re-organizing process during knowledge construction. Students can save their projects at the end of each project session to provide electronic records of their thinking process. Each project's structural representations or outlines then can be captured into image files to trace changes attempted by students, and to identify faulty construction or misrepresentation of concepts. This portfolio idea enables students, parents, and teachers to follow the development of understanding and to discuss problems along the way. To promote intentional use of thinking strategies, criteria for assessing both domain knowledge and cognitive skills should be clear and available to the students. You may also want to include your students in brainstorming and making decisions about assessment criteria.

In sum, a general rule of thumb for designing cognitive PBL is visualize, visualize, and visualize the thinking process.

Conclusion

What we have been proposing is an approach to PBL in which the goal is to focus on thinking, making thinking processes visible to teacher and students. Ideas and understandings can be evaluated and revised much more easily if there is something to see, something that can be shared, discussed, and revised. We have tried to give you both a conceptual framework for understanding exactly what the learning issues are and some examples of principles, guidelines, and technologies that can assist you in your cognitive PBL projects.

Write and tell us what strategies you have tried to encourage higher-order thinking, and let us know if any of these ideas are helpful in your projects.

Resources

For links from this and other PBL articles in this series, go to Diane McGrath's PBL Web site at http://coe.ksu.edu/PBL/.

Supplement to these articles: http://coe.ksu.edu/PBL/supplement1204.html

Articles

Bruce, B. C., & Levin, J. A. (1997). Educational technology: Media for inquiry, communication, construction, and expression. *Journal of Educational Computing Research, 17*(1), 79–102. Available: http://www.lis.uiuc.edu/%7Echip/pubs/taxonomy/.

McGrath, D., Sylvester, A., & Chen, P. (1999). *At risk: Traditional teaching. Bring in the learners and the Web!* Presented at the National Educational Computing Conference, Atlantic City, NJ, June 22–24. Available: http://coe.ksu.edu/mcgrath/NECC/NECC99.htm.

Perkins, D. (2003, Dec.). Making thinking visible. *New Horizons for Learning.* Available: http://www.newhorizons.org/strategies/thinking/perkins.htm.

Web Sites on Making Thinking Visible

Concord Consortium's Making Thinking Visible—Promoting Students' Model Building and Collaborative Discourse, an NSF project: http://mtv.concord.org/

Harvard's Making Learning Visible: http://www.pz.harvard.edu/mlv/

Thinkofit's Conferencing on the Web: http://www.thinkofit.com/webconf/

WISE (Web-based Inquiry Science Environment): http://wise.berkeley.edu/. (You must register to use these online tools.)

Pearl Chen is an assistant professor of instructional technology at California State University, Los Angeles, where she enjoys working with students from diverse cultural and linguistic backgrounds. She has focused her teaching and research on using technology to create significant and memorable learning experiences and has written and published on the topic of learning by designing hypermedia documents.

Diane McGrath is an associate professor of educational computing, design, and online learning at Kansas State University. She is former editor of two ISTE journals, JCSE and JRTE, and has written a number of articles related to technology and higher-order thinking for ISTE periodicals.

visit www.iste.org/LL

author's update
Pearl Chen

Since the publication of this article, we have looked more deeply into three critical features of project-based learning (PBL): (a) PBL artifacts, (b) student collaboration, and (c) community of inquiry. We have also looked at recent research efforts on scaffolding strategies for PBL environments and approaches to design project experiences that promote deep learning and sustained engagement. To understand the process of knowledge transformation in cognitive PBL, we focus on conditions that promote complex thinking, inquiry, and knowledge building within the project-based learning community (Chen, 2006). In particular, we are interested in how group collaboration, dialogues, and creative work with ideas can be mediated, enhanced, and enriched by the construction of "milestone artifacts," a form of collaborative representation in which group members instantiate their developing knowledge in text, graphics, digital products, or physical artifacts. We suggest that structuring an extended inquiry process around various milestone artifacts can provide more opportunities for students to deal with the typical learning difficulties as we described in our article. Furthermore, milestone artifacts completed by different groups can provide a rich resource for the whole-class knowledge building discourse, which can motivate the community of inquiry in producing higher level knowledge work.

Scardamalia and Bereiter (2003) define knowledge-building as "the production and continual improvement of ideas of value to a community." Similar to the PBL approach, the process of knowledge building can be enhanced by working on an external artifact or a communal database in which collective discussion and synthesis of ideas are made visible. Knowledge-building tools such as CSILE and its current version, Knowledge Forum (www.knowledgeforum.com), have been used to unfold cognitive processes, making the knowledge building/thinking process visible for both teachers and students. Without using such a tool, PBL may be less structured, and this may be problematic for students engaging in intentional and focused collaborative efforts. Notably, research on providing activity structures such as action-based activities and discourse-based activities, and the use of dialogic activity structures can help educators design effective scaffoldings not only for the inquiry process and content-area learning, but also for the dialectical process in a PBL knowledge-building community. Although action-based activities engage students in coordinated construction and representation of knowledge, discourse-based activities such as communication, interpretation, evaluation, and reflection can help students make connections among concepts, projects, and their actions and goals.

Incorporating structured activities and appropriate technology tools should be considered important scaffolding strategies in the design of cognitive PBL experience. Moreover, cognitive PBL can be designed from an epistemic perspective to encourage different ways of knowing, expression, and evaluation. Epistemic tasks such as explanations, arguments, critiques, and assessments can be incorporated into group learning tasks. In our research, students are asked to keep a notebook to monitor and evaluate his or her own epistemic process throughout the PBL experience. This can make their development of understanding visible and thus may open ideas, thought processes, and structures of knowledge for critical examination and assessment. As instruction is moving more and more from a physical location to a cyberspace environment, we have also begun to look at online PBL communities (Chen & Chen, 2007). Our goal is to accelerate current research on PBL and to develop a conceptual framework of project design that is essential for developing 21st-century skills for all students.

Resources

Chen, P. (2006). Learning by building knowledge with peers. *Journal of Instruction Delivery Systems, 20*(2).

Chen, P., & Chen, H. (2007). Knowledge building and technology dynamics in an online project-based learning community. *Special Issue of International Journal of Technology in Teaching and Learning, 1*(1/2), 1–16.

Kolodner, J. L., & Gray, J. (2002). Understanding the affordances of ritualized activity for project-based classrooms. In P. Bell, R. Stevens, & T. Satwicz (Eds.), *Keeping learning complex: International Conference of the Learning Sciences* (pp. 221–228). Mahwah, NJ: Lawrence Erlbaum Associates.

McGrath, D. (2005). Invited Conference Speaker, Edunova, San Jose, Costa Rica. Technology-supported PBL as a key strategy to develop 21st century student skills.

Polman, J. L. (2004). Dialogic activity structures for project-based learning environments. *Cognition and Instruction, 22*(4), 431–466.

Scardamalia, M., & Bereiter, C. (2003). Knowledge building. In *Encyclopedia of Education* (2nd ed.). pp. 1370–1373. New York: Macmillan Reference USA.

chapter 10
Connected Classroom

Connected Classroom started out as Mining the Internet, which was an offshoot of Judi Harris's successful book series of the same name. Whereas earlier it was a collection of what was new and useful on the Internet, the column evolved into a discussion of how interactive tools could enhance classroom instruction. This evolution was based on the needs of the classroom teachers. When the network-based tools were new, maverick teachers needed a forum to share the best for the classroom. But as technology use became more commonplace and sophisticated, the need to share specific sites lessened. In fact, the volatility of the Internet made it hard.

With the retirement of the Mining the Internet concept, we changed the name to Connected Classroom and shifted the focus to how the tools enhanced learning and what new tools and uses are on the horizon. The common thread among the articles collected here is their forward-thinking approach. Our Mining the Internet/Connected Classroom authors have really had their fingers on the pulse of emerging technologies that are useful in the classroom, writing about them long before many other authors in the field.

In our first entry, Sara Kajder and Glen Bull discuss the emerging use of blogs in language arts ("A Space for 'Writing without Writing,'" March 2004). I've made no secret throughout this collection of my love for the blog as tool for personal and professional development. However, without my work on *L&L*, I probably wouldn't have found out about them until much later. Here, Sara and Glen reported on an early adopter of the the technology. Teacher Emily Van Noy started using paper journals with her students, but she found little success; ready writers enjoyed the assignment, and reluctant writers wrote as little as possible. She later abandoned journals, but said she felt disconnected from her students' writing process. With the advent of greater technology access and after a survey to ensure that students had adequate Internet access outside of the classroom, Emily decided to have students write their journals on private blogs. As with many technology interventions, blogging seemed to increase student engagement and enjoyment. The exciting thing about this article is seeing how ahead of the game Sara, Glen, and Emily were. Blogging is still an important classroom tool, and with our ever-increasing focus on user-generated content, I believe blogging will continue to be important.

Next up is a discussion of the early stages of the user-generated web ("Folk Taxonomies," Glen Bull, September 2005). Glen believed that these early user-control tools represented both the future of the web and its true potential. When Tim Berners-Lee created the concept of the web, he envisioned a loose collection of interlinked items under no central control. He points to Google as a prime example of the next step in this concept: a search engine based on searching the links among files rather than on the opinions of expert catalogers. The power of the web and the newer developments on the web lie in its decentralization, the ability of the lay population to create and share their own content. The rise of YouTube, MySpace, Facebook, and other popular tools since this column was published shows how right Glen was.

The idea of user-generation goes even farther in the final article here ("Educational Crowd-sourcing," Glen Bull, November 2007). Web users are not just creating, sharing, and discussing content. They are now the experts solving problems. By asking for help from a large group of people, you gain the power of collective wisdom. Think of it as your Ask the Audience lifeline, if your classroom were an episode of "Who Wants to Be a Millionaire." The lesson for educators is not that you will have to loosen the reins on classroom learning and allow random people from the Internet to teach your students. Rather, you will want to be open to collaboration with the larger world, in a manner that works for you and your students.

March 2004

A Space for "Writing without Writing"

Blogs in the Language Arts Classroom

By Sara Kajder and Glen Bull
With Emily Van Noy

Subject: Language arts, English

Audience: Teachers, teacher educators, library media specialists, tech facilitators

Grade Level: K–12 (Ages 5–18)

Technology: Internet, Weblogs

Standards: *NETS•S* 3, 4; *NETS•T* II (http://www.iste.org/standards/). *ELA* 6 (http://www.ncte.org/standards/standards.html).

We first introduced use of Weblogs in the classroom in the September and October 2003 issues of *L&L*. Weblogs are a relatively new innovation, consisting of Web-based journals facilitated by software that generates chronological entries.

Weblogs, commonly shortened to blogs, have become enormously popular. At last count, several million users have engaged in the practice of blogging. This has led to increased levels of public discourse and discussion. It provides new channels through which news and information are disseminated outside the conventional mechanisms of traditional news media.

The long-term effect of blogs is yet to be determined. The phenomenon is so recent that its overall place on the Internet cannot be reliably assessed, and it is still evolving. However, teachers are already exploring instructional uses in innovative ways.

Starting Points

In Emily Van Noy's seventh grade English/language arts classroom in Charlottesville, Virginia, blogs are allowing student writers to come into their own. Students are using blogs as personal journaling spaces. Using Blogger.com, a free blog site, they set up individual accounts that offer inviting, immediate journaling spaces for both class content and, in some cases, related student interests and literacies. Initial prompts from Emily focused on class content and students' work as readers and writers.

In an August 13, 2003, *New York Times* column called "Can Johnny Blog?" Pamela O'Connor wrote "this may be the year that school blogs come into their own." In this column, we review some of the practical steps

Continued

Continued

involved in using blogs with Emily's students, as well as some of the instructional reasons for bringing blogs into her classroom.

Blogs developed through tools such as Blogger.com require no knowledge of HTML and provide students with the opportunity to publish through the stroke of a key. Blogs have led to a resurgence in journaling, through their accessibility, their audience, and their immediacy.

Bringing Journals Back

Our collaborator Emily is an experienced English/language arts teacher who is using blogs with student writers in the hopes of bringing informal journaling back into her English curriculum. In reflecting about her previous experiences as a writer and a teacher, Emily shared,

> For the past three years, I have included a composition book as one of the supplies for my language arts classes. In my first year, this book was used for journaling. Twice a week the students would write for 15–20 minutes. I would give the students a choice of two prompts that usually required them to explain their opinion about a topic.
>
> As the students were developing their moral selves, I wanted them to put the time and effort into thinking about what they believed and why. Some students thrived off of this writing time and used it to pour out their thoughts on the pages; others continued to hate writing, wrote as little as possible, and filled the remaining space with doodling.

As an idealistic first-year teacher, I planned on collecting the 80 journals, reading and responding to the students, making them explain further, think deeper. After I lugged the crates full of journals from school to car to home, I would spend a whole weekend, once a month, doing nothing but reading and grading journals.

Although in the beginning I did respond to the journals and form relationships with students through that exchange, I eventually looked for length and checked the pieces accordingly. I was becoming the type of teacher I dreaded becoming, grading on quantity rather than quality.

By her third year teaching, Emily abandoned journaling, refocusing her instruction around the writing domains in the Virginia Standards of Learning. She offered,

> Twice each quarter, I would walk the students through the writing process, have them peer edit, and then grade their final products. My students became better writers, but I did not feel the personal connection that I did with my first group. Many of my students' end-of-year surveys reflected that they wished we had done more free writing.

I was left with many questions. How could I include informal journaling in my writing program? How could I save time, yet give meaningful responses to my students' journal entries? How could I reinforce correct capitalization and punctuation in my students' writing, especially when typed?

Emily first began using blogs in a Digital Storytelling Institute at the University of Virginia. Participating English and language arts teachers used blogs to detail their experiences in writing and developing a digital narrative. This led Emily to reemerge as a journal writer and to consider what role blogs could play in her students' writing.

The Nuts and Bolts of Getting Started

Good teaching requires effective planning, especially with the introduction of a new online writing technology. Bringing blogs into her classroom required Emily to manage student accounts and postings while developing compelling journaling activities that were essential to students' work in class.

She began with a parent survey in an effort to learn about the realities of students' access at home. In school, she worked to track down the status of her students' Web permissions forms. She explained,

> Blogs have led to a resurgence in journaling, through their accessibility, their audience, and their immediacy.

Continued

Continued

LANGUAGE ARTS

Language Arts 03-04

Wednesday, September 17, 2003
========================FINISHED BLOG========================

Links
Google News
Edit-Me
Edit-Me

Describe yourself as a reader.
What are your strengths/weaknesses?
What are your likes/dislikes?

Archives
09/01/2003 - 09/30/2003

When I read, I am taken into a world of adventure. I read whenever I can, because it puts me into someone else's world, and shows me creativity to spark my day. I use reading to give me ideas for schoolwork, to give me a time to rest from the daily grind, and to help me fall asleep in the night. I usually read 30 minutes before I go to sleep, and it puts pleasant thoughts in my head for sleeping. I read when I'm bored, or when I have nothing else better to do. I use reading to help with many things.
I am a very fast reader, able to do 40-50 pages of a near 12-point typed book in a night of reading. I can also read aloud fast, which I've noticed that not many people can do. I usually understand most of the words, or if I don't, I use context clues. If I still don't understand the word, I usually skip it, which is not a good habit. I know I should use a dictionary, but usually since I am reading before I go to sleep, (and usually groggy,) I don't feel like getting up for a dictionary. Other than that bad habit, I consider myself a strong reader.
I like many types of books, fiction or nonfiction. The only thing I don't read much of is anything related to history (for example; historical ficiton.) I can't get too fixed to historical works; history is not one of my favorite subjects in school. Other than that, I will read any type of book. I don't like when at school, the language arts teacher picks **what** book the class should read for the unit. (Sorry Ms. VanNoy!) I am fine when the teacher says what type of book we should read, but when the teacher picks the book, I have never liked the teacher's decision to do that. Other than those, I love reading, no matter what book. I read to calm myself, to have adventure, and to complete school assignments. Reading is great!
posted by Andrew : 8:56 AM

POWERED BY
BLOGGER

My school streamlined the process this year and had all parents fill out permission forms for their children. This information was then put into a database that all teachers could access. Because I had explained the purpose behind blogging and the safety rules we were employing, some parents, who originally had not given consent, allowed their children to publish using Blogger. Plan B for students who still could not publish on the Web was word processing at home or school.

Step two involved setting up the actual student blog accounts. Though she originally planned to enter the information for each student account herself, plans quickly changed. She offered,

The first account I made took five minutes, and I soon realized that it would take me hours, if not days, to set up accounts for all 80 of my students. Blogs were something that were going to help me save time, not take up more of it. So, I took the students into the lab and walked them through the process.

Students established their accounts using a combination of their initials and numbers from their school ID. Emily advised them to use her school e-mail address instead of entering personal e-mail addresses. This was done both to avoid sharing personal information and to aid in trouble-shooting when students forgot logins or passwords.

The final decision on Emily's part was whether to publish the students' blog addresses, making public what could be used as a private writing space. Because students were already equipped with a public writing tool through their use of Blackboard.com for threaded literature discussions, she chose to keep the blogs private.

Once the accounts were active, the remaining step was to meaningfully integrate journal writing into the curriculum. Early exercises were designed to encourage students to reflect on the work of an effective reader in their postings. Additional prompts focused students on exploration of themes and essential questions within the literature studied by the class. Subsequent activities challenged students to use the blogs as reflective space following literature circle discussions and other class activities.

Student Responses

After their initial blog posts, students were asked to complete an exit survey, examining their response to using Blogger.com as a journaling space and offering ways to make the experience more helpful. We expected the open-ended responses to be helpful in determining how we would proceed both with journaling assignments and our use of Blogger.com.

Students were unified in responding that they were drawn to writing in this new space. As Felisha offered, "it isn't boring—something different from pencil and paper." Students are writing more in their blogs because of the speed and ease of typing. They are also quick to emphasize that the blog is a way to regularly communicate with their teacher, something that the monthly grading of paper journals can often prevent. One student referred to the blog as a place for "writing without writing."

Volumes of writing research indicate that student writers, no matter how savvy, are often blocked by the intimidation of the blank page. This does not seem to be the case when students are writing within blogs. As Eric wrote, "using a blog is more fun, and I think it doesn't cause a writer's block."

Writing in blogs can lead to sharing ideas and work within communities, something students appeared hungry for within their posts. As Andrew wrote, the blogging experience would be made better if "a list of blogspot Web addresses were provided for classmates who want to share so that others in the class could read their opinions on different topics." Though Emily's design is for students to use the blog to express ideas they might not want to share with an entire class, the archiving feature does leave open the possibility to view by entry. Later assignments could allow students to gain public response, as

Continued

Continued

in the use of blogs outside of the classroom.

Bumps in the Journey

As with the introduction of any new technology into a classroom, the transition to working with blogs has not been without challenges. Though it is under what appears to be continual development, Blogger.com is still a relatively young tool. Student writers have come to it expecting the features found in conventional word processors, especially when it comes to spelling checkers. Emily explained,

> With the first blog posting, I struggled to find spell check for the students to use. The version I had used in the spring had it, but that had all changed. The help menu showed me a picture that matched the old Blogger, and the Blogger listserv said it was only available on Blogger Pro, which cost money. I presented this problem to the students and made an interesting discovery. The Blogger page they were seeing at home on their PCs was different than what we were seeing at school on the

Macs. When I loaded Blogger using Netscape Navigator instead of Internet Explorer, I saw what my students were seeing at home: what I had considered the "old version" of Blogger. No spell check to be had.

Students have identified the need for online access to also be a sticking point when it comes to using blogs in a way that meets their needs as students and as writers. Daniel wrote that "having Internet access all the time" would make a significant difference in how he used the tool as a writer. To post to a blog, the student must be logged on to their Blogger.com account. Students have worked around this problem by typing entries in a word processor and posting from a bank of four computers in the classroom. However, the goal of posting to communicate and share ideas quickly is lost when students do not have ready access.

> Several of my students are much more tech savvy than I could ever hope to be. I am going to rely on those students to teach me about the ins-and-outs of

Blogger as well. I set up a forum on Blackboard for my students to post their questions about Blogger as well as any tricks they had discovered for changing templates, adding pictures. And so on. Over time, I hope this forum will serve as a "Blogger how-to" for my classes.

Next Steps

Blogs are becoming an essential writing space in Emily Van Noy's classroom, both in terms of unique capacities of the tool and the instructional frame provided by compelling journal prompts. We're only just getting started and are at a place where questions far outweigh answers. Emily's list is long and reflective of our early stage: "How often will my students blog? How am I going to assess my students' blogs? What will the rubric look like? What is the most convenient and meaningful way to respond to my students?"

We are convinced that, as we continue to work with blogs in language arts, they will expand the possible ways in which we engage and lead student writers in the classroom.

Sara Kajder is a graduate fellow in the Center for Technology and Teacher Education within the Curry School of Education at the University of Virginia.

Glen Bull is the Ward Professor of Education in the Curry School of Education at the University of Virginia.

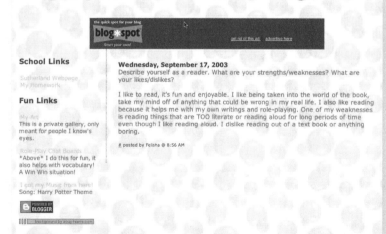

Language Arts - Felisha's Blogs

the quick spot for your blog

blog spot
Start your own!

get rid of this ad   advertise here

School Links

Sutherland Webpage
My Homework

Fun Links

My Art
This is a private gallery, only meant for people I know's eyes.

Role-Play Chat Boards
Above I do this for fun, it also helps with vocabulary! A Win Win situation!

I got my Music from here!
Song: Harry Potter Theme

POWERED BY BLOGGER

background by soup-teens.com

Wednesday, September 17, 2003
Describe yourself as a reader. What are your strengths/weaknesses? What are your likes/dislikes?

I like to read, it's fun and enjoyable. I like being taken into the world of the book, take my mind off of anything that could be wrong in my real life. I also like reading because it helps me with my own writings and role-playing. One of my weaknesses is reading things that are TOO literate or reading aloud for long periods of time even though I like reading aloud. I dislike reading out of a text book or anything boring.

posted by Felisha @ 8:56 AM

September 2005

CONNECTED CLASSROOM

Folk Taxonomies

By Glen Bull

Glen Bull is co-director of the Center for Technology & Teacher Education in the Curry School of Education at the University of Virginia and editor of Contemporary Issues in Technology and Teacher Education *(http://www. CITEjournal.org). Glen serves as a volunteer columnist for L&L.*

Early in the 1990s, Tim Berners-Lee had a powerful idea—the concept of the World Wide Web. He describes its origins in *Weaving the Web,* observing that "What was difficult for people to understand was that there was nothing else beyond URLs and HTML. There was no central computer controlling the Web … not even an organization that ran the Web." The Web simply consisted of, in the felicitous title of David Weinberger's latest book, *Small Pieces Loosely Joined.*

The success of this vision produced an unparalleled explosion of information. This resulted in a parallel problem that everyone has encountered—how to locate the right piece of information. A 2005 study by Hanson and Carlson, published by the Educational Development Center identified the time required to locate resources as the number one factor affecting teachers' use of the Web. (***Editor's note:*** For this and other URLs, see Resources on p. 23.)

There are several strategies for identifying useful information. One of the more interesting approaches is based on the ability of the Web to aggregate patterns of information contributed by many individuals. A number of Web-based tools currently under development rely on this approach.

The social bookmarking tool del.icio.us and the image site Flickr are two examples of this emergent technology. These tools allow users to assign their own descriptors to links (in the case of del.icio.us) and images (in the case of Flickr). The patterns that emerge can be described as a *folk taxonomy* or collective categories created by the lay populace. Thomas Vander

Wal employed the term *folksonomy* to describe the type of collaborative categorization that becomes possible under these conditions.

A Taxonomy through Social Bookmarks

Del.icio.us allows users to store their bookmarks on a central site. This allows them to access their bookmarks from multiple computers at different locations. A number of past bookmarking services have offered this capability.

However, the del.icio.us bookmarking tool goes a step further. It allows users to assign labels known as tags to stored bookmarks. Rather than creating a hierarchy of folders in the manner of the local Favorites folder in Internet Explorer, users can recall bookmarks through searches on sets of tags. This is a significantly different way of organizing and accessing bookmarks.

The del.icio.us site employs choices that users themselves create rather than attempting to establish uniformity through an official list of descriptors that professional catalogers assign. The Web site aggregates the user-generated choices. Users can view popular Web pages for any given topic or area on the site.

The distinction between the top-down hierarchical view in the Internet Explorer Favorites bookmarks and the flat view of bookmarks accessed through tag searches in del.icio.us parallels the top-down Yahoo hierarchy and the Google search mechanism, but at a personal level.

The patterns that emerge can be described as a folk taxonomy or collective categories created by the lay populace.

Continued

Continued

Joshua Schachter, creator of the del.icio.us tool, decided to allow other users access to the data generated in this manner. As a result, dozens of user-generated tools are being developed, with names like populicio.us and trendalicio.us. Many of these are listed on the Absolutely Delicious Tools site and are well worth exploration.

A Taxonomy of Tagging Images

The Flickr photosharing site applies the same concept of collaborative tagging to images that del.icio.us employs for collaborative bookmarks. Like del.icio.us, it also provides third-party access to the tags. A similar industry of user-generated tools that make use of the Flickr tags is flourishing. For instance, a word tool developed for Flickr allows students to enter words that are spelled out using letters drawn from the image collection.

Teachers in all classes now can have access to countless instances of signs for any letter. Another tool, Mappr, allows users to search on a tag and see a geographic distribution of images that have been taken by Flickr users. For example, students in a botany class could click on the name of a plant such as "oak" and see an array of images of oaks taken in sites across the country. Many of these Flickr tools are listed on The Great Flickr Tool Collection site. They also merit exploration.

Transcending the Card Catalog

In the case of both Flickr and del.icio.us, the combination of user-assigned tags and third-party tools makes it possible to transcend the limits of a physical catalog. By aggregating the cataloging decisions of many individual users, useful patterns of information can emerge.

Clay Shirky, a professor at New York University, has written extensively about the implications. An exemplary podcast captures his perspective on the transition of the card catalog from physical atoms to electronic bits.

The most popular search engine, Google, was based on a precedent-breaking approach. Rather than hiring expert catalogers to organize an exponentially growing mass of online information, the developers created a search engine based on the way that documents are linked to one another. Google used the structure of the Web itself as a mechanism for accessing information within it.

Google, Flickr, del.icio.us, and the very Web itself are fundamentally about implications of loose connections among information. The Web offers the capability for aggregating independent decisions made by diverse groups of individuals. Dozens of experiments are now taking place that capitalize on this capability. It takes time to adjust to the implications of removing the physical catalog. However, the promise of the Web will be realized as we begin to make this transition.

Resources

Absolutely Delicious Tools: http://pchere. blogspot.com/2005/02/absolutely-delicious-complete-tool.html

Clay Shirky Podcast—Ontology is Overrated: http://www.itconversations.com/shows/detail470.html

Delicious Bookmarking Tool: http://del.icio.us

Effective Access: Teachers' Use of Digital Resources by K. Hanson & B. Carlson. (2005). Educational Development Center, Inc. Available: http://www2.edc.org/GDI/

Flickr Photosharing Site: http://www.flickr.com

The Great Flickr Tool Collection: http://pchere. blogspot.com/2005/03/great-flickr-tools-collection.html

Mappr: http://www.mappr.com

Spell with Flickr: http://metaatem.net/words.php

Thomas Vander Wal: http://www.vanderwal.net/

November 2007

CONNECTED CLASSROOM

Educational Crowdsourcing

By Glen Bull

Glen Bull is co-director of the Center for Technology & Teacher Education in the Curry School of Education at the University of Virginia and editor of Contemporary Issues in Technology and Teacher Education *(http://www.CITEjournal.org). Glen serves as a volunteer columnist for L&L.*

Crowdsourcing refers to a process that draws on the talents of a diverse group to accomplish a task or goal. James Surowiecki's 2005 book *The Wisdom of Crowds* popularized the notion that under certain conditions diverse groups can collectively solve problems that even experts might find challenging.

The following year *Wired* magazine contributing editor Jeff Howe coined the term *crowdsourcing* to describe the process of outsourcing a task or problem to a crowd. For example, Inno-Centive (http://www.innocentive.com) provides a site on which a corporation can post a problem to be solved, together with a reward or incentive for the first person or team to solve the problem. Prizes offered typically range from $10,000 to $100,000.

Innovation and Diversity

In a number of cases, scientists and problem solvers from diverse backgrounds are solving problems that have eluded companies' internal research teams. Companies do not pay unless the problem is satisfactorily solved, extending their capabilities without adding additional overhead.

The problems posted on InnoCentive are typically complex ones that require specialized expertise or scientific knowledge to solve. An Amazon beta project, the Mechanical Turk, offers problems within the capacity of anyone to solve. For example, a typical task might involve tagging a set of images (i.e., assigning appropriate cataloging terms).

The original *Wired* magazine article is available on Jeff Howe's Crowdsourcing blog at http://crowdsourcing.typepad.com. A shorthand defi-nition provided on the blog defines *crowdsourcing* as "the application of Open Source principles to fields outside of software." Crowdsourcing frequently involves financial incentives, but can encompass volunteer efforts as well.

Exploration of crowdsourcing solutions is taking place in fields as varied as the electronics industry, biotechnology, the creative arts, and journalism. Could crowdsourcing be applicable to the field of education?

Upon first consideration, the answer appears to be that it might be applicable under the right conditions. Millions of volunteers contribute to education and schools in many different ways. These individuals come from all walks of life—parents, retired educators, businessmen who would like to give something back to the community, etc. Many of these individuals would be willing to participate in an educational crowdsourcing project if a mechanism were provided.

Research Findings

Crowdsourcing has now become the focus of a serious field of academic research. Some of the initial findings might be helpful in understanding conditions under which crowdsourcing might be effectively implemented in education. A professor in the Harvard Business School, Karim Lakhani, published some of his conclusions in the May 2007 issue of *Harvard Business Review*. He based his findings on an analysis of solutions submitted in response to challenges posted on InnoCentive.

1. *Rewards are necessary but insufficient.* Participants were initially attracted to the site by the rewards—financial, in the case of commercial ventures. However, the enjoy-

Continued

Continued

ment of solving a puzzle or novel problem seemed to play an important role as well. There did not seem to be a correlation between the size of a reward and the likelihood that the problem would be solved.

2. *Knowledgeable experts are still important.* The engineers inside the company played a crucial role in determining which problems should be broadcast, and in identifying the best solutions.

3. *Diversity matters.* In many cases the problems were ultimately solved by individuals with differing backgrounds who were able to apply methods from their own fields. Lakhani concluded that innovation often occurred at the intersection of disciplines, observing that "the more diverse the problem-solving population, the more likely a problem is to be solved."

Assignment Zero

The editors of *Wired* magazine decided to apply the methods of crowdsourcing to learn more about crowdsourcing in Assignment Zero. This project linked volunteer citizens with experienced journalists for investigative assignments. Several hundred volunteers participated, ultimately producing 80 interviews and seven articles. The interviews provide perspectives from James Surowiecki, Alpheus Bingham (the co-founder of InnoCentive), Karim Lakhani, and many others.

Jeff Howe ultimately described Assignment Zero as a "satisfying failure"—a failure because it did not fulfill the expectation of producing dozens of finished articles, but satisfying because the process yielded insights into lessons that may lead to more successful ventures in the future.

Many of the lessons appear to relate to availability of knowledgeable experts and organizers to manage a project. Initially the onslaught of more than 500 volunteers overwhelmed the organizers. This was compounded by the fact that some of the editors were not experienced with the Internet or online organization, according to David Cohn, one of the project leaders. Another organizer, Tish Grier, commented in a blog posting, "One of the first things I noticed … was the inability of many of the journalists to understand the importance of organizing and staying in constant contact with volunteers."

In a summation in *Wired* magazine, Jeff Howe concluded, "The plain fact is that in the future, journalists will have to develop these skills if they want to succeed in a future in which their readers are also their writers… . The crowd does not contribute in a vacuum. They do so as part of a community of other contributors."

Another key lesson can be derived from the fact that many of the topics identified by the organizers failed to attract volunteers, according to Howe. In other words, the work that can be accomplished lies at the intersection of the needs of the organizers and the interests of the volunteers.

The project was also hampered by some technical issues. Some participants appeared to find the Web site layout and organization confusing, although this was updated and revised as the project progressed.

Despite the problems encountered in this online experiment, the result was one of the largest compendiums of information about crowdsourcing available on the Web—a useful resource that must be counted a success despite the problems encountered in compiling the repository. These resources are made available under a Creative Commons license so students are free to analyze, remix, and write

their own stories to create their own synthesis and conclusions.

The Challenge to Education

What might be concluded about opportunities to apply these concepts to education? One commonsense observation is that the topics that citizen volunteers may wish to teach will not always naturally align with the areas of greatest need in schools. For example, a thriving community of amateur astronomers exists who doubtless would be willing to assist schools, but astronomy is typically a small portion of the overall science curriculum.

A corollary is that educators will be crucial in identifying project directions and working with volunteers in an educational crowdsourcing initiative. In an interview with Randy Burge, Alpheaus Bingham comments that one of the most crucial elements in crowdsourcing is to "get a problem into right 'chunk-sizes'" and sequence a series of tiers of increasing complexity. In education, the task is to identify areas that present the greatest difficulty to students, and structure requests for assistance from volunteers in ways that they can make contributions.

Jeff Howe's observation that in the future journalists will have to become experienced in electronic collaboration with their readers in order to be successful might apply equally well to educators. If we wish to join other disciplines that are taking advantage of the wisdom of crowds, we will need to become increasingly adept in learning how to collaborate in this manner.

Wired magazine provided leadership for an interesting experiment in journalism. Educational associations such as ISTE and SITE would be natural leaders for a "highly satisfying failure" in educational crowdsourcing. Assignment Zero set the bar high. Our challenge is to conceive and implement an equally satisfying experiment in education. ■

chapter 11

Miscellaneous Columns

Often, issues come up that require treatment in the magazine, but that don't fit perfectly into the current structure. When the issues seem ongoing, as was the case with Project-Based Learning and Media Matters, we can create a column and a regular schedule. But when they appear to be one-offs, we need a flexible area in which to place them. The Guest Editorial is one good place, and I included one of those here.

The rest of this chapter includes the columns that were too new by the end of volume 35 to occupy an entire chapter on their own but that we did deem worthy of an ongoing regular column. ISTE in Action is one example. Created as an adjunct to the new ISTE News section, ISTE in Action covers the work ISTE is doing in the field, from CEO Don Knezek or former President Kurt Steinhaus outlining the broad goals of the organization to a behind-the-scenes look at putting together NECC, now known as ISTE's annual conference and exposition. Another example is our advocacy column, Voices Carry. I'd happily put all of the columns in here, as I see this column as my baby. My educational background is in both magazine journalism and political science, so ISTE's recent focus on advocacy was a wonderful synergy of two of my professional fascinations. Director of Government Affairs Hilary Goldmann took on the task of inspiring burgeoning ed tech advocates and keeping the general membership informed of important federal policy issues.

We open with Doug Johnson's "Proposal for Banning Pencils" (Guest Editorial, February 2006). People still talk about this article in courses and on the blogs. Some see the humor and take away the intended lesson: banning new technologies ensures that education will never see their potential benefits. Students will never see models of appropriate use or benefit from a discussion of the ethics of, for example, Internet-capable devices in the classroom. Teachers will never challenge themselves to adapt to current technologies and create materials that take advantage of the inherent student engagement. Other readers take it too literally and miss the opportunity to think about the rules they have enacted in their classrooms and schools. Now even after looking at the potential power of a new technology, a responsible educator may still decide that the best option for his or her situation is to ban that technology. And, although I would prefer that educators embrace technological developments, I support them in making what they believe is the best decision for their situation.

Next, we move to an ISTE in Action entry that describes the genesis and purpose of the ISTE Institute, a professional development offering ("Systemic Leadership," Idelma Quintana, August 2007). I selected this one because I think the ISTE Institute is a wonderful and important offering that not a lot of people understand. That is the real value of the ISTE in Action column: sharing the good works that ISTE is doing. ISTE is a very active membership association, but it hasn't always had the best PR campaign among its membership. A lot of people see an Institute session in the program at NECC, and plenty of eligible members receive notifications of upcoming Institute programs. But the average member doesn't really know what the Institute is and why it is so important. After reading this article, those members who were not familiar with the Institute can see the potential effects of the training and, I hope, rush to get their district involved.

We close our look at the miscellaneous columns with a piece that educates about the importance of well-thought-out legislation ("Reframing the Debate," Hilary Goldmann, December/January 2007–08). In a rush to deal with current issues, legislators sometimes move too fast on legislation that doesn't truly meet the needs of the country. The example Hilary gives is the Deleting Online Predators Act, passed by the U.S. House of Representatives in 2006. Most people would agree that the Internet increased the opportunities for sexual predators to connect with children and young adults. And we would agree that preventing that is important. But in the rush to protect children, legislation that unduly limited educational access to online materials almost became law. Legislators had to support the bill, even if they saw the fatal flaws. Why? Because a vote against legislation aimed at protecting children would be career suicide. ISTE worked with other groups who opposed the law and key Senators to ensure that the law did not pass the Senate. After the demise of this bill, a new bill was introduced that met the needs of educators while adequately protecting children. The focus was on education, not restriction. At the time of the column, the bill had not been made law, but its introduction was a victory for ISTE and like-minded groups in reframing the issue.

February 2006

A Proposal for Banning Pencils

EX ABUSU NON ARGUITUR IN USUM.
(The abuse of a thing is no argument against its use.)

GUEST EDITORIAL

By Doug Johnson

Doug Johnson has been director of media and technology for the Mankato (Minnesota) Public Schools since 1991. He is a veteran author whose works have appeared in books, journals, and magazines. Johnson serves on ISTE's board of directors and as a volunteer columnist for L&L.

When it comes to "technology" use in schools, every responsible educator's first concerns should be student safety and educational suitability. I am suggesting that we ban one of the most potentially harmful technologies of all—the pencil. We must eliminate them from schools because:

1. A student might use a pencil to poke out the eye of another student.
2. A student might write a dirty word or, worse yet, a threatening note to another student, with a pencil.
3. One student might have a mechanical pencil, making those with wooden ones feel bad.
4. The pencil might get stolen.
5. Pencils break and need repairing all the time.
6. Kids who have pencils might doodle instead of working on their assignments or listening to the teacher.

Oh, sure, kids might actually use a pencil to take notes or compose a paper—but really, what's the chance of that?

Sounds pretty absurd, doesn't it? But listen to the reasons teachers and administrators on our district technology committee gave for banning iPods and MP3 players from the classroom:

1. They might get stolen.
2. They make kids who can't afford them feel bad.
3. Kids might listen to them instead of to the teacher.
4. Who knows what kinds of lyrics the kids might be listening to?
5. Kids might listen to test answers.

Oh, sure, kids might actually use them to study, to replay their French vocabulary lesson, or to listen to audio books, an NPR broadcast, or a teacher-created lecture—but really, what's the chance of that?

I cringe whenever I hear a district or school "banning" cell phones, student blogs, e-mail, flash drives, chat, personally owned laptops, or game sites. Student access to the Internet itself was hotly debated in the mid-1990s. Each of those technologies can and does have positive educational uses. Each of those technologies is a big part of many kids' lives outside of school. And yes, each of these technologies has the potential for misuse.

One of my biggest worries has always been that by denying access in school to technologies that students find useful and meaningful, we make school more and more irrelevant to our "Net Genners." (One of our students on the advisory board had the courage to say he concentrates better in study hall and the library when his digital music player drowns out other distractions.) When are we going to learn to use the kids' devices for their benefit rather than invent excuses to outlaw them?

My experience is that the more familiar educators are with a new technology, the less likely they are to restrict its use by students. When we old-timers experience a technology's benefit ourselves, the more we understand its benefit to students.

Is an iPod on your wish list? Add it—for your students' sake.

What do you think about allowing the use of personal technology devices (e.g., cell phones, MP3 players) in the classroom? Tell us at letters@iste.org. Include a photo of yourself to accompany your response, and you might just see your smiling face in a future issue of *L&L!*

*Originally printed in Education World, December 2005. Reprinted with permission.
Available: www.educationworld.com/a_tech/columnists/johnson/johnson004.shtml.*

August 2007

Systemic Leadership

Idelma Quintana, outgoing ISTE Institute Program Director, describes how a comprehensive professional development model benefits an entire district.

ISTE has partnered with the Illinois State Board of Education (ISBE) to bring an ISTE Institute to nearly 50 districts across Illinois. An EETT grant, referred to locally as TECH-IL, made it possible for each participating school to purchase the following equipment:

- teacher laptop with wireless card and docking station
- teacher workstation
- five to seven student computers per classroom
- interactive whiteboard
- digital projector
- digital still camera
- color laser printer
- scanner

Glenda Bequette, Principal Education Consultant, Curriculum & Instruction at the Illinois State Board of Education, knew that the equipment alone would not be enough to support effective technology integration for improved teaching and student learning. She set about coordinating a matrix of professional development opportunities that would prepare recipients to maximize the effect this grant would have on their schools. Glenda sees the ISTE Institute as "the professional development component that ties together

all of the training recipients have received." The focus of the ISTE Institute is to build systemic leadership for improving teaching, learning, and leading through the effective use of technology.

This hybrid professional development model (three days of face-to-face meetings coupled with ongoing, personalized online mentoring from experienced practitioners) had its opening session in Springfield, Illinois, in December 2006. The session was attended by nearly 200 participant members of school leadership teams. Each leadership team comprises an administrator, a technology coordinator, a lead teacher, and a classroom teacher. The role each of these team members plays in their school is essential to achieving school-wide systemic change.

Teams worked intensively during the opening session to engage in an assessment of their strengths and areas that need attention to effectively integrate technology in teaching, learning, and leading. The cornerstone of this program is a project that each team designs to address those areas that need attention. Each school project focuses on the specific priorities of that particular school in terms of capacity for technology infusion and

student learning. Two examples of the focus different schools chose are:

Increase teacher practice of "student centered learning" by effectively using technology to develop and implement student based learning projects relating to the Illinois curriculum standards. (Pope County Elementary, Pope County School District)

Increase student reading fluency skills with an emphasis on vocabulary and comprehension by effectively integrating technology into instruction. (Columbia Elementary, Peoria School District)

At the end of the intensive two-day opening session, participants returned to their schools with a concrete plan of action and a system for collecting and analyzing data that will allow them to gauge the effects of their efforts. Teams are co-mentored over a five-month period through the process of implementing their project. They work online with an ISTE mentor with national experience and expertise and receive onsite mentoring from locals with expertise in technology infusion within the local context.

In May, the leadership teams and the teachers and students in their schools exhibited their work, celebrated their accomplishments and refined their plan for building on and sustaining those accomplishments beyond this grant. Interviews with participants are available online via podcast at http://istepd.groups.vox.com.

For additional information on the ISTE Institute, visit the Institute Web site at http://www.iste.org/Institute/ or contact Debren Ferris at institute@iste.org. ■

December/January 2007–08

Reframing the Debate

VOICES CARRY

By Hilary Goldmann

Hilary Goldmann, ISTE's director of government affairs, has 20 years of experience in public policy and advocacy, and serves as a volunteer columnist for L&L.

Don Knezek, ISTE's CEO, recently spoke at a congressional briefing on Internet safety. The purpose of this briefing was to inform Senate staff about empowering parents and leveraging educational opportunities to keep kids safe online, and to highlight legislation recently introduced by Senators Daniel Inouye (D-HI) and Ted Stevens (R-AK), S. 1965, "The Protecting Children in the 21st Century Act." From my perspective, however, the focus of this briefing indicated the success ISTE and our community is having on changing the terms of the Internet safety debate from one of locking up the Web to one of education.

It was only last summer that the Deleting Online Predators Act (DOPA) zoomed to passage in the U.S. House of Representatives. The bill was introduced in May 2006, and in almost unheard of speed passed the House in August 2006. DOPA would require schools that participate in the E-Rate program to bar access by minors to commercial social networking Web sites or chat rooms unless used for an educational purpose with adult supervision. Voting against DOPA labeled a policymaker as soft on child Internet safety, and with the upcoming congressional election at the time policymakers could not afford to vote against DOPA. Fortunately, ISTE and others opposing DOPA were able to work with key U.S. senators, and this legislation never passed the Senate and did not become law.

As the new Congress convened in January 2007, the issue of Internet safety was still a priority, but this time the messages from the education, library, and industry community opposed to DOPA had effectively guided policymakers' approach to this important policy issue. Members of Congress are now focusing legislative initiatives on educating students on how to stay safe online and to be responsible digital citizens rather than handcuffing access to social network sites at schools and libraries. It is evident that policymakers heard our concerns and tailored their legislative initiatives to limit as much as possible the federal intrusion and monitoring and reporting burdens on schools and libraries to comply with these pieces of legislation.

Under the Protecting Children in the 21st Century Act, school E-Rate recipients will be required to certify, as part of their Internet safety policies, that they are "educating minors about appropriate online behavior, including interacting with other individuals on social networking Web sites and in chat rooms as well as cyberbullying awareness and response.

Responding to a reporter's question about S. 1965, Knezek stated, "We now see a bill that asks schools to take their proper role in teaching safe and responsible use of the Internet, rather than trying to block emerging communication and social networking systems with great potential for positively engaging students and improving learning. One of a school's primary functions is to ensure safety and build responsible citizens, and trying to block every threatening activity that goes on in society is not a formula for effective education."

This legislation has not been passed by the Congress, but its mere introduction indicates our voices were heard. This is a first step in reframing the debate on how to keep kids safe online. ∎

Art

As an editor, much as I like to think that only the words matter, I know that the art direction of an issue can be just as important. To that end, I've collected the best cover designs and feature art treatments over the past five volumes of *L&L*. This special color insert provides the opportunity to share five of the most intesting covers as well as five of the best article layouts the *L&L* artists created. You may notice that *L&L*'s cover title treatment changed, as did many of the design parameters for the features. I do think it is safe to say that what didn't change is the creativity and skill the designers put into every issue.

Covers

The most interesting covers, for me, were visually arresting. They brought something different to the table, and they caught people's eyes while they were reading.

May 2004

This one was really fun, and it seemed to start a trend, because we on staff kept seeing this type of image made up of smaller images in ads and magazines for the next few months. The cover image is made up of all of the images used throughout the issue. Because this issue got bonus distribution at NECC, we worked hard to make sure we had a cool image that would get people unfamiliar with the magazine interested in opening it.

Learning & Leading with
Technology

October 2004   Vol. 32 No. 2 $7.75

Manage the Data Deluge

Use Handhelds for Teaching Literacy and Math

Bring Digital Archives to Your School

iste

October 2004

This simple image really speaks to the concept of the article it is tied to: Manage the Data Deluge. It is a little edgy, and it was a real conversation starter. And the art must have worked, because it's hard for even staff to get a copy of this issue.

November 2005

This image is so cool. The green harkens back to the early monochrome monitors. (I know a lot of people had amber. My first was green.) And the hatching egg with the circuit board overlay would be a neat graphic even if it didn't tie so nicely into the tagline for the feature it accompanied (New Hardware Standards Hatching).

Learning & Leading with
Technology

Facing the Future
New Hardware Standards Hatching

Computer Tutors Get **Personal**

Podcasting Classroom

November 2005   Vol. 33 No. 3 $7.75

iste

Learning & Leading

WITH TECHNOLOGY

Thinking **Differently** Online

Developing an **Ed Tech** Agenda

Get Your **MUVE** On

Is It Time for a National Student Tracking System?

May 2007 Vol. 34 No. 8 $7.75

iste.

May 2007

Another NECC issue. This image is a great take on the MUVEs featured in the issue. It bends reality just enough that you know it is a virtual world, not just a nice illustration.

September/October 2007

This was a nomination from the blog that I totally agreed with. It made me do a double-take when I first saw it, and I know that it made people ask, "What are you reading?"

Learning & Leading

Celebrating **35** Volumes   WITH TECHNOLOGY

Bound by Security

Rushing into Online Policy

Motivation that Works

iste.

September/October 2007 Vol. 35 No. 2 $7.75

Features

The very best feature article layouts must not only draw a reader in, they also should tie a multipage story together. Additionally, the art and layout should let readers know at a glance, "this is a special part of the magazine."

"And the Readers Say..." *by staff*

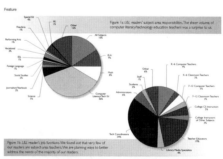

October 2003

The lead image combined an aerial photo from the most recent NECC with a pie chart. We used pie charts later in the article to illustrate some of the results of the reader survey, which makes for nice continuity throughout the layout. I also like how the quotes from the open-ended portions of the survey are used to increase the visual interest.

"Are You the Copy Cop?" *by Doug Johnson and Carol Simpson*

April 2005

The traffic violation imagery worked so well to communicate an added level of interest in this article. Doug and Carol discussed how the role of the media specialists had morphed to include policing teachers' use of copyrighted materials. The image of the traffic cop illustrated an implication that perhaps this was not the most comfortable or pleasant role for media specialists to take on. The design was tied into the rest of this issue's series on copyright, but this layout really stood out to me.

"Identifying Key Research Issues"

by Gerald Knezek, et al

May 2006

This is a beautiful abstraction of the keys to technology success, and the design staff did a great job tying together so many pieces by using snippets of the main image on each companion piece. An article with this many components can be a nightmare to pull together visually, but the team was up to the challenge here.

"From Toy to Tool"

by Liz Kolb

From **TOY** To **TOOL**

By Liz Kolb

Audioblogging with Cell Phones

Imagine asking your students to bring their cell phones to class. As educators we often reject cell phones in the classroom, considering them destructive and distractive "toys." As a former technology coordinator, I used to think cell phones were harmful for the classroom environment.

I wanted to ban cell phones from my school. I thought it was too easy for students to use cell phones to cheat on tests and text message during class. Over time I have come to realize that cell phones are part of our students' everyday existence. Today students use cell phones to communicate and collaborate with the world around them. I think something so integral to our students' lives outside of school deserves some consideration for potential use inside the classroom.

I would like to propose that cell phones can be learning tools. As educators we can help students learn how to use their everyday "toy" as a "tool" for constructing knowledge. With the new audio input feature of many Weblog sites such as blogger.com and blogzy.com, students can use their cell phones to create blogs, collect and store data, and develop multimedia projects. (***Editor's note:*** See Resources on page 19 for these and other URLs.)

An audioblog is similar to a podcast; it is a voice message from a phone that immediately posts to a blog site. Students can post audioblogs anytime from anywhere. I will explain how to create audioblogs using cell phones (see How to Audioblog, page 17) and give some examples of how cell phones and audioblogging can be integrated into the classroom.

Audioblogging with Students

Audioblogging with a cell phone creates opportunities for students to conduct interview activities (inside or outside of school). Instead of lugging microphones, tape recorders, tapes, and digital recorders to interviews, students have an instant recording and storage device with their cell phones. Because most students have their cell phones at all times, they can immediately conduct interviews outside of school.

For example, students in an English literature class conducting local author studies could just pull out their cell phones to conduct interviews when they meet the author. They can dial in to Gabcast, set their cell phone down and ask their questions. When they finish their interview they press a button and their interview is immediately posted to a blog site. Also, as many cell phones have camera and even camcorder features, and sites such as blogger.com also have the ability to post pictures taken with cell phones, they could interview, snap a few pictures, and take some quick movies all with one simple device. Once the interview is complete, students do not have to worry about storage problems (such as tapes going bad or accidentally erasing information) because the interview is instantly saved online.

Once the interview is posted, students can perform various activities with the audioblogs. They can download the video files, put them into a video editor such as iMovie or Movie Maker and edit the interview clips, insert the pictures from their cell phones, and insert the movie clips to create a video journal of their author study. If the students did not want to use the video editors, they could further develop their blog around their interview clips.

How to AUDIOBLOG

Setting up audioblogging for your blog from start to finish takes about 15 minutes. First, set up your own blog using a site such as blogger.com (although with Gabcast you can use many different Web-based blog sites). Once the blog is set up, create an audioblogging cell phone account with Gabcast. Here's how:

1. Log on to Gabcast.com.
2. Click on the blue link that says "Sign Up Now."
3. Follow a quick tutorial asking for a login and password, a primary phone number, and a Screen Name.
4. Once you create your account, you are ready to set up your own channel. This is where your audioblogs will post. Click on "My Channels," then click on "Create a New Channel." You will be asked to give your channel a title and description, and type in a numeric four-digit password (you will use this number when you call in to Gabcast to create your audioblog).
5. To post your audioblogs automatically to your blog site, click on the "Add New Blog" button. Enter the login and password for your blog site. Also include your blog site ID. Now every audioblog you record from your cell phone will automatically post to your blog! Click on "Add." When you submit, you will receive a message to click on your My Channels options.
6. Click on "My Channels." There, pay attention to the channel number and password. You will need to know these when you call Gabcast. Now you are ready to audioblog!
7. Dial the toll-free Gabcast number (1.800.749.0632). Follow the verbal instructions, and then you will be given time to dictate your audioblog entry.
8. When you finish, you are given the choice of immediately posting this audioblog, listening to the file, or creating another audioblog.
9. Once you post the audioblog, you can immediately access the file by logging on to your blog, where the audioblog should appear as an audio file.
10. Your post will also show up in Gabcast under My Channels, where other people can subscribe to your channels and you can delete audioblogs.

November 2006

I love the juxtaposition of the kid with the can and string phone and the kid with the cell phone. And the use of lettering that looks like old refrigerator magnets really shows a progression from the old to the modern. This abstract representation of progression from old to new is an interesting way to tie the art with the feature content. I also really like the fun colors. The design has a playful feel to it.

"Fitting the Pieces Together"

by Patricia A. Yost

Fitting the Pieces Together

>> Successful Technology Integration with Laptops

By Patricia A. Yost

Two and a half years ago, our middle schools (State College Area School District, State College, Pennsylvania) embarked on a student laptop initiative that began as a pilot program and has continued to develop into a model for successful technology integration. Although we were entering uncharted waters as far as laptop technology is concerned, there were some known principles that have guided us to success.

We knew that truly successful technology integration would require a pedagogical focus rather than a technology skills focus. Our professional development, therefore, would reflect that focus. We knew that our teachers and students already possessed substantial technology skills. Our objectives, therefore, were to help students use technology as a tool for higher-order thinking and learning and to help teachers use technology as a tool for promoting higher-order learning. We knew that teachers need time to get comfortable with new technology, that they need time to develop new applications of technology for instruction, and that they need time to collaborate and share with peers. Our strategy, therefore, was to provide the time and appropriate supports to allow our teachers to become comfortable and competent technology integrators.

Two and a half years into the journey, we are pleased to observe a wide variety of high-quality technology integration happening daily in our classrooms.

- Rather than focusing on topical research, teachers are beginning to pose research questions that require students to gather information for a purpose: to make a decision, to decide between alternatives, to answer a why, which, or how question.
- Rather than using their video projectors to lecture from presentation slides, teachers are beginning to create interactive, hyperlink-infused, self-paced presentation documents that students can use to learn new content or to collaborate on a team project, in much the same way that they can use a WebQuest.
- Instead of showing full-length feature films in the classroom, teachers are beginning to use 2–3-minute video segments to illustrate a point or to show a comparison.
- Instead of limiting students to texts available on the classroom shelves,

teachers are beginning to find online materials that allow them to differentiate content to meet different students' needs.
- Instead of being the "sage on the stage," teachers are directing students to high-quality Web sites, and are asking students to create meaning from what they find and to demonstrate their understanding by creating multimedia presentations.
- Instead of using word processors only as smart and efficient typewriters, students are using word processing tools to become better writers. They use the spell and grammar checkers, as well as the embedded dictionary and thesaurus, to improve their word choices and sentence construction. Because editing with a computer is less laborious than editing with a pencil, students are becoming more adept at editing as they write; they are willing to read, and re-read, write, and re-write while their work is in progress.
- Provided with options for how to demonstrate their learning, students are increasingly choosing audio, video, and image-laden projects. Where appropriate, students are selecting spreadsheet projects to illustrate points best explained through organized data.
- Increasingly, teachers facilitate electronic chats and discussions among their students, and communication through e-mail and teacher Web sites has become an accepted standard.

November 2007

I find that I am drawn to simple designs for the features, and I really like the lime green tones. The broken Rubik's cube is fun, and I like how the color and shapes are drawn through the entire article. There are times that the opening design doesn't relate to the following pages, but this one is obviously the same article all the way through.

chapter 12

Product
Reviews

Reviews are an important part of *L&L*, with a rich history and a high level of importance. It's not enough to provide educators with integration ideas and tools to ensure proper use of technologies. We must also let them know whether the new hardware and software products live up to the hype. After years of focusing mainly on software, we recently began including hardware and open source reviews to fit the needs of our readers.

We start with one of the first hardware reviews, a review of a student response system ("GTCO CalComp InterWrite PRS RF," J.V. Bolkan, May 2006). Although Jeff was the writer of this review, like many of the in-house hardware reviews, the testing process was a group effort. We editors played with the tools, testing the response units for usability and comfort. We took a simple test that Jeff created to test both the hardware and the included software. The art staff milled around us, taking pictures of the units in use to illustrate the article. Then Jeff went back to his computer to write the review. We got quite a bit of positive reader feedback on the inclusion of hardware reviews at NECC that year, so we knew we were on the right track. In his author's update, Jeff gives a little background on reviews and what he is doing with ISTE and reviews now.

Next, we review EMTeachline Mathematics Software (David K. Pugalee and Margaret Adams, October 2006). This is a suite of software tools that teach math at all levels and includes practice software, problem-solving software, and testing software. David and Margaret were impressed by the level and amount of information provided. However, they were less impressed with the interface and the relationship between the information provided and its application to particular problems and solutions. They also found that the program would be of limited use to students needing remediation because of its reliance on mathematical symbols and jargon. Much teacher support and separate scaffolding would be required. This information about a potentially expensive set of mathematics modules can save school systems money and teachers headaches as they try to integrate a tool unsuitable for their needs. David and Margaret did a good job of identifying the settings in which the modules work.

We conclude with a look at a robust web-based art program ("GeeGuides geeArt16," Savilla Banister, August 2007). As *L&L's* curriculum specialist in the visual and performing arts, Savilla Banister has a lot of experience with technology tools that support art instruction. Savilla focuses on the power of the tool in teaching art fundamentals and storing individual progress and portfolios. She points out the drawback of the web interface, which requires a tremendous amount of bandwidth. The great thing she does is point readers to a demo so they can experience the software and see if, based on the information she provided in her review, it will work for them. The addition of motivated and capable curriculum specialists has been a huge boon to the magazine. In addition to helping us round out Learning Connections by writing and mentoring authors for their curriculum areas, they also serve as a resource for the Product Reviews section, allowing us to ensure broad coverage there too. Savilla provides further ideas for using the software in her author's update.

May 2006

PRODUCT reviews

- GTCO CalComp InterWrite PRS RF
- **Sony Super Duper Music Looper**
- **Sony Acid Music Studio**
- **Epson PowerLite 82c**

GTCO CalComp InterWrite PRS RF

By J.V. Bolkan

GTCO CalComp's InterWrite PRS RF personal response system is a high-end radio frequency solution for college classrooms and some high schools. Most K–12 environments will probably be better served by a lower cost infrared PRS system from GTCO CalComp or one of its competitors. But the InterWrite PRS RF is a great choice if you need a powerful system that can handle slightly more than 2,000 response units, or you need the flexibility of "clickers" that don't require direct line of sight with the receiving unit, and you need enhanced interaction between students and the system.

The hardware portion of the system is simple, consisting of a USB receiver just slightly larger than a deck of playing cards and the clickers. The receiver plugs into standard power and has a single LED status light that confirms power, and USB connection to a computer. Because it is a radio device, you can hide the device under, or even in your desk, and that might be a good thing because in addition to a massively uninspired design (it is ugly) the device's plastic case appears only slightly more durable than your average model airplane.

Conversely, the clickers, or response units are, if not gorgeous, at least attractive in an industrial, utilitarian way. Better yet, they feel durable, solid,

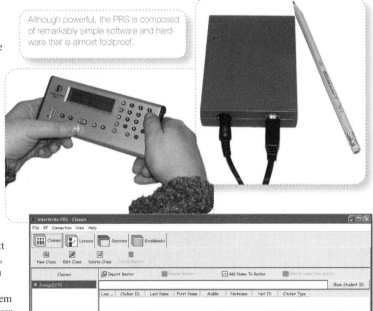

Although powerful, the PRS is composed of remarkably simple software and hardware that is almost foolproof.

and well built. A two-line text screen adds a degree of interactivity that the less expensive infrared devices simply can't provide. The radio technology enables the handheld clicker to receive as well as send, so students know if their response has been recorded. Five alpha buttons (A–E), true and false buttons, and a simple 12 button numeric array (1–0 with a decimal and minus button) provide flexibility in answering multiple-format questions. A recessed on/off switch, up and down scroll, back, setup, and a larger return button complete the controls. The tiny buttons are well spaced, so

even ham-fisted senior editors can easily press just the right choice. The devices run on AAA batteries and, according to the company, should power a unit through a typical semester before replacement. The miserly battery usage may come in part from the default settings for sleep mode—the clickers put themselves to sleep in about two minutes. Most people will want to change that setting right away.

Naturally, the hardware really isn't the heart and soul of the system. The software, its power and usability, is what makes a response system work. GTCO CalComp seems to understand

Continued

Continued

this completely. The PRS software is Java-based, so it runs and appears essentially the same on Macintosh, Windows, or any other Java-enabled platform. This cross-platform openness is also evident in the format of the data gathered by the system. The gradebook data can be exported in basic Excel format, and you can import data into the gradebook.

Instant feedback, colorful graphs, and a host of configuration options make a personal response system an incredibly powerful tool in the classroom. A powerful system such as the InterWrite PRS RF only makes it better.

InterWrite PRS RF System
Receiver and 32 response units: $2,400
http://www.gtcocalcomp.com

author's update   J.V. Bolkan

I'm a technology review geek who once started a technology review business, Bolkan-Nelson Media Labs, where I designed benchmarks, evaluated products, and wrote an awful lot about gadgets, software, and computers.

Naturally, I set about convincing the rest of the staff that *L&L* should have an expanded products and services section, including reviews. The electronic whiteboard review was one of the first hardware reviews to ever appear in *L&L*. I left *L&L* in September 2007 to become ISTE's book acquisitions editor. I'm sure I'd miss the Reviews section, except that even after it stopped being my job, I'm still volunteering to do occasional reviews in the magazine.

October 2006

- **EMTeachline Mathematics**
- **Fourier Nova 5000**

PRODUCT reviews

EMTeachline Mathematics Software

By David K. Pugalee and Margaret Adams

EMTeachline is a software company specializing in educational products, including mathematics software focusing on arithmetic, pre-algebra, algebra I, algebra II, trigonometry, and hyperbolic trigonometry with a database of nearly 5 million math examples with 11 levels of problem complexity from basic through advanced.

The mathematics software modules are intended for school-age students, math teachers, and others who are interested in solving math problems. The software is a learning and teaching tool for students, math teachers, and tutors working with all ages and skill levels. It supports both English and German interfaces. There are three primary program lines available with different options available to the user. EMTask is a math test preparation program allowing the user to develop tests, variant tests, quizzes, exams, and homework on a variety of topics at multiple levels of complexity. EMSolution is a problem solving software that expands problem solutions step by step, including objective, grounding definition, rule, and math formula. This program also includes all options of EMTask. EMMentor is an interactive program focusing on problem-drilling skills. The program provides guidance in solving math problems, evaluates performance, finds errors, and generates exercises for correcting them. It includes all

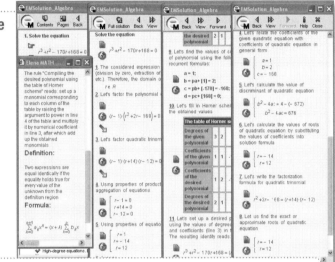

Each problem is solved step by step, with the in-depth substantiation of each step.

options of EMSolution and EMTask. Descriptions of programs and trial versions can be found at the company's Web site.

The program provides an extensive database of mathematics problems, allowing users to select a topic and one of 11 levels of complexity. Teachers can arrange problems from the database by topic, complexity level, solution method, and type of task. The problems are challenging and demonstrate the application of the steps necessary to arrive at a correct solution to the mathematics problem. The presentation of the problem solving process step by step is perhaps the greatest strength of the program. The performance analysis and the ability for students to work at their own pace are positive features of the program, making it appealing for individual as well as classroom applications.

Overall, the software provides very detailed components within each category of topics and subtopics. For example, the Solution Mentor offers detailed definitions of mathematical terms and operations; however, this information may be somewhat difficult for users to apply in understanding the solution process for the problems. Though the program provides a differentiated avenue for developing concrete skills in solving mathematical problems, the interface did not provide for easy navigation through a particular problem with information in language that is easily accessible to many users, particularly students who are struggling with understanding mathematical concepts and procedures. Although the problems are not overly complex for the topics covered, the language used to develop a theoretical base for the execution of pro-

Continued

Continued

cedures is very technical. The use of technical mathematical notation and symbols may also pose problems.

Although the developers state that the programs are geared for a wide audience, from elementary to secondary students as well as teachers, the level of presentation raises questions about the appropriateness of the software for some student audiences. It should be noted, however, that the comprehensive body of mathematical language is very good, and the logical and consistent use of the language throughout the program is remarkable. Yet the software would be very limited as a source for remediation for middle or secondary-level students, or for typical undergraduate students needing help in math courses. The technical nature of the language and the symbolic level of definitions and formulas would likely be problematic for many students without careful teacher support. There is a student audience for this type of program, but students would need to understand technical mathematical language and symbol use. Many would find the detailed step-by-step development of solutions a helpful guide in building and developing procedural problem solving skills. Teachers would find the program to provide a useful database of mathematics problems.

Pricing for the EMMentor ranges from €350 ($415) for the trigonometry module to €157 ($170) for the algebra proof inequities module. EMTask modules range from €23–€64 ($27–$76).

EMTeachline Mathematics
Pentium 2 or higher
64 MB RAM
Windows 98 or higher
Internet Explorer 5.5 or higher
EMTeachline
http://www.EMTeachline.com

David Pugalee is an associate professor at the University of North Carolina Charlotte. His research focuses on communication in mathematics including the role of language in mathematics teaching and learning. He is currently serving as interim director of the Center for Mathematics, Science & Technology Education at UNC Charlotte.

Margaret Adams is a doctoral student in curriculum and instruction at The University of North Carolina at Charlotte, concentrating in mathematics education. She holds a Master of Arts Degree in Experimental Psychology from Brooklyn College, The City University of New York, and a Bachelor of Arts Degree in Psychology from Pace University.

August 2007

PRODUCT reviews

- **GeeGuides geeArt16**
- **Travels with Music**
- **NewSoft WMS 100 Image**

GeeGuides geeArt16

By Savilla Banister

G eeGuides provides online, interactive, well-designed lessons in art theory, art history, and art creation. The Web site requires a login for students and for teachers. It stores individual student progress through the 16 lesson modules, including student portfolios of their digital art creations. GeeGuides purchase includes the license for Corel Painter Essentials Paint Software, which students may use to create various art products.

GeeGuides is easy to navigate, once one logs in as either a teacher or a student. Besides the main menu that allows access to the 16 modules, a Glossary, a Gallery of Art, and a My Portfolio section can be accessed on the left-side tab menu. Each of the 16 modules offers an overview of the topic covered (The Language of Art, Color, Line, Portraits, etc.), activities, movies and "challenges," interactive quizzes that ask students to apply the information covered in the module.

These challenges allow students to manipulate art materials in a digital environment, in a way that might be too expensive and messy, otherwise. For example, in the module on color and value, students can sample various hues and add black or white paint to change the value of the colors, without actually using real paint. This type of experimentation can assist a student in being more thoughtful and deliberate about the colors mixed and applied on an actual canvas.

The well-designed interface is appropriate for most K–5 students. Here, the GeeGuides Color Movie is activated in the module, providing students an introduction to the topic.

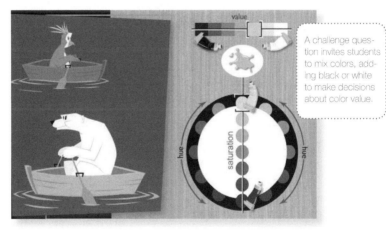

A challenge question invites students to mix colors, adding black or white to make decisions about color value.

GeeGuides materials are well designed and provide a nice balance of animated, interactive, audio, and video elements to maintain student attention. Art teachers and elementary classroom teachers could use GeeGuides to supplement their fine arts curriculum. If a teacher uses a computer projection system, the GeeGuides material could be shared as a full-classroom experience. However, the power of GeeGuides is its ability to provide individualized interaction and maintain records and art portfolios for the users.

Teachers are provided with a variety of hands-on art activities, as well as digital art experiences. These lesson plans and art activity descriptions may be downloaded as PDF files to print or to save.

As a Web-based resource, GeeGuides is dependent on a fast Internet connection. If several teachers are using this

Continued

Continued

program or other streaming products (such as United Streaming), a school might find that their bandwidth won't support such use.

Although the GeeGuides site doesn't specifically say that the program is targeted toward K–5 students, I made that assumption based on the cartoon character guides, the Corel tutorial structure, and the pace of the 16 modules. Younger students might require assistance from an adult while navigating the program. Older students should be able to work independently.

To get a better feel for the program, access a full lesson at http://www.gee guides.com/demo/. I would encourage an exploration of the items provided before purchasing. If you are looking for a resource that will stimulate student interest and competence in art fundamentals, GeeGuides may be for you. Cost is $69.95 for a family or homeschool license ($34.95 for additional students) or $995 for a school site license (includes unlimited student logins for 12 months).

GeeGuides, LLC
GeeGuides geeArt16; $69.95
http://www.geeguides.com
1.888.375.0560, FAX 1.970.375.0566

Travels with Music

By Savilla Banister

Travels with Music is an interactive environment inviting the user to explore the world via music. The interface opens with a world map noting 10 regions (soon to be 15) available for "travel." Once a region is selected, a variety of media are presented, including video and audio clips, images of the artists and their instruments, and explanatory text. A glossary and multiple games are also included that support the users in developing aural skills in identifying the musical instruments highlighted. An excellent preview of the program is provided online at http://www.travelswithmusic.org/preview/TWM.php.

The content provided is of high quality and further engagement with the artists, their music, and their countries is encouraged with e-mail addresses provided. Of course, if hundreds of students began e-mailing these artists every day, they might not be able to respond quickly, but the opportunities for dialogue could meet the needs of teachers targeting multicultural awareness through asynchronous communication.

As noted above, the application can be purchased on DVD, in which case a computer with a DVD drive is required, or via Internet subscription. Using a high-speed connection, I had no trouble navigating the program and quickly accessing the video and audio content. This would not be the case if high speed and high bandwidth were unavailable. Flash Player and Quicktime Player are also both needed for the application to run. These are free downloads for any operating system.

The Web site notes that educational discounts are available, but apparently these need to be negotiated, as an exact discount price was not noted. Although the program could be a welcome addition to K–12 music classrooms, or any classroom where diversity and multicultural understanding is an emphasis, teachers should check with their school tech support staff before purchasing. If Internet subscriptions are purchased, school network systems must be robust enough to handle the streaming media and open enough not to block the elements within the site with local firewalls. If DVDs are purchased, teachers should be sure they have DVD drives on all workstations that would handle the program.

PassportM, Inc.
Travels with Music; $99 (DVD), $80 (online)
http://www.travelswithmusic.org/twmlive/
1.510.540.8136

High-quality content on the Travels with Music DVD helps students discover the arts and music of various world cultures and regions.

Savilla Banister is an associate professor of classroom technology at Bowling Green State University. Banister taught visual arts and music in elementary schools prior to her tenure at BGSU. She continues to work with K–12 teachers as they integrate multimedia technologies into their classroom. She serves as L&L's curriculum specialist in the visual and performing arts.

author's update
Savilla Banister

geeArt16, with its emphasis on high-quality arts education, provides teachers and students with an excellent resource to target specific domains within ISTE's National Educational Technology Standards for Students (NETS•S). The Creativity and Innovation standard is an obvious one that can be demonstrated through the use of geeArt16 tools and experiences.

Students can:

- use the knowledge they have about primary colors to create color palettes for projects and blend/mix colors (virtually) to learn about secondary colors, hues and shades.

- create original pieces of digital art (and hard-copy artwork) by engaging in the geeArt16 learning modules.

- use the geeArt16 simulations to explore concepts of color, shape and design.

- identify trends that they discover in manipulating the artistic tools in geeArt16 and predict what will visually occur based on their acquired knowledge of the principles presented.

In addition to its wonderful tools and curriculum, GeeGuides also hosts an online GeeKids area (www.geeguides.com/geekids/), providing students with a venue to design electronic postcards, download movies starring Gee characters, or create new computer desktops using the geeArt16 tools. GeeKids is yet another way that geeArt16 is providing opportunities for children to grow into artists.

chapter 13

Buyer's Guide

Buyer's Guides round out the Products & Services section, which also includes product reviews and new technology product announcements. These staff-written pieces compare products within a tight category that fits the needs of educators. The buyer's guides are based on manufacturer's reports of their products' capabilities. The goal is to do the beginning legwork for you so that you can compare products and narrow down the list of items to research further.

We start with a review of current "Student Response Systems" (May 2007). The guide discusses some of the uses of response systems and one of the biggest obstacles: cost. Reassuring readers that the cost is within reach and then backing it up in the comparison table, the guide makes the case for bringing response systems into the classroom. The value of instantaneous feedback on student understanding is worth much more than the cost of the systems.

We move to another technology category: "Multimedia Laptops" (September/October 2007). We compared laptops in the *November 2006 Buyer's Guide*. The models and price-point change frequently, and the need for affordable, high-performance laptops is ongoing, so we believe it is important to revisit this category every so often.

In our final guide, we profile multi-user virtual environments ("Virtual Worlds," December/January 2007–08). After profiling MUVEs in the May 2007 issue ("Get Your MUVE On," Ross A. Perkins and Cathy Arreguin), we provided a sampling of the different MUVEs available for use with students. We typically focus on hardware for the Buyer's Guide because you can find enough items for comparison even with a restrictive set of criteria and because the items are comparable on standard criteria; often, software programs have such specific strengths that comparing them on a standard set of criteria is not really useful. But, in this guide, the staff did a good job comparing a non-standard set of items on criteria that are useful to educators.

May 2007

BUYER'S guide

Student Response Systems

Instant polling—what teacher doesn't sometimes want to stop class and quiz the students to see how much they are absorbing? Traditionally, this simply wasn't practical. By the time you've converted into quiz mode, supplied the appropriate questions, given the students ample response time, collected the answers, and assessed and compiled the results, well, you're probably at least a day or two later. Student response systems can change that dynamic dramatically.

You've seen them in action on television shows such as "Who Wants to Be a Millionaire?" The basic concept is simple—each student has a *clicker*, a device similar to a television remote control that they use to answer your questions. A receiver connected to your computer tallies the answers automatically and nearly instantly. If nearly everyone gets the right answers, you might proceed with the lesson. If most don't, you may need to go over the lesson again.

Every one of the products in this buyer's guide provide at least this level of functionality and thus can be a huge advantage in the classroom. Most have features well beyond simple aggregate polling. A typical response system has at least 5 buttons for multiple choice responses, the more sophisticated can handle short text answers as well. Many are truly interactive, capable of showing that the user's answer was received, and even if it was correct or not.

As with most technologies, student response systems have become affordable enough for the typical classroom because the technology has become common in the corporate and higher education arenas. Although the basic clickers and base technology are essentially the same, the support software can vary from mere hardware drivers to deep and rigorously developed and tested curriculum. Naturally, price reflects this.

Other major factors affecting price are the sophistication of the clickers and the communication type (infrared or radio frequency). Radio frequency (RF) devices are the more expensive. They, unlike the television remote-style infrared devices, don't require line-of-sight to operate, can handle many more users, and have more robust interactivity. Infrared devices are best suited for smaller classes (some can handle as few as 30 users dependably).

Most of the systems profiled here come in sets. A set includes a base unit, a number of clickers, and software for the base computer. Most of the clickers require batteries, but like a typical remote control, the batteries last for a considerable time.

Pricing and evaluating the system that will best fit your school's needs is beyond what a two-page article can hope to provide. However, these are among the leading and most popular choices currently available for K–12 and higher education.

Company/URL/Phone	Model(s)	Communication Type
eInstruction http://www.einstruction.com 1.888.707.6819	CPS IR; CPS RF	Infrared; Radio Frequency
GTCO CalComp http://www. interwritelearning.com 1.866.496.4949	PRS; PRS RF	Infrared; Radio Frequency (2.4 GHz)
iClicker http://www.iclicker.com 1.866.209.5698	iClicker	Radio Frequency (915 MHz)
Qwizdom http://www.quizdom.com 1.800.347.3050	Qwizdom Q4 and Qwizdom Q5 RF	Radio Frequency
Renaissance Learning http://www.renlearn.com 1.800.656.6740	Classroom Response System	Radio Frequency
Turning Technologies http://www. turningtechnologies.com 1.866.746.3015	ResponseCard IR; ResponseCard XL; ResponseCard RF	Infrared; Infrared; Radio Frequency

Pricing*	Base Unit	Clicker(s)	Requirements	Software	Feature Notes
Sold in classroom packs including clickers, base, and software from $1,495 (24-clicker IR) to $3,745 (40-clicker RF) Additional parts pricing: $250 IR, $350 RF Base Units; $63 IR clicker, $95 RF clicker	IR and RF units both USB (powered) IR base maximum of 64 remotes, with 60' range; RF base maximum of ~1,000 remotes, 200' range	Both types use 2 AAA batteries. IR unit has 8 alphabetical buttons, requires line-of-sight to base unit. RF unit has 3-line LCD screen allowing as many as 12-character responses	Win XP/Mac OS X	REAP (real-time evaluation of academic progress) gradebook, data management	RF clickers have strong input features, good for middle and high school users. Strong suite of curriculum software available for K–12. IR solution relatively limited
Sold in classroom packs including clickers, base, and software from $1,725 (32-clicker IR) to $2,250 (32-clicker RF) Additional parts pricing: $249 Base Units; $45 clicker	RS-232/USB (requires power supply), IR base maximum of 64 remotes, with 60' range; RF base maximum of 2,000 remotes/base, can chain as many as 4 bases, 150' range	Both types use 3 AAA batteries. IR unit has 10 alphabetical buttons and two programmable keys; RF unit has 2-line LCD screen, 18 input keys	Win XP/Mac OS X	InterWrite PRS gradebook, data managment	Powerful interactive clickers, RF models very strong for the price. GTCO CalComp offers great curriculum support and deep content, especially for elementary and middle school
$100 Base Unit; $35 Clicker (free base unit with purchase of 100 clickers)	USB (powered), LCD displays voting data (timer, vote count, and % of responses for choices A–E, as many as 1,500 remotes, 200' range. Includes flash drive with software, also used for storing student data	Five keypad choices, unique ID, LED vote status, power, and battery displays, 3 AAA batteries	Win XP/Mac OS X	Open source iclicker floating menu software (enables you to use the system over any application), igrader gradebook software	Among the most popular systems in higher ed, robust and simple five-button clickers ideal for multiple choice, but not flexible. 915 MHz frequency won't conflict with Wi-Fi networks. Relatively sparse K–12 curriculum support
Sold in classroom packs including clickers, presenter clicker, base, and software from $1,680 (16-clicker Q4) to $3,290 (24-clicker Q5)	USB (powered), 1,000 remotes, 1,000' range.	Q4 uses batteries, Q5 is rechargeable. Both include full numeric 18-button keypads, the Q5 adds a help button and a rocker pad for text input. Q5 has backlight capabilities	Win XP/Mac OS X	Interact data management (includes control, content, and learning game software)	One of the deepest sets of curriculum, unique Instructor Remote, highly interactive clickers with private "assistance request" button. Despite complex capabilities, suitable for younger readers
Sold in classroom packs including 24 clickers, base, and software $2,199. Individual clickers $79	USB (powered), 1,000 remotes, 1,000' range	2 AA batteries, 5-line LCD display, onboard memory for self-paced testing, multifunction calculator capacity	Win XP/Mac OS X	Classroom Response System software and AccelTest 2.2 gradebook	Low-cost RF system with high-end feature set including large LCD screen, onboard RAM and calculator function
Customized classroom pack pricing, contact vendor. $395 base unit with software, $34 IR clicker; ~$50 XL; $64 RF clicker	USB (powered), IR and XL models use same receiver. IR can handle 50-60 clickers with 90' range; RF 1,000 clickers, 400' range	12 keypad choices on all models, XL model includes onboard memory (as many as 99 answers can be stored) for self-paced testing mode. All models use coin-type batteries.	Win XP/Mac OS X	TurningPoint classroom management software	Self-pace mode is a powerful feature. Turning Technologies also offers a "virtual" clicker system for classroom with networked computing devices

*Pricing in this category is extremely volatile, and custom bids are the norm.

September/October 2007

BUYER'Sguide

Multimedia Laptops

Although laptop prices have lev-
eled out recently, they continue
to become more powerful.
The budget laptops profiled here—
priced less than $900*—boast good-
sized hard drives, fast processors, solid
graphics performance, and often flash
memory card readers. They all include
DVD recording drives (which can also
burn and read CDs).

All come standard with wireless
networking capability. This feature
raises the price slightly, but it dramatically increases the versatility of the
machines. Students and teachers won't
be tied down with wires just to navigate the network, allowing computers to be useful in the library, during
lunch breaks, on field trips, and even
potentially from the student's home.

Laptops aren't typically as upgrade-
able as desktops, but most of these can
easily accept more RAM at the least.
Nearly every one of these systems can
also be ordered with a bevy of upgrades and options such as larger hard
drives, faster CPUs, as well as software
bundles and OS upgrades.

Nearly all the Windows laptops are
capable of running Microsoft's Vista,
but you might want to specify at least
1 GB RAM, or better yet, 2 GB for full
functionality.

As always, size is also a price factor
in the laptop category. Small, lighter
units typically command a premium,
except when it comes to the screen
size. However, larger screens typically
drain batteries faster.

Prices are basic, educational pricing
can be significantly lower.

* The cost of the Apple machine included
here is higher than the upper limit of $900.
We included it to help Apple users find a
low-cost laptop.

Vendor	Model	URL	Price	Size (in.)
Acer	Aspire AS3100-1868	http://www.acer.com	$610	10.6 × 14.1 × 1.3
Apple	MacBook	http://www.apple.com	$1,299*	8.92 × 12.78 × 1.08
Averatec	AV2370-HM1E	http://www.averatec.com	$799	11.69 × 8.38 × 1.44
Dell	Inspiron 1501	http://www.dell.com	$639	10.45 × 14 × 1.44
Gateway	NX570X	http://www.gateway.com	$699	10.5 × 14.2 × 1.33
Hewlett-Packard	Compaq Presario V6000Z	http://www.hp.com	$575	10.12 × 14.05 × 1.56
Hewlett-Packard	Pavilion dv9000z	http://www.hp.com	$899	11.65 × 15.16 × 1.57
Lenovo	3000 c200	http://www.lenovo.com	$699	10.9 × 13.1 × 1.3
Sony	VGN-N320E	http://www.sony.com	$899	10.4 × 14.3 × 1.4
Toshiba	Satellite A200/205	http://www.toshiba.com	$739	10.5 × 14.3 × 1.55

Weight (lbs.)	CPU Speed	CPU Brand	RAM	Hard Drive	Screen size (in.)	Graphics	Drives	Special Features
6.2	1.8 GHz	AMD Sempron 3400+	512 MB	80 GB	15.4	ATI Radeon Xpress 1100	DVD±R/ RW/CD-R	MS Vista Home Basic, 5-in-1 media reader
5.1	2.16 GHz	Intel Core Duo	1 GB	120 GB	13.3	Intel GMA 950	DVD±R/ RW/CD-R	iSight video camera, OS X v 10.4
4.08	1.6 GHz	AMD Turion 64 X2	1 GB	100 GB	12.1	nVidia GeForce Go 6100	DVD±R/ RW/CD-R	4-in-1 media reader, MS XP Media Center Edition
6.7	1.87 GHz	AMD Turion 64 X2	1 GB	80 GB	15.4	ATI Radeon Xpress 1150	DVD±R/ RW/CD-R	3-in-1 card reader, MS Vista Home Basic
6.25	1.73 GHz	Intel Pentium dual core	1 GB	80 GB	15.4	Intel GMA 950	DVD±R/ RW/CD-R	6-in-1 media card reader, MS Vista Home Premium
6.6	1.7 GHz	AMD Athlon 64 X2	1 GB	80 GB	15.4	nVidia GeForce Go 6150	DVD±R/ RW/CD-R	Multi-format card reader, Vista Home Basic
7.8	1.7 GHz	AMD Turion 64 X2	1 GB	120 GB	17	nVidia GeForce Go 6150	DVD±R/ RW/CD-R with	Multi-format card reader, Vista Home Premium
6.13	1.73 GHz	Intel Celeron M	512 MB	80 GB	15	Intel GMA 950	DVD±R/ RW/CD-R	MMC, SD, and Memory Stick card reader, Vista Home Basic
6.3	1.6 GHz	Intel Core Duo	1 GB	120 GB	15.4	Intel GMA 950	DVD±R/ RW/CD-R	Memory Stick, Memory Stick Pro card Reader, Vista Home Premium
6.29	1.73 GHz	Intel Pentium dual core	512 MB	80 GB	15.4	Intel GMA 950	DVD±R/ RW/CD-R	IEEE-1394 port, Vista Home Basic

December/January 2007–08

BUYER'S guide

Virtual Worlds

Multi-user virtual environments, also known as virtual worlds, have become mainstream. Mattel's Barbie Girls surpassed three million registered users in its first 60 days after launching in July 2007 and is growing at the rate of 50,000 new users a day, according to a report from *Scientific American*. To put that in perspective, Second Life took three years to get to a million registered users. In August, the Walt Disney Company purchased New Horizon Interactive's popular Club Penguin site for $700 million. The Virtual Worlds Conference and Expo in San Jose, California, in October boasted 35 virtual world publishers.

Most virtual worlds share basic traits in common. Users create a customized avatar, a representation of themselves in the virtual environment. "In world," they can chat with other users through instant-message style texting or, in some worlds, voice over Internet protocol. Users can take part in various activities and obtain accessories and other items (including homes and furnishings!) with in-world currency, which they acquire either

through participation, through winning games or contests, or through purchasing from the world's publisher. Some worlds allow users to create, develop, and sell items within the world.

In addition to worlds such as Whyville and Quest Atlantis created specifically for educational purposes, educators are colonizing existing virtual world platforms as a means to extend and enhance teaching. Many educational institutions, including ISTE, run virtual classrooms and discussion and workshop forums in Second Life. Active Worlds, Inc. created Active Worlds EDU specifically for educators.

Interaction with various types of people and experimentation with different identities and social groups is a formative part of adolescence, and new worlds are launched on a regular basis. The list at right is merely representative; each world outlined is worth hours of exploration. As online social networking becomes more commonplace and sophisticated, virtual worlds will become a rite of passage for students, and a necessary tool for educators.

	Publisher	Target Age Range
Active Worlds EDU http://www.activeworlds.com/edu/	Active Worlds	Educators
BarbieGirls http://www.barbiegirls.com	Mattel	Girls 6–16
Club Penguin http://www.clubpenguin.com	New Horizons Interactive/Disney	6–14
Gaia http://www.gaiaonline.com	Gaia Interactive	Teens
Habbo Hotel http://www.habbo.com	Sulake	11+
Quest Atlantis http://www.questatlantis.org	Center for Research on Learning & Technology, Indiana University	9–12
Teen Second Life http://www.secondlife.com	Linden Labs	13–17
There http://www.there.com	Makena Technologies	13+
Toontown Online http://www.toontown.com	Disney	7+
Whyville http://www.whyville.com	Numedeon	8–15

Cost/Membership Types	Media	In-World Activities	Control and Safety Features	Number of Users	Developers Tools	Platform
Free basic account $650/year for 20 student licenses See AW Web site for complete details	Download	Chat, games, shopping, virtual construction	Code of conduct in public areas	Unknown (1,000+ worlds)	Software Development Kit	Windows 98, Me, 2000, or XP
Free basic account	CD, MP3 player	Chat, accessorizing Mattel marketing throughout	Language filter	3 million	No	Windows XP or Vista
Free basic account Subscription plans starting at $5.95/month	Web-based	Chat, games	Language filter, in-world moderators	5 million/month	No	Flash 6-enabled browser
Free basic account Extras require Gaia Gold	Web-based	Chat, forums, games, auctions	Optional language filter, in-world moderators	2 million/month	No	Java-enabled browser
Free basic account Extras require Habbo Coins	Web-based	Chat, games	Language filter, in-world moderators	7 million/month	No	Shockwave-enabled browser
Memberships restricted to teachers and other facilitators. See QA Web site for complete details.	Download	Quests	Access restricted to authorized users Communication is recorded	Unknown	Teacher Toolkit and professional development workshops	Windows XP
Free basic account Additional basic or premium accounts starting at $9.95/month Extras require Linden dollars	Download	Chat, games, virtual construction Campus:TSL Public and private educational projects	Age verification, community standards, in-world moderators	Unknown	Yes	Windows XP sp2, Mac OS X 10.3.9+, Linux i666
Free basic account Extras require Therebucks	Download	Chat, games, auctions	Customizable profanity filter, "PG-13" content standards	Unknown	Yes	Windows 2000, XP, Vista
Free basic account Subscription plans starting at $9.95/month	Web-based	Chat, playgrounds, teamwork against Cogs	Predefined chat phrases, profanity filter, parental controls menu	1.2 million	No	Windows 98, ME, 2000, or XP with Internet Explorer v. 5.1+ Mac OS X 10.4.6 (Tiger) with Safari Browser
Free basic account Extras require Clams	Web-based	Educational quests and games	Language filter	2.27 million/month	No	Flash-enabled browser

chapter 14
Member Profiles

With the increased focus on *L&L* as the membership magazine, we decided to begin creating community among our members. In addition to the reader forums we provided in the magazine, we also wanted to celebrate our members. We began by focusing on individuals, later expanding the focus to include all categories of membership. I focused on one profile of each category here, to provide a broad representation of what we achieved with the column.

In one of our first profiles, we captured the energetic personality of a teacher from Louisiana ("Hungry Minds," September 2004). Daphne Griffin walks a fine line with her young students, providing developmentally appropriate activities while also harnessing the power and excitement of technology. She gives her kindergartners a high level of responsibility, trusting them to direct their activity and take attendance. She knows that her students have a high comfort level with technology, and she takes inspiration from them when she integrates technology into the classroom. But it's not all self-directed learning and digital tools. Daphne keeps things light and fun, using props such as a wind sock whale that students can pretend is eating them. Seeing Daphne in person, with her dynamic attitude and vibrant personality, I am impressed with how well her persona shone through in the text.

Next is a profile of an ISTE affiliate, the Northwest Council for Computer Education (February 2007). The more than 70 affiliates provide a network of like-minded educators that can help support ISTE's work. In return, ISTE supports its affiliates through networking assistance, representation in ISTE initiatives and leadership, and discounts for affiliate members. Featuring affiliates in *L&L* is a valuable means of increasing each affiliate's profile in the field. In this profile, we focus on NCCE's history and success and learn that NCCE has actually been around longer than ISTE, which is an interesting fact.

We move to a profile of one of ISTE's corporate members, Texas Instruments (November 2006). Texas Instruments (TI) is one of the original members of the ISTE 100, and a strong supporter of educational technology. The ISTE 100 provides a connection between educators and companies that provide educational products and services. That connection enables educators to help shape the future of ed tech by providing feedback on the companies' offerings. This profile focuses a bit on the products TI offers for education, but mainly provides information about future directions of the company.

Our final profile is of the Special Interest Group for Teacher Education ("Teaching Teachers to Create 'Sticky' Learning," September/October 2007). The SIGs provide an important means for educators to gather with their colleagues for discussion and targeted professional development. For example, teacher educators need vehicles in which to publish their research, and SIGTE's *Journal of Computing in Teacher Education* provides a respected peer-reviewed source. As the profiles of the SIGs move into their second round, we are able to focus less on the who, when, and where and more on the how and why for each SIG. Here, we profile SIGTE's communications officer, who shares a bit about what brought her to ISTE, where she is focusing her research, and where she sees the need for increased focus in teacher education.

September 2004

Member Profile

Hungry Minds

Daphne Griffin Feeds Off the Energy of Her Young Students

Name: Daphne Griffin

Job Title: Teacher

Location: St. Joseph Catholic School Ponchatoula, Louisiana

ISTE Member Since: June 2002

Famous/Historical Person She'd Bring to Her Classroom:
"I'd bring one of the Apostles into the classroom. Next, I'd bring Susan B. Anthony. I'd want someone who could teach a lesson. I can teach them facts, I can't teach them acts."

Daphne Griffin has a lot in common with her kindergarten students, by design. The young learners are just getting started and almost everything is new. Daphne is always looking to start something new in her classroom.

"I don't hold onto projects. I put them in a folder when we're done—I don't want to be a 'folder teacher' who just does what I did last year because its easy," she says earnestly.

Daphne doesn't take shortcuts, tangibly or pedagogically. She strives to create a developmentally appropriate learning environment that engages her students as well as herself. "My students don't even touch a pencil the first six weeks of school. We work on developing fine motor skills and coordination," she explains. She also trains the students in being students. "By January, my classroom is pretty much self-run. They come in, know to let me know who's there and who's not. They sit at their desks, pull out their work folders, and do what they're supposed to be doing."

Daphne's belief in developmental appropriateness doesn't blind her to the possibilities technology can bring to her classroom. "I entertain five-

year-olds all day. They're coming from video games, interactive computer games, and videos. You ask them to sit at a desk and pull out a zipper bag with scissors, some pencils, crayons, and some glue. They're having some fun," she adds with heavy sarcasm.

"Kids are not intimidated by the technology. I had 17 kindergarteners [in 2002–03], and 15 of them had computers at home. I have to know that these kids use the remote at home ... you can't just read a book to them all the time. You need something that'll come out at them.

"I literally gave the kids a $300 digital camera. We did plenty of projects where they go and shoot three pictures then tell me a story about the pictures. We also paired up with eighth grade buddies who helped them find objects to photograph with names that started with different letters. We took all the photos and put them into a presentation program to create the Crusader Alphabet."

Naturally, it isn't just technology that Daphne relies on. Sometimes she'll be nearly as zany as her students. "I made a big ol' snake that you pull up while the students are reciting the boa constrictor poem ... oh

no! It's got my knee, oh gee, oh gee!"

The key, according to Daphne, is keeping the attention level high, whether technology is involved or not. In some ways, she admits, the technology is as much a motivation for her as it is for the students. "I've been an educator for 13 years. You slowly lean toward the technology, dabble in it, then you get better.

"When you get better, you get faster and you can do more. It took a while when I first brought the digital camera in class, then after a while it was faster—now I want to do digital video. It keeps you fresh."

Making an impression on her students is a recurring theme with Daphne. One of the few projects she repeated was a wind sock whale. It was 57 feet long, blown up with a fan, and intricately detailed inside. The kids could walk through and even sit inside it.

Evidently, there's nothing better for grabbing a youngster's attention than having them be devoured by a snake or a whale, unless it is having a highly motivated original such as ISTE member Daphne Griffin as your teacher.

Photos and story by L&L staff

February 2007

MEMBER profiles

Promoting Ed Tech Use in the Pacific Northwest

The Northwest Council for Computer Education is a nonprofit organization of educators that strives to support and advance the use of computers and related technologies at all levels of education in the U.S. Pacific Northwest.

For more than 36 years, NCCE has brought teachers, technology specialists, and administrators together to discuss and learn about the issues facing technology in education today.

Heidi Rogers, NCCE executive director, says that their affiliation with ISTE, and similar organizations that champion the appropriate use of technology in the classroom, is invaluable to their mission and to their membership.

"Together with our affiliate colleagues from around the world we

Northwest Council *for* **Computer Education**

http://www.ncce.org

share a common mission which is to support and advance the use of educational technology," says Rogers. "NCCE's circle of influence expands and continues to promote effective uses of technology to increase student achievement and to enhance the educational system."

NCCE has held a regional conference focused on technology in education for nearly 20 years. The 2007 conference, themed "Agents of Change," kicks off at the Spokane Convention

Center March 6–9. The event features an intriguing lineup of keynote speakers, practical workshops, and a large hall of exhibitors.

"Our conferences continue to grow in numbers because we strive to rise above your expectations and listen to our members' needs," says Rogers.

Currently, NCCE's nearly 3,200 members represent 14 states and two Canadian provinces. Members of NCCE receive advance notification for conferences and workshops, and share the opportunity to interact with other educators who have similar interests. Yearly dues are $10.

President: Jeff Allen, jallen@oesd.wednet.edu

Executive Director: Heidi Rogers, hrogers@ncce.org

President Elect: Vince Ruggiano, vince_ruggiano@beavton.k12.or.us

November 2006

MEMBER profiles

Texas Instruments Strategies Add Up

Texas Instruments (TI) has been a bedrock member of ISTE's corporate membership program and the Ed Tech landscape in general since the very beginning.

Even though company representatives are careful to point out that more than 85% of the company's business is in semiconductors, they also readily admit that almost everyone thinks of them as the ubiquitous graphing calculator manufacturer.

Melendy Lovett, president of TI's Educational & Productivity Solutions (E&PS) business and senior vice president of TI, explains that it is her business unit that is the actual member of the ISTE 100. "We value the relationship we have with ISTE and the ISTE members because we believe

TEXAS INSTRUMENTS
http://www.education.ti.com

that working with them allows us to continue down the path of improving student achievement with technology.

"It's a tradition at TI to work closely with educators. We want to better understand what tools they need to teach the most difficult concepts in math and science, and that's been a guidepost of ours from the very beginning."

TI's flagship education products are the TI-83 and TI-84 graphing calculators for high school students and the TI-73 for middle school use. However, in 2004, TI added the TI-Navigator, "a classroom, network, and formative assessment product," says Lovett. The TI-Navigator enables teachers to network all the TI graphing handhelds in the classroom and provides numerous

tools to help teachers better understand how their students are working through problems.

TI continues to look for ways to both increase the effectiveness of existing products and to develop new ones. "We are very committed to research, using it to guide our product development and then using third-party effectiveness research once we've introduced it to the market," explains Lovett.

Recently, TI has begun interventions in selected school districts based on the company's systemic view that math and science education involves professional development, curriculum, and other factors, not just TI products. "This is a new arena for us, we're really pleased [with initial results] and see them more as a beginning than a place to stop."

September/October 2007

MEMBER profiles

Teaching Teachers to Create "Sticky" Learning

Teresa S. Foulger is an assistant professor in the College of Teacher Education and Leadership at Arizona State University. She is also the new Communications Officer for ISTE's Special Interest Group for Teacher Education.

"I was introduced to ISTE when I worked as a grant coordinator with five districts and many technology coaches to support," Foulger says. "This was a very challenging job for me, and ISTE provided the foundation for my work, including the NETS for Students as a primary focus for promoting a new vision for including technology in the classrooms. Of course, the NETS for Teachers was invaluable."

sigte
http://www.iste.org/sigte

Foulger's current research agenda focuses on technology supports to teaching and learning. "I'm especially interested in collaborative environments—both online and face-to-face. I teach using hybrid or blended techniques because I'm a believer in the synergy that can be created by the intentional combination of face-to-face with online work. I mostly promote asynchronous tools. In our college we're working hard to make sure that hybrid methods use technology in ways that provide us with interactions that couldn't be available

otherwise. We shouldn't use technology unless it enhances what we do."

According to Foulger, the biggest challenge for teacher educators promoting technology integration is the backlash K–12 teachers perceive because of the emphasis on teaching to the standards. "Technology integration normally occurs in more interactive, project-based environments," she explains. "Teachers who see the standards push as a move to be more directed have a hard time seeing the benefits of technology. How do we get teachers to trust that a well-created process that is student-centered can create some magical learning, the kind of learning that is 'sticky' and won't need to be recalled right before the standardized test is administered?"

chapter 15

The Future
of *L&L* by Kate Conley

Over the past 35 years since ISTE first began publishing an educational technology magazine, we have seen changes that the early adopters of that technology might never have conceived of in their wildest dreams. These changes have both inspired and challenged educators, and educators have continued to do what they always do with these kinds of challenges. They have risen. They have dreamed. And most important they have learned how to use these tools to improve teaching and learning.

Learning & Leading with Technology has changed right along with those educators. It has provided valuable information. It has challenged assumptions. And it has supported the vision of a world in which every student has what she or he needs to achieve by supporting those educators and education leaders who have promoted the effective and appropriate use of technology to improve teaching and learning.

Despite all of these changes, *L&L* has never lost its primary focus. *L&L* is and always has been about the sharing of knowledge and information. It is about committed educators doing innovative things with technology in schools and being willing to share their experiences with others. It is about exploring the issues that concern us, evaluating the tools that inspire us, and pursuing the dreams that engage us. It is about people who share their successes and failures, their ideas and knowledge, and their profound belief in the power and importance of using technology to improve teaching and learning.

Despite how much technology itself has changed in the past 35 years, ISTE's message has remained simple and constant: effective technology integration is key to improving teaching and learning to help ensure students' success in this new century.

L&L is the voice of ISTE. It is the organization's official membership publication.

L&L is a powerful forum for educators and education leaders, members or non-members, willing to share their experiences and advances in the field as a whole. The magazine is a valuable resource to readers who make use of *L&L*'s content in classrooms across the globe on a daily basis.

L&L has evolved and changed over the years as the needs of educators have evolved. As early adopters we may simply have needed to know what this new technology was and how to get it to work in our classrooms. When 8 mg of memory was more than one could ever imagine needing, our lives were perhaps a little less complicated but our dreams were also a little less ambitious. Our need to understand, apply, and evaluate new technologies has increased as our needs have become more pressing. Like most educators, *L&L* readers strived to use these new, increasingly complex tools to address increasingly complex problems.

Additions of new columns and departments such as Bloggers Beat, Voices Carry, Point/ Counterpoint, Reader Polls, and ISTE in Action are direct results of our keeping up with the constantly changing times. Most recently, *L&L* has added a digital edition, providing readers with an online opportunity for anytime, anywhere reading, an easy-to-search archive, and broader sharing. The print edition remains a welcome addition to our members' mailboxes eight times a year.

L&L will continue to provide a place where professionals across all levels of the teaching and learning enterprise can find valuable information, tips, tricks, and resources to enhance their teaching experience. We are also expanding our abilities to connect readers using ISTE's new Ning (www.iste-community.org/group/landl) and will expand opportunities for greater distribution and accessibility of *L&L* content through the ISTE website (www.iste.org).

As ISTE celebrates its 30th anniversary and I my 10-year anniversary in 2009, I know that *L&L* will continue to grow and evolve to meet the ever-changing needs of educators as they seek to integrate new technology effectively to improve teaching and learning. The technologies that we will publish articles about may not have been invented yet, but I know that the need to provide solid information about how they can be used in education will continue. So we will continue to provide a venue in which educators can share their experiences and read about what their peers are doing to prepare students for careers that might also not have been invented yet. Visit www.iste.org/LL to see how we're doing.

Many thanks to the numerous authors, curriculum specialists, and columnists who generously volunteer their time by sharing valuable information to enrich the education community as a whole and to the readers who benefit from and expand upon that information to enrich the learning experience for students of all ages everywhere.

Kate Conley is currently the Periodicals Director at ISTE. She has been the editor of Learning & Leading with Technology since 1999. She holds a master's degree in journalism and has edited a variety of trade periodicals. Before coming to ISTE, she taught English language arts and writing at the secondary level in the San Francisco Bay Area for eight years. She still remembers the smell of the mimeograph machine, which represented high tech when she earned her teaching credential back in the late 20th century. You can reach her at kconley@iste.org.